tornadoes • hibernating bears • galaxies • rainbows • honeybees •

# How Come?

By Kathy Wollard • Illustrated by Debra Solomon

WORKMAN PUBLISHING, NEW YORK

comets • talking parrots • tipped-over planets • ball lightning •

*Library of Congress Cataloging-in-Publication Data*
Wollard, Kathy
How come?/ by Kathy Wollard; illustrations by Debra Solomon
p. cm.      Includes index.      ISBN 1-56305-324-1
1. Science—Miscellanea—Juvenile literature [1. Science—Miscellanea. 2. Questions and answers.]
I. Solomon Debra, ill.  II. Title
Q163.W59 1993
500—dc20   93-25471 CIP AC

Workman books are available at special discounts when purchased in bulk for premiums and sales promotions as well as for fund-raising or educational use. Special editions or book excerpts also can be created to specification. For details, contact the Special Sales Director at the address below.

Workman Publishing Company, Inc.
708 Broadway
New York, NY 10003

Manufactured in the United States of America

21   22   23   24   25   26   27   28   29   30

# Acknowledgments

*This book is dedicated to Evan Morris, Aaron Wollard, and Alexander Gorlin, with love.*

We would like to thank former and current *Newsday* people: B.D. Colen, who shaped the column at the beginning; Anthony Marro, who believed in it; Liz Bass and Jacqueline Segal, for expertise and encouragement; and Michael Muskal, who pushed and prodded us to turn "How Come?" into a book. And finally, we express our gratitude to Roy Hanson, the column's first editor, who did not live to see this book. Kathy Wollard would also like to thank her husband, Evan Morris; Karen Fitzgerald; Juliette Ayisi-Agyei; Jeff Coleman; Steve Kelly; and Jennifer Wehman, for assistance and support of every description. Special thanks to Jearl Walker, who never fails to return calls, and always gives wonderfully understandable answers to questions on every aspect of physics. Thanks also to our agent, Meg Ruley. Finally, at Workman, we are grateful to editor Suzanne Rafer, art director Robbin Gourley, and most especially our editor, Margot Herrera, for the many hours she spent working to make the book a reality.

—*Kathy Wollard and Debra Solomon*

# Contents

# The Great Beyond ....71

# The Solar System ....95

## Our Home Planet .................153

## How's the Weather? ............181

## At the Zoo ......................................203

## Why We Are How We Are 255

# Where did *How Come?*

**H**ow Come? began as an idea kicked around in the Melville, Long Island, offices of *Newsday,* one of New York's liveliest and most popular daily newspapers. What about a weekly column aimed at kids that explained everyday mysteries? And why not have the kids ask their own questions? Within weeks of the first appearance of "How Come?" in *Newsday*'s Discovery section in June 1987, a flood of mail appeared, full of questions from both children and adults. Shortly thereafter, Debra Solomon became the illustrator, adding a new element of inspired craziness. Today, the column is syndicated to newspapers in the United States and around the world.

One of the joys of writing the column is opening the hundreds of letters that pour in, many accompanied by drawings, from children with endless wonderful questions about the world. (Some that don't appear here: If glass is transparent, why does it cast a shadow? When someone you love dies, why do you feel the pain in your heart?)

Sometimes, kids send in their own theories after a column appears, suggesting, for instance, that it was lightning that caused the extinction of the dinosaurs. Other times, they ask questions about the future: They worry about having enough space to live in and air to breathe when they grow up. And every so often, seemingly simple questions prove to be unanswerable: "How does a moving bicycle stay up?" is just one of many that scientists are still puzzling over.

Each column was originally meant to be read as a self-contained whole, and we have tried to preserve that form in the book. That necessarily means some redundancies, but it also means that you, the reader, can open the book to the middle, and jump from topic to topic at whim. However, as you do, you will probably begin to notice the connections between seemingly unrelated topics, such as skin color,

# come from?

strange designs in spider webs, and how stars work.

Sometimes, the 500-word space allotted to the column in newspapers cramped a full explanation. The book's format allows more complete explanations, and the addition of sidebars and "Fast Facts." But none are meant to be encyclopedic. Hopefully, they will send a reader off to another book, a science museum, or a friendly science teacher.

I have tried to make **How Come?** as accurate, error-free, and up-to-date as possible. This meant revising the book until the last moment to include the latest findings about the thin atmosphere of Mercury, the temperature of the Earth's core, and the impact crater in Mexico that may mark the beginning of the end of the dinosaurs. But science is constantly reevaluating, retesting, and rethinking. Next year may bring the news, for example, that the asteroid theory of dinosaur extinction has serious holes.

Fortunately, science is less a collection of carved-in-stone facts than a method of finding out about the world, an open-minded process that will go on as long as we do. The very first "How Come?" column was "Why is the sky blue?" It is still the most frequently asked question. Although the commonly accepted theory was worked out by John Rayleigh in 1899, "How Come?" still gets mail from people who don't agree with his answer. And that's as it should be.

Finally, just so we don't forget, every question, including why the sky is blue, retains an element of deepest mystery. Science, after all, attempts only to represent the world. The world itself always stands apart, just a bit out of reach.

*Kathy Wollard*
*New York City*

# Color & Tricks of Light

Light is made of tiny particles of energy called photons, which travel extremely fast—186,000 miles a second in a vacuum. Science tells us that nothing can travel faster than light.

Although light is a particle, it also acts like a wave, and comes in a variety of wavelengths. Our eyes can see only light in a certain range of wavelengths—those of visible light (the kind we see coming from the Sun, or a lamp). But gamma rays, X-rays, and ultraviolet light are also types of light—ones with photons too energetic (and too short-wavelength) for our eyes to see. Likewise, photons of infrared light, microwaves, and radio waves are too low-energy (and too long-wavelength) for us to see.

Visible light comes in a rainbow of colors, and white light, such as sunlight, is simply these colors combined. Put a prism in a beam of bright white light, and the light will split into its constituent colors, or wavelengths. First comes longer-wavelength red, and then orange, yellow, green, blue, and finally violet, the shortest wavelength of visible light. (The rainbow appears because the prism bends the light of each wavelength a little differently from the next, so they each emerge on their own.) A second prism to catch the rainbow light, placed upside down, will recombine the colors into a white beam.

# Why is the sky blue?

**S**ometimes the simplest questions are the hardest to answer. Scientists have come up with many explanations over the years for why the sky is blue. But the best came from Lord John Rayleigh, a British scientist, almost 100 years ago.

First things first. The sunlight that lights up the daytime sky is white—so the sky should be a brilliant white, right? In order for the sky to look blue, something must be happening to the light as it passes through Earth's atmosphere.

White light is made of a rainbow of colors. We can see this rainbow when we look at light through a prism. The prism breaks light up into bands of color: red, orange, yellow, green, blue, and violet. Together, these make up the light we see as white.

So as white light streams in from the Sun, something must be splitting the light up into its colors. Then, somehow, the blue part of the light must be drowning out all the other colors.

What could cause this? There are several possibilities.

The air surrounding the Earth is made of gases—nitrogen, oxygen, argon, and others—mixed with water vapor and ice crystals. There are also dust and chemical pollutants, and, high up, a layer of ozone. All of these parts of the air have been accused of making the sky blue.

For example, both water and ozone tend to absorb reddish light, letting bluer light pass through. Maybe, some scientists thought, this explains blue skies.

## *White light is made of a rainbow of colors.*

But it turns out that there simply isn't enough water and ozone to absorb the amount of red light that would make the sky blue.

In 1869, John Tyndall, a British physicist, suggested that dust and other particles in the air scatter light, and

# Bored with Blue?... Suggestions for the summer sky.

What about plaids...

or animal prints...

... how about mile-long paisleys crawling through a sea of stripes?

blue emerges strongest. To prove his idea, he made some smog and then shone a beam of white light through it. Looked at from the side, the smog turned a deep blue.

Tyndall decided that if the sky were filled with perfectly clear air, white light would pass through without breaking up. Pure air should produce a bright white sky.

At first, Rayleigh believed this, too—but not for long. In 1899, he published his own explanation: The air itself, not dust or smog, Rayleigh said, turns the sky blue.

Here's what happens:

Some sunlight passes through the empty space between gas molecules in the atmosphere, reaching the ground as white as when it started out. But the sunlight that runs into gas molecules, such as oxygen, is absorbed, then scattered every which way.

The atoms in the gas molecule get excited by the absorbed light, and re-emit photons of light in all wavelengths—from red to violet—out the "front," "back," and "sides" of the molecule. So some light heads on toward the ground, some is sent out into the sky, and some speeds

back towards the Sun.

What Rayleigh discovered was that the brightness of the emerging light depends on the color. Eight photons of blue light emerge for every one of red. So blue light shooting out of the molecule is eight times brighter than red light.

The result? Intense blue light floods at us from all directions in the sky, from zillions of gas molecules. The sky isn't "pure" blue, because the other colors reach our eyes, too. But they are very faint, drowned out by the bright, bright blue.

# Why do the leaves change color in the fall?

Leaves get their ordinary green color from chlorophyll, a pigment found in plant cells. (A pigment is any substance that absorbs visible light.) Chlorophyll absorbs sunlight and uses its energy to make food for the plant. But in the fall, tree leaves lose their bright green color. Poplar leaves turn golden, sugar maples flame red. These color changes mean chemical changes are occurring in the leaves: Something is happening to the chlorophyll.

As summer turns to autumn, each tree begins to prepare for winter. Nutrients move slowly out of the leaves and into the tree's branches, trunk, and roots, where they are safely stored against the deep freeze ahead. When spring comes, the tree will draw on these nutrients to grow new leaves.

As the nutrients depart, the leaves stop making chlorophyll. The chlorophyll remaining in the leaves grad-

*Chilly weather causes chemical reactions that make radish-red pigments in some leaves.*

ually disintegrates, which allows other pigments to come out of hiding. In some trees, yellow and orange pigments emerge. (These include carotenes, the chemicals that make carrots orange.) So the leaves of birch trees and hickories turn buttery yellow as their chlorophyll fades away.

The leaves of other trees turn beautiful shades of red. The scarlet, wine-red, and purplish colors of some leaves are created by pigments called anthocyanins. These pigments also tint radishes and red cabbages, roses and geraniums.

Unlike the carotenes and

other yellowish pigments, the anthocyanins are not even present in the leaves until fall. These chemicals form when the weather turns chilly.

The color that leaves turn is mostly inherited, like our hair color. But whether these colors are dull or bright depends on the weather.

The deepest, most brilliant shades develop after weeks of cool, sunny fall weather. For example, when the temperature drops to between 32° and 45°F, more anthocyanin forms. The ideal weather for stunning foliage is found in places like Vermont. In England, where fall weather is rainy and milder,

**FAST FACT**

Trees store up food for winter, just like chipmunks and squirrels do. Only instead of burying nuts in the ground, trees store nutrients in their branches, trunks, and roots.

leaves may turn muddy yellow or brown.

As autumn fades to winter, colors fade, too, and leaves loosen from their moorings. Leaves are held to branches by their stems. As the weather cools, the cells at the end of each stem fall apart. Eventually, each leaf is held to its branch only by the thin veins through which water and nutrients once flowed. A light wind or rain can break these flimsy threads, sending the leaves drifting to earth in a carpet of color.

The yellow and red pigments may stay in the leaves for days after they have fallen to the ground. Gradually, though, the colorful pigments disintegrate. All that's left is the tannins—brown chemicals that also color tea.

The now-brown leaves, cut off from their water supply, dry up. Picked up by the wind, they whirl through the air in leafy cyclones, and crackle underfoot on Halloween.

# Where do rainbows come from?

**W**illiam Wordsworth, an English poet who lived in the 1800s, wrote:

*My heart leaps up when I behold*
*A rainbow in the sky. . .*

Something about seeing a rainbow gives us a shivery feeling. The bands of color, dipping down from the sky, are so beautiful and rare.

People once thought rainbows were signs from the gods. It's not surprising. A rainbow appears in the sky, seemingly out of nowhere. Then, just as mysteriously, it vanishes.

Today, we know something about how rainbows are made, but that should not make us appreciate them any less. Scientists who unravel rainbow mysteries use math.

• • • • • • • • • • • • • • • • • • • • • •

They say that even the math that explains a rainbow is special and lovely (although it's also very complicated).

The colors of a rainbow always come in the same order: first red, then orange, yellow, green, blue, and violet. Red is the brightest band of color, running along the top of the bow. Then come the other colors, each paler than the last. Violet, the inner band, is dimmest and hardest to see of all.

What are rainbows made from? The recipe is simple: droplets of water in the air, light, and someone to look.

It is not enough, how-

ever, for the Sun to come out during a shower. Everything must be lined up just right. The Sun must be low in the sky, or even just below the horizon. And you must be standing with the Sun behind you, looking toward where it is raining or where it has just rained.

Here's how a rainbow happens: A beam of sunlight, making its long journey from space, plunges into the heart of a raindrop. As the beam pierces the outside of the drop, it bends a little. Acting

### FAST FACT

**You don't always need raindrops to make rainbows. Light can be refracted by fog or spray from the sea, too.**

like a prism, the raindrop bends (refracts) each color hidden in the white light a little more or a little less than the next. So as it enters the raindrop, the white beam suddenly splits apart into beautiful rays of color.

*Inside* the raindrop, the colored rays collide with the inside wall. This wall acts like a mirror, and bounces the light rays off it. Now, bent still more, they shoot back out of the raindrop through

*Raindrops can act like tiny prisms, splitting white light into the spectrum of colors.*

the same side they entered.

The sunlight had originally come from behind you. Now the changed light is coming back at you. Your eyes see a rainbow of colors in an arc across the sky— light bent and reflected by thousands and thousands of tiny raindrops.

Once in a great while, you may have the rare pleasure of seeing two rainbows appear at once. The second, larger and so pale it can barely be seen, has its colors reversed. The outer band is violet, and the inner band is red. A double rainbow is caused by beams of light being reflected twice inside each raindrop.

Because they are tricks of light, rainbows aren't "things" in the sky, like birds or clouds. Each person present sees a different rainbow (or, if he's lucky, double rainbow) made from the light rays streaming in from behind him and the raindrops in front of him. The rainbow you see is yours alone.

# Why is the color of a flame usually orange?

lames come in all colors. A wood fire in a fireplace dances with yellow, orange, red, white, blue. Colors in a flame depend on two things: the temperature of the fire and what material is being burned.

To see how color depends on temperature, picture a burner on an electric stove. Before it is turned on, the burner's round coils are cool and black.

Now imagine you want to heat some soup. You turn the burner on. The coils heat, and they begin to glow dull red. As they get hotter, they get redder. Finally, as the burner reaches its highest temperature, the coils turn bright orange-red.

Of course, the burner is not *really* burning—it's not on fire. It's just getting very hot. If it could get even hotter, it would change color even more dramatically. Instead of stopping at orange-red, it would become yellow, and then white, and then blue.

Blue would mean it was hottest of all.

Something similar happens in a flame. Take, for example, a candle flame. A candle flame flickers in several different colors, as the wick burns down through the melting wax.

Fire needs oxygen. (If you put a jar over a candle, the flame will die out.) When a candle is burning, the middle of the flame, near the bottom, isn't getting much oxygen. So it looks darker.

*A wood fire burns at a lower temperature than a candle.*

But the outside and top of the flame are getting lots of air. There, the flame burns brightly. As the wick burns down, and the candle's wax melts and sputters, tiny

Another Romantic Moment Spoiled by Fire Appreciation

I love candles too, but how about looking for the reflection in my eyes?

pieces of carbon—bits of candle burnt to a crisp—fly up. (Charcoal is a kind of carbon.) These teeny pieces of carbon are so hot, they glow—just like the burner on your stove.

In fact, they're hotter than the burner—more than 2,500°F. So instead of glowing red, they glow yellow. This is what makes candle flames mostly yellow. Near the burning wick, the flame is blue. That's because it's even *hotter* there, where the action is.

In a fireplace or campfire, we may see even more colors. A wood fire burns at a lower temperature than a candle. So it is usually more orange than yellow. Some carbon particles

in the fire, however, are very hot, and add yellow. (We can see them afterwards, when they've cooled, as black soot inside the chimney.)

Other colors in the fire come from the different chemical elements in the burning wood. There may be some sodium in the fire, for example. (Sodium is part of

---

**FAST FACT**

Minerals and metals, such as calcium, sodium, and copper, heated to high temperatures, are what give fireworks their color.

---

what makes up salt.) When sodium is heated, it gives off a clear yellow light.

And there may be some calcium, a mineral, in the fire. (We all know calcium—there's lots of it in milk.) Calcium gives off a deep red light when it is heated. If there's any phosphorus (another mineral), it will give off greenish light. All of these elements may be in the wood or in other materials thrown on the fire.

Finally, the mixing together of all these different colors in the fire can make white—just as a rainbow of colors put together makes up the white light from the Sun.

# Why are some oceans green and others blue ?

· · · · · · · · · · · · · · · · · · · · · · ·

**B**lue oceans. Green oceans. Colorless, clear drinking water. What color *is* water, anyway?

The surprising answer: Pure water is blue. But since there is so little water in a drinking glass, the color is too faint to see. Fill a clear glass building with the very same water, and we would see its true blue hue.

The color depends mainly on how water molecules absorb and reflect light. White light, such as sunlight, is made of a rainbow of colors, called a spectrum. Water molecules absorb much of the red-through-green part of the spectrum that travels through them. The blue part is reflected back out. So we see blue.

But not all water is the same color. Way out in the middle of the oceans, water is deep blue, almost purple.

Near land, however— along the Earth's coastlines— water color shades from blue to green to yellow-green. Why the difference? The answer has to do with what's floating in the water and how deep it is.

Near coastlines, ocean water is filled with tiny plants and bits of organic material washed off the land. Like green plants on land, these tiny plants, called phytoplankton, contain a chemical called chlorophyll. Chlorophyll absorbs most red and blue light, and reflects most green light. So some ocean water near coastlines appears green.

Seen from space, the colors of the oceans, like the colors of the land, show where Earth's life is concentrated. Green waters are like the tropical rainforests on the continents, full of life. Deep blue waters, with little life, are like the continents' empty white deserts.

# "We all live in a _____ Submarine...?"

The way water and the material floating in it absorb light changes colors underwater, too. Imagine you are piloting a yellow submarine. Near the water's surface, your submarine looks perfectly yellow. However, the deeper you dive, the more water light must pass through before it strikes your sub. By the time the sub is 100 feet below the surface, most of the yellow, orange, and red in the sunlight streaming down

*Deep blue ocean waters are like the continent's empty white deserts—there's not a lot of life in either.*

through the ocean has been absorbed by water molecules. What's left is mostly blue and green light. So instead of yellow, your submarine looks blue-green. Descend even farther, and most of the green disappears, too, leaving only a dim blue light.

Turbid ocean water—water with more material floating in it—absorbs more light than clear water. So cloudy waters get darker faster as you descend.

# Why do the Moon and the Sun seem to change colors?

Seen from space, as photographs taken by the astronauts show, our Moon is a gray-white ball, brilliantly lit by the Sun. And, glowing against the inky black of space, the Sun itself appears nearly white.

But when we look at the Moon from Earth, its color depends on where it is in the sky. When the Moon first peeks over the horizon, it may appear bright orange. Gradually, as the Earth turns and the Moon rises higher in the sky, its color steadily fades. The orange changes to yellow, then pales to a yellow-white, until finally, when it is directly overhead, the Moon is more nearly its true gray-white.

Similar tricks happen with the Sun. In the middle of the day, the Sun normally looks yellowish-white. But at sunrise and sunset, it may turn red or orange or pink. How come?

Our Moon and Sun are not really changing colors hour by hour, way out there in space. The clue is that the colors appear to change only when you look at either body through the Earth's atmosphere. Looking at the Moon or the Sun through air is like looking through a veil. Light, which has to pass through the air before it reaches our eyes, is changed by its trip.

*Dust, smoke, and pollutants redden the light that reaches our eyes.*

Nitrogen, oxygen, and other gases that make up our air, plus the tiny particles of dust, smoke, and pollutants that are always floating through, redden the light that reaches our eyes.

How does this work? The light that is produced inside the Sun is white. And moonlight, of course, is simply

COLOR & TRICKS OF LIGHT

**FAST FACT**

During forest fires, when smoke billows into the air for days, the rising Moon is often blood-red, and the sunsets and sunrises are spectacular.

reflected sunlight.

But, white light contains within it many colors—all the colors of the rainbow.

So sunlight is invisibly full of color as it zips through space at 186,000 miles a second. When it enters the Earth's atmosphere, some of the light slices cleanly through, reaching the ground without encountering a single air molecule—staying white.

But since the Earth's air is made of gas molecules, some of the light will run into these molecules on its way down. And when it does, light is scattered.

It is mostly bluer light that is scattered out of the beam of white light. (Why? See page 2.) So by the time sunlight reaches our eyes, the colors that are left in the beam are the warm ones. This makes the Sun look yellower to us than it actually is

The Sun looks closest to its true color when it is overhead. Then, its light must pass through only the air above us—air that becomes thinner and thinner higher up. So much of the sunlight reaches our eyes unscathed.

But when the Sun is near the horizon, its color changes dramatically. Then, its light must pass through the heavy blanket of air near the ground that extends from us to the horizon. Encountering many more air molecules than usual, as well as more dust and pollutants, even more of the blue end of the spectrum is scattered out of the light beam. This leaves mostly orange and red light in the beam by the time it reaches our eyes. And so we see the Sun as a fiery orange ball at sunrise and sunset.

# Make Your Own Harvest Moon

To see for yourself how the Moon or Sun changes color, try this. Fill a large, clear glass bowl, such as an empty fish bowl, with water. Now get a flashlight. Darken the room, switch on the flashlight, and shine it through the water. You should see the light as normal, nearly white.

Now pour a little milk into the water. Shine the light through. You should see the light redden through the swirling milk. Something similar happens when we see the Moon or the Sun through a layer of thick or polluted air.

The same thing happens with the Moon. This explains why we can go out early in the evening, when the Moon is near the horizon, and marvel at its bright-orange, harvest-moon color. Then, as the night wears on and the Moon climbs high in the sky, it pales to white. We are seeing more of the entire spectrum of moonlight—and that makes white.

The more polluted the air, the more spectacular the colors of the rising and setting Sun and Moon. (That's one advantage of living in a smoggy city, such as Los Angeles.)

# Where do stars get their colors?

ur star, the Sun, is the palest yellow. But stars come in a stunning array of colors. One cluster of stars is called "The Jewel Box." Set against the black velvet of space is a field of sapphire-blue stars, with one orange star glowing in their midst.

The different colors of stars depend on their very different temperatures. Here's how it works.

Light is radiation that travels in waves. The distance between the peak of one wave to the peak of the next is called (not surprisingly) the wavelength. Light waves are *very* short. How short? Imagine dividing an inch into 250,000 infinitesimal parts. A few of these parts, strung together, are the length of a light wave.

Even though a wavelength is impossibly tiny, a lit-

Where do Stars get their Color?

on the beach.... FABULOUS makeup artists... Tanning Salons?

tle more or less wave makes a big difference to what we see. That's because our eyes see different-length waves as different colors. Waves of red light, for example, are about one and a half times as long as waves of blue light. (White light is made up of many different wavelengths, or colors.)

---

**FAST FACT**

**Our yellowish sun is about 10,000°F at its surface. The exteriors of the hottest blue stars may be more than 60,000°F.**

---

We know from everyday experience that the color of an object may change as its temperature does. Take an iron poker put in a fire. As the cool black iron heats up, a faint reddish glow spreads over its surface. As it heats up further, the iron gets even redder. If you could heat the iron still hotter without melting it, the poker would turn from red to orange to yellow to white, and finally to blue-white.

Scientists have figured out the natural laws that tell how color and temperature are linked. As a material gets hotter, most of the radiation coming from it has more energy and shorter wavelengths.

We know that blue light has a shorter wavelength than red light. So a heated object giving off blue light should be hotter than one glowing red.

The atoms of the hot gases in a star emit particles of light, called photons. The hotter the gas, the higher the energy of the photons—and the shorter the wavelength of the light. So the hottest, youngest stars emit blue-white light. As stars use up their nuclear fuel, they tend to cool off. Consequently, elderly, cooling stars usually give off red light. Middle-aged stars, such as the Sun, glow yellow.

Our Sun is only 93 million miles away; we can easily see

*You can estimate the age of a star by its color.*

what color it is. But stars beyond the Sun are trillions and more miles distant, and it's hard to tell—even through the most powerful telescopes—exactly what color they are. So scientists let incoming starlight pass through special filters, or through an instrument called a spectrograph. These reveal how much light of each wavelength is coming from a star.

Astronomers determine the overall color of the star by noting which wavelength of light registers as most intense. Once they know the color, they can figure out the surface temperature, using a simple mathematical formula. And from the temperature, they can also get a good idea of the star's age.

# What is the aurora borealis and what causes it ?

An *aurora* is a multicolored glow in the night sky. A typical aurora is a shimmering curtain of blue-green light, with patches of pink and red. These ribbons of color may be more than 100 miles wide, and can stretch for 1,000 miles. Dancing like flames in the dark sky, an aurora is a planet's own light show.

Auroras appear on Earth, but are triggered by events on the faraway Sun. Here's how it works.

The Sun is a glowing ball of gas made mostly of hydrogen and helium atoms. All atoms have particles called protons at their centers. These are orbited by other particles called electrons. Protons have a positive electrical charge, while electrons

*You can see an aurora almost every night at the North Pole.*

are negatively charged.

The halo of superhot gas surrounding the Sun—called the *corona*—is constantly expanding into space, sending bits and pieces of atoms off in every direction. This is what we call the solar wind, made mostly of protons and electrons zipping along at up to 600 miles a second. Meanwhile, solar flares shoot violently out of the Sun now and then, releasing a gust of new particles into the "wind."

When the solar particles near Earth, they start to feel the effects of our planet's strong magnetic field. The Earth is like a giant magnet, with lines of magnetic force curving out into space and converging near the North and South poles. (Its magnetism is be-lieved to be caused by electric currents created by the rotation of the Earth's iron core. To see how magnetic fields work, hide a bar magnet under a piece of paper. Now sprinkle iron filings or tiny iron nails onto the paper. They should line up in curving lines around the magnet, showing the shape of the magnet's force field.)

The Earth's magnetic force lines attract passing charged particles from the

Sun, pulling them in. Pulled-in particles travel in "beams" along the lines, which bend back to Earth at the magnetic poles (which are near but not at the North and South poles).

As the particles travel along the invisible lines, they are unceremoniously dumped into Earth's atmosphere in the far north and south. Now the fun begins.

Our atmosphere is made mostly of nitrogen and oxygen. When electrons and protons stream in from the Sun, they collide with nitrogen and oxygen atoms high up in the air. Some of these atoms lose some of their own electrons, and others get "excited," gaining energy.

Aurora Borealis (Suggested Improvements)

① Add Music (all good light shows are orchestrated.)

② Refreshments (what's a show without something to eat?)

③ Timing (Regularly scheduled solar flares - preferably on weekends.)

When these atoms return to normal after their run-in with the solar protons and electrons, they give off photons of light. Nitrogen that has lost electrons emits violet and blue light. And excited nitrogen glows a deep red. Excited oxygen gives off green and red light. So the charged particles from the Sun cause the air to shimmer in many colors. This is the aurora. The glow near the North Pole is called the *aurora borealis* (it's

*Charged particles from the Sun cause the air to shimmer in many colors.*

also known as the Northern Lights). The glow near the

South Pole is named the *aurora australis* (and also called—you guessed it—the Southern Lights).

An aurora appears almost nightly at the North Pole, and 20 to 200 times a year in northern Scandinavia and North America. There are even five to ten auroras each year near latitudes as far south as those of London, Paris, and Seattle—and the ghostly lights have even been seen in Mexico.

# On hot days, why do we of water on the road

A patch of water shimmers on the road ahead, only to disappear as your car nears. A freighter appears to hang upside down in the sky over Lake Michigan. A medieval castle, complete with turrets, towers over the ocean.

What do these visions have in common? All are mirages. And all are caused by the peculiar dance of light and air. Mirages can be simple, like the familiar pool of water on a hot highway. Or they can be startlingly elaborate.

In 1643, an Italian priest named Angelucci described an incredible vision he had seen at the ocean. At first, he said, the ocean stretched out calmly to the horizon. But as

he watched, a dark line of mountains suddenly rose up out of the water.

## Mirages are not imaginary; they've even been photographed.

In front of the mountains, thousands of dirty white columns sprang up from nowhere. Soon, the columns shrank, and finally curved over into Roman arches. Then, in a kind of grand finale, giant castles, studded with windows and towers, grew on

top of the arches.

What the priest saw was a kind of towering, complicated mirage called a *fata morgana*. (Fata means "fairy" in Italian. In legend, Morgan le Fay was King Arthur's sister. Her special talent was creating castles that hung suspended in the air.)

Air is indeed the magic ingredient in all mirages. Air molecules bend light. How sharply light bends depends on the air's thickness. For air at roughly the same pressure, thickness depends mainly on temperature. Hot air is usually thinner than cold air, because its molecules are more energetic and spread further apart. (Molecules move less as the temperature drops.)

Images glimpsed through the lens of our atmosphere

# see an imaginary patch ahead?

can be badly out of focus, out of place, magnified, shrunk, or even upside-down. This is because light rays curve as they travel through warm, then cool air, or vice versa.

The water on the road is a good example. Heat rising from sun-baked asphalt warms the air above the road. Sunlight streaming down from the sky passes from a layer of cooler, thicker air into the hot, thin air just above the road.

Thinner air means fewer gas molecules for light to run into. As the leading edge of a light wave enters the hotter air, its way is clearer, so it speeds up. But the rest of the wave, still in the thicker air, lags, making a kink in the wave. The light wave has bent so it is now traveling along

FATA CASTLE Straight ahead

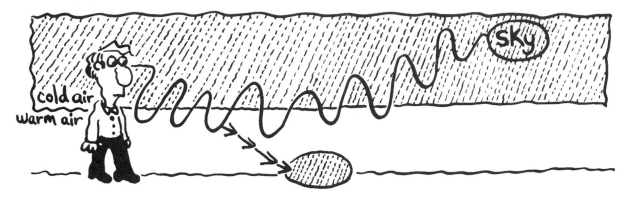

the ground, with the bottom half of the wave in hot air and the top still in cool air. The dragging of the slower top half makes the wave kink again, bending it upward—toward your eyes.

Since the light was carrying the image of the sky, you see sky where asphalt should be. And since hot air is full of movement, the "sky" appears to shimmer and looks like water. But as you drive nearer, the image moves down the road, always out of reach.

Mirages can work backwards, casting images from the ground into the sky. This can happen on a lake or ocean, where a cool, thick layer of air often hangs under a heated layer. In this case,

*Light waves curve as they travel through warm, then cool air.*

light rays bouncing off the water may bend up into the sky and then back down to us. A real sailboat hidden below the horizon may suddenly loom gigantic in the sky, sailing by in the clouds.

Fantastic images can be created even out of a flat,

calm sea, as light bending this way and that throws pieces of the ocean into the sky. The mountains, columns, and castles that appeared before Father Angelucci were really shimmering slices of the sea, cast up in a hodge-podge of angles.

Hazy, air-borne castles, as well as many other mirages, have even been photographed. Mirages, after all, are not imaginary; they are images, sometimes distorted, of real objects. So the thirsty desert traveler is not hallucinating when he "sees" an oasis of water just ahead. But crawling toward it, he will find it ever retreating, a ghost of the sky brought to the desert floor.

# Why do stars twinkle?

Actually, stars themselves don't twinkle. Stars appear to twinkle when they are very far away *and* when their light must pass through air on its way to our eyes. If we happened to be someplace where there is no atmosphere, even the stars that are the farthest

*As starlight passes through thicker then thinner air, it appears to shimmer.*

away wouldn't twinkle.

For example, astronauts on the Moon, which has no atmosphere, saw a sky filled with stars, all shining with a steady light. But back here on Earth, which is covered with a thick blanket of air, starlight bends this way and that as it makes it way down to the ground.

Why? Above and around us, masses of air are always moving. Warm air rises, and cold air sinks. Air bends light to differing degrees depending on its thickness. So as starlight passes through thinner then thicker air, it appears to shimmer. This makes the image of the stars larger, less sharp. And it makes starlight change quickly in intensity: First bright, then dim, then bright again, as though the star were sparkling. This change in intensity is called *scintillation*. We call the whole effect twinkling.

Not all objects in the night sky twinkle, however. Planets reflect sunlight, and they seem to shine with a steady light. Venus and Mars, for example, look like big, bright stars—without the twinkle.

Why? Because the planets are closer to Earth, we see them as tiny disks rather than as single points of light. Light coming from all parts of the disk is still bent by the air. But the disk is made of so

*One way to distinguish a planet from a star: Planets don't twinkle.*

many individual points of light, some of them brightening while others dim, that the total average intensity doesn't really change. So the planets seem to shine steadily. In fact, that's a good way to tell that you are looking at a planet, not a star. Only when its light passes through very turbulent, thick air will a planet appear to twinkle.

Our Sun is a star. But since it is so much closer to us than the stars we see at night, we see it as a large, steadily shining disk. If the

Sun were to move trillions of miles away, it would be lost among all the other stars in the night sky. And we would see it twinkling, just like the rest.

Twinkling may be beautiful, but it is a real headache for astronomers. Even if the sky is clear, the air can be very turbulent. The work of observing and photographing the stars is made very difficult when their bright images dance this way and that.

Good nights for studying the stars come when the air calms down. When the atmosphere above a telescope holds nearly steady, astronomers say "the seeing is good tonight."

The problem of twinkling is one reason why astronomers are so excited by telescopes orbiting high above the Earth, such as the Hubble Space Telescope. Free of the Earth's atmosphere, such telescopes can send back clear images of the stars from the steady light they receive.

# Forces & Particles

Everything—you, this book, the stars—is made of atoms. An average atom is about eight-billionths of an inch across. To get an idea of how small that is, a page of this book, which feels so thin, is about 500,000 atoms thick.

In each tiny atom, whizzing electrons orbit a bundle of protons and neutrons, rather like planets orbit a star. The atom is held together by the electromagnetic force, one of four basic forces in the universe. Negatively charged electrons are attracted to positively charged protons, so they tend to stay in orbit. (The same electromagnetic force makes lightning zig-zag down through the sky.)

Gravity, the attraction of matter to matter, is the force that keeps planets in orbit, and makes your shoe drop to the floor when it falls off your foot. We notice gravity more than electromagnetism, but the electrical force is by far the stronger. The force attracting (or repelling) charged particles in an atom is 1,000,000,000,000,000,000,000,000,000,000,000,000 times as strong as the gravitational force between particles in the same atom.

In an atom's center, an even more powerful force, called the strong force, binds protons and neutrons into a tight clump. A fourth force, the weak force, plays a role when an atom's center falls apart in a burst of radioactivity.

# Why are bubbles round?

 e've all admired bubbles—especially soap bubbles, with their perfectly round shape and shimmery colors. One British scientist, C.V. Boys, was so intrigued that he wrote a 200-page book called *Soap-Bubbles, Their Colours and the Forces Which Mould Them.*

Boys called bubbles "magnificent objects," and pointed out that the force that holds bubbles together is present in all liquids—you can't pour tea, turn off a dripping tap, or wade in a pond without encountering it.

Imagine filling a balloon with water. The rubbery skin of the balloon stretches and stretches as more water is added. It can only stretch so far, however, until it bursts.

Now think about a drop of water. Picture a drop collecting at the end of a faucet. It hangs, growing bigger and bigger. Finally, after it has reached a certain size, it falls off. Why, Boys asked, does the water hang at the end of the faucet at all? It is as if, he said, the water were hanging in a little elastic bag, like the balloon. Then, it is as if the elastic bag breaks or tears away when too much water fills inside.

There isn't really a bag around a water drop. But something, Boys said, must be holding the drop together in much the same way as an invisible skin would.

This "something"—a property of water and other liquids—is called surface tension. Take water. Water molecules under the surface are strongly attracted to each other. Surface water molecules, however, are not attracted to the air molecules above them. They are only attracted downward and inward, toward the rest of the water. This "surface tension" creates the effect of a skin on the water.

The "skin" keeps the water hanging on the end of the faucet—until finally, it gets so heavy it breaks off.

Different liquids have "skins" that are stronger or weaker, Boys pointed out. Alcohol, for example, has a weaker surface tension than water, and doesn't form drops as well. But liquid mercury, which skids across the floor in beads from a broken thermometer, has six times the surface tension of water.

## *Liquid mercury has six times the surface tension of water.*

Surface tension also holds soap bubbles together. When you dip a wand into a soapy solution and then pull it out, you see a thin film stretched across the wand. Blow into it, and surface tension makes the soapy film stretch like an elastic skin. The film closes around the air, and the bubble pops out and floats away.

Because of the elastic "skin" of a bubble, the air inside a soap bubble is under pressure—like the air inside a balloon. The strength of the pressure depends on how tightly the bubble is curved. The tighter the curve, the smaller the bubble, and the more force on the air within. Boys did experiments that showed that air, rushing out of a soap bubble like air jetting out of a balloon, can blow out a candle flame.

But why is the bubble round? The answer is that the surface tension causes the liquid film to pull itself into the most compact shape possible. The most compact shape in nature is a ball (and not a rectangle, for instance). So the air inside is held neatly in by the same force all around the bubble. (At least until the bubble bursts.)

But, Boys noted, with effort bubbles can be made that are not perfectly round. For example, if you take a soap bubble between two rings and tug on either side, you can pull the bubble into the shape of a cylinder. The bigger such non-round bubbles are, the more unstable. A long cylinder will soon develop a "waist" and break apart into two spherical bubbles.

# When you turn a wet some drops stick to the

What do drops clinging to a glass, insects walking on water, and icicles forming under your house's eaves in winter have in common? Stay tuned.

First, a look at how liquids behave: Like people in a crowd, the molecules in a liquid, such as water, slip and slide around each other. This is what enables liquids to flow into all the nooks and crannies of a container, taking its shape. While they move more freely than molecules in a solid, molecules in a liquid are nonetheless attracted to each other. (However, water molecules are not as strongly attracted to one another as the molecules in some other liquids, such as honey. That's why honey is thick and syrupy, and flows slowly, while water is thin and moves quickly.)

*Water is very attracted to glass, but it flees from waxed paper.*

Since the molecules in a liquid share some attraction, liquids, like solids, have surfaces. (The molecules in gases, on the other hand, fly apart in all directions. When water turns to steam—a gas—it no longer has any surface.)

On the surface of a liquid, the way molecules are held together by their mutual attraction is called "surface tension." (Surface tension is the reason certain insects can walk on water. Their bodies are very light, and the surface tension of the water keeps them from breaking through.)

Surface tension is also what draws water into rounded drops. Water molecules are attracted to other water molecules, but not to the air molecules around them. So a small amount of water can form a springy ball. (For more on surface tension, see page 26.)

When you have finished your glass of water, leftover droplets tend to stay in the glass when you turn it over because the water molecules,

# glass over, why do bottom and sides?

while not attracted to air, are *very* attracted to the molecules in the glass. The biggest drops may slide out anyway, as gravity drags them earthward. But the smallest and lightest drops will stubbornly cling, their

*Adding soap to water reduces its surface tension.*

surface molecules and the glass's locked in a kind of electrical embrace. In fact, water is so fond of glass that it often spreads out, wetting the glass, rather than converging into drops. When you try to shake it out, it may run

## Drip, Drip, Drip: Icicle

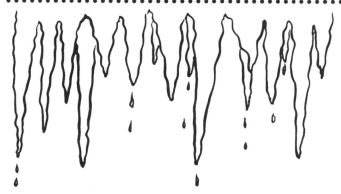

**B**ecause of surface tension, and because one water molecule is attracted to the next, beautiful icicles can form in winter.

How? Water from melting snow collects in drops on the edge of a gutter. It is held together by surface tension and is also attracted to the metal gutter. As the temperature drops, some of the water

freezes solid there.

Other drops, pulled down by gravity, run down the ice. But because they are attracted to their fellow water molecules in the ice, only the heaviest fall to the ground. The rest collect at the tip, and freeze there.

Ice adds to ice, drip by drip. Soon, there is a long, pointy icicle, shining in the sun.

around the edge of the glass, holding on for dear life. (Water is not attracted to just any old solid. It will bead into drops and slide right off waxed paper, for example.)

*Surface tension is the reason certain insects can walk on water.*

There is one way that you can get nearly all the water to come out of a glass: Use some soap. Soap and detergent reduce water's surface tension. In the washing machine, detergent prevents water from beading up on the surface of clothing. The water soaks into the clothes, so the soap can sink in, too. If you add a little soapy water to your glass, fewer drops will form and more will slide out.

# How come the planets, the Sun, and other stars are round?

Our sky is filled with round objects. During the day the Sun's face is a circle. At night our Moon is a silver ball, and we know the planets and stars are spheres, too. The thousands of round shapes make us wonder: Why aren't stars really pointy, as they appear to be when they twinkle? Or why isn't there at least one planet shaped like a cube, or a pyramid?

The reason? There is a force that smoothes worlds into balls everywhere in the universe. That force is gravity.

Gravity is the attraction of every bit of matter to every other bit. It's what pulls base- balls down from the sky, and holds whole planets together. The more matter an object has, the stronger its gravitational pull. However, compared to other forces, such as electromagnetism, gravity isn't very strong. That's why we don't detect the gravitational attraction between two people, or between your hand and your pencil. There's just not very much matter in a pencil—or in a person.

However, drop your pencil, and you'll see gravity in action. The pencil falls down towards the Earth—not up, and not sideways. That's because the Earth's gravity is pulling it. Compared to a pencil, the Earth is an enormous body, a lot of matter in one place with a lot of pull.

To feel the force between you and the Earth, just jump into the air. Tugging you back down is the attraction of your body to all the matter in the Earth.

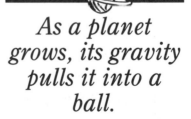

*As a planet grows, its gravity pulls it into a ball.*

Gravity pulls things together. Our nine planets formed from collisions of bits of material, about 4.6 billion years ago. As they got larger, their gravity tended to pull in smaller pieces of material and add them to the mass. (You can see this happening still when a meteor streaks down from the sky, tugged toward the Earth.)

As a planet grows, its gravity tends to pull it into a ball. The bigger the world gets, the stronger its gravity. New bits get pulled in—and flattened down. Eventually, there is a rounded body.

*On Mars, the gravity is one-third as strong as on Earth, and the mountains are up to three times as tall.*

Although gravity makes ball-shaped planets, they are still bumpy. From space, the Earth looks like a nearly per-fect blue-white sphere. But as we get closer, we see that there are high mountains poking up from the surface. Get closer still, and we notice buildings, and people.

The Earth doesn't have enough mass to flatten a per-son—or a mountain. But there is a limit on just how big mountains can grow, since a planet's crust must be able to support the weight.

One of our next-door neighbors, Mars, is a smaller planet, with only one-third the gravity of Earth. In part because the pull of Mars is less, said James Pollock, a NASA planetary scientist, nat-ural structures can get very high. For example, Olympus Mons, one mountain on Mars, is 78,000 feet tall. That's almost as high as three Mt. Everests piled on top of each other. (Olympus Mons, or Mt. Olympus, is named after the mythical Greek mountain so high that it was home to gods.)

On a much more massive world than Mars or Earth,

New and Different Sunset

with, say, 10 times the gravity of Earth, surface features would be flatter. And tall ani-mals, such as long-necked giraffes, wouldn't do well. Short, squat animals might roam the landscape.

Sometimes, the gravity of one object in space can change the shape of another nearby. One blue supergiant star, scientists think, has an invisible companion circling it—a black hole. A black hole (sometimes formed by a collapsed star) is an object whose gravity is so strong that not even light can escape.

Pulled by the black hole, a stream of gases pours out from the star—and into the hole. As the invisible black hole orbits, the star's bulk is tugged this way and that, distorting its round shape. (For more on black holes, see page 86.)

On the other hand, small, lightweight objects in space are often not even remotely round to begin with. With so little mass, their gravity isn't strong enough to pull them into a ball. So some asteroids look like flying mountains. And Phobos, one of the moons of Mars, is shaped like an Idaho potato.

# Gravity, Gravity Everywhere

Even though the gravity we feel most strongly is the Earth's, other bodies are tugging at us from the sky—the Moon, the Sun, the other planets, and even the distant stars. Although gravity's effect diminishes with distance, distant bodies visibly affect the Earth. The Moon's gravity makes tides in the oceans, and the Sun's gravity makes the Earth circle it year after year.

In fact, scientists think there is no limit to gravity's range. Even at an infinite distance, there is still a miniscule attraction between two objects. We can get so far out into the emptiness of space that we are almost weightless. (Weight is actually a measure of the force gravitiy exerts on something.) But since every bit of matter pulls on every other bit, we would still be imperceptibly pulled this way and that by some distant star or planet.

# How come stars don't fall?

Look up: There's the ceiling, or the sky. Look down: There's the floor, or the Earth. "Up" and "down"—we use the words every day without thinking.

We say "what goes up, must come down." A ball soars into the air, but soon falls back to Earth. Yet we see stars high in the night sky. Why don't they tumble down, like the ball?

But wait a minute. Are "up" and "down" really what they seem? If we fly to the South Pole—Antarctica—we won't be hanging upside down. No matter where we go on our round planet, the sky will still be up above our head, the ground down beneath our feet.

What we call "down" has a lot to do with gravity. Things fall towards the Earth—what we call "down"—because they are attracted by the Earth's gravity.

But when we get away from the Earth, directions like up and down lose a lot of their meaning. Floating in space, there is no up or down—just the vast, empty distances between the planets and stars.

Because there is virtually no gravity tugging him down, an astronaut in a space shuttle is weightless. He can walk on the roof of the shuttle or walk on the floor, and neither will seem like "up" or "down." These directions depend on how we are oriented in a gravitational field. When there is little gravity, there is little or no sense of "up" and "down."

That all changes, however, as the astronaut prepares the shuttle for landing, and

*"Falling" or "shooting" stars are actually meteors, rocky or icy fragments tugged in from space by Earth's gravity.*

Why Don't Stars Fall?

oh!

extra strong Scotch tape

PURE STAR

PURE EPOXY

willpower

Invisible String

the craft is pulled in by the Earth's gravity. As the shuttle begins falling towards the surface of the planet, the astronaut will remember what "down" means.

Just as each planet has its force of gravity, so does each huge star in space. This enormous gravity is what keeps the nine planets in our solar system, including the Earth, orbiting our star, the Sun. (For more on how gravity affects orbits, see page 102.)

The stars in the night sky are so far away—trillions and trillions of miles—that the attraction between them and the Earth is very tiny. But if

*In space, there's no such thing as up or down.*

they were somehow moved closer, it would be the Earth that fell towards them, and not the other way around.

Stars don't fall to Earth, but meteorites sometimes do—those rocky or icy objects tugged in from space by the Earth's gravity, often doing a spectacular burn as they plunge through the atmosphere. That's what people—mistakenly, but romantically—call "falling stars."

# How do scientists know there are such things as atoms ?

The idea that everything is made of atoms has been around since at least the 5th century B.C., when a Greek philosopher named Democritus suggested that matter was made up of tiny, moving particles. But there was no way to know whether atoms existed; the idea just seemed to make sense.

For centuries afterwards, the notion of atoms was kicked around, but it wasn't always very popular. Then in the 1800s, atoms once again appeared on the scientific hit parade.

Scientists come up with models that help to explain reality. The atom was such a model. Even though no one could see atoms, the idea of them kept popping up because it helped explain what scientists were seeing both in their experiments and in the natural world.

The model *worked*—even if no one could prove it was true. For example, in the early 1800s, the British chemist John Dalton was studying chemical reactions, and he found that when two substances combine in a reaction, they do so in certain fixed proportions. For example, one part oxygen to two parts hydrogen makes water.

*Scientists believed in the existence of atoms a long time before they could prove it.*

This suggested that there were identical, equal-weight atoms of one substance linking up with different equal-weight atoms of another substance. (In the case of water, one atom of oxygen bonds to two hydrogen atoms.) The atom model helped explain

If it jiggles, it has atoms...

Pollen in a glass of water...

dust in a beam of light...

Kids five minutes before the final bell.

what Dalton was seeing in his chemistry experiments.

And there was more evidence for atoms: If you look at tiny particles in water, such as pollen grains, through a microscope, you will see them jiggling. Why? Well, scientists reasoned, maybe because they are being bombarded by moving atoms, or atoms grouped into molecules (in this case, water molecules).

Scientists who believed in atoms thought they were little balls of electrically charged particles—positive and nega-

tive particles nicely mixed together, making the whole atom neutral. But then a New Zealand scientist, Ernest Rutherford, did some experiments in 1907 that showed that this model wasn't quite right.

Rutherford shot high-speed, positively charged particles at gold foil. He assumed they would travel right through. And some of them did. But others ricocheted back at the experimenters— as if they had been powerfully repelled by something in the foil. Rutherford was amazed.

He said it was like firing a mortar shell at a piece of tissue paper—and having it bounce back and hit you!

Rutherford's experiment helped further prove the existence of atoms and what they must be like. It showed that positive and negative charges weren't mixed together in homogenous balls. Otherwise, his positive particles wouldn't have been repelled, since they would have encountered only nice, neutral balls.

Instead, there is a clump of particles at the center of an

# Seeing Atoms—and Pushing Them Around

While scientists have long known that atoms exist, they were frustrated because they couldn't actually see them. Now, scientists can call up images of actual atoms on a computer screen, and move the real atoms around on a surface, by using a special instrument called a scanning tunneling microscope (STM).

It's impossible to see atoms using ordinary microscopes, because atoms are so tiny—about 4 to 16 billionths of an inch across. A hair on your arm is a million times wider than an atom. Nor can we use visible light to illuminate an atom—a wavelength of ordinary light is about 2,000 to 5,000 times wider than the atom itself.

But an STM is not something you look through. It's a computerized tool with a tip that can be moved ever-so-carefully just above a material's surface. As the tip moves, electrons jump across the gap between the tip and the surface, creating a tiny electric current. This current changes as the distance between the tip and the surface changes. A surface that looks smooth is actually bumpy at the atomic level. The tip passes over individual atoms, which are like hills on the surface. The computer maps the surface of the material, creating an image of its atoms. Voilà; we can "see" atoms.

Scientists have also been able to use STMs to manipulate atoms. First, they cool atoms to about 453°F below zero—near what scientists call "absolute zero," when atoms barely move. Using the STM tip like you could use a magnet to move a pin—without touching it—scientists have nudged atoms into patterns that spelled words. The words were a kind of Braille, which could only be read by using the STM.

atom, where positively charged protons—and neutral neutrons—are located. Negatively charged electrons orbit this nucleus, at a considerable distance. Since the positive and negative charges balance out, the whole atom is indeed electrically neutral—it has no charge.

But the nucleus itself is a clump of positive charge. And some of Rutherford's positive particles had passed too near to the gold atoms' positive centers. Since positive charges repel each other, the

*Protons and neutrons, small as they are, are thought to be made up of even smaller particles, called quarks.*

particles that came near atomic centers bounced back

at Rutherford—telling him something important about the way atoms are made.

Today, scientists think that protons and neutrons are made of even smaller particles, called quarks. Quarks are a newer model to explain how an atom works. And just like the scientists who tried to get evidence for the atom model, today's scientists are trying to prove quarks exist.

# How small are air molecules?

When we think of the Earth's air, we think of oxygen. However, our planet's atmosphere is a mixture of many gases. Grab an air molecule at random, and chances are, it's a nitrogen molecule—about 77 percent of the air is made of this gas. Oxygen makes up about 21 percent more. Traces of other gases, plus water vapor, make up the rest.

These other gases include carbon dioxide (used to make soda fizzy), neon (used in electric signs), helium (used in balloons), methane, krypton, nitrous oxide (the "laughing gas" used by dentists), hydrogen, ozone, and xenon.

The gas molecules, from the common to the exotic, are

*Imagine dividing one inch into a billion parts. One of those parts is about the size of an air molecule.*

fairly evenly mixed in the air (although much of the ozone is concentrated in a thin layer about 15 miles up). They whiz around us at from 700 to more than 3,000 miles an hour, way too small for the naked eye to see. Even as you read this, a molecule of kryp-

ton may zip up your nose.

Molecules are bunches of atoms, rather like bunches of grapes. The more atoms glommed together, the bigger the molecule. (A molecule of water has two hydrogen atoms and one oxygen atom. But some large molecules, such as the DNA found in body cells, are made of tens of millions of atoms.)

Most air molecules—of whatever variety—are very, very small. For example, an oxygen molecule is made up of two oxygen atoms, and a nitrogen molecule is made of two nitrogen atoms. Each of them measures a few hundred millionths or billionths of an inch across. It's very hard to imagine dividing an inch into a billion parts. But we can get some sense of the

If the Atoms in your body were as big as grains of salt... would you be...

Tall enough to touch the moon?

with a step ladder, maybe...

Bigger than New York?

including the boroughs, possibly...

Able to walk cross country in fifteen minutes...?

California

In between

New York

at a fast pace, perhaps...

size of air molecules by comparing them with salt crystals, as scientists Gerald Feinberg and Robert Shapiro did in their book *Life Beyond Earth.*

Spill a little salt on the table in front of you, then try to separate out one tiny crystal. Now imagine yourself shrinking down, down, down, like Alice in Wonderland. The single crystal of salt seems to grow before your eyes until it becomes the size of a baby's block. As you shrink more, the salt crystal grows to the size of a house. Go on shrinking, and the salt crystal towers above, stretching into the sky like the Empire State Building.

But you still haven't shrunk enough to get an idea of how the size of an air molecule compares with a grain of salt. As you feel yourself getting smaller and smaller, the top of the salt crystal disappears from view. Now the grain of salt is as tall as 100 Empire State Buildings, one on top of the other.

Suddenly, you see what looks like a gumball speed by your head. Reach out and grab it, if you can. In the palm of your hand, rattling around, is the gumball—really an air molecule. Compare it to the grain of salt, 100 skyscrapers high. That's how small an air molecule is.

# If solids, like glass and packed molecules, how

First, a few words about solids, liquids, and gases: In a solid, the molecules are *very* attracted to each other—they really stick together. That's why solids have definite shapes, such as a block or a ball. But even though the molecules in a solid hold tight to each other, they are always vibrating a little. (Nothing in nature stands completely still.)

In a liquid, the molecules are held more loosely together. They slip and slide past each other. That's why a liquid flows, and how it can spread out to fit its container.

But in a gas, molecules are not attracted to each other. They fly off in all directions, zipping around at high

*Glass absorbs photons, then emits photons traveling in the same direction.*

speeds. (The average speed of hydrogen atoms in air at 32°F is 3,600 miles per hour.) And there's a lot of empty space between the molecules. You can walk right through a gas, and not even notice it's there.

Temperature is mainly what determines whether a material will take the form of a solid, liquid, or gas. At the everyday air pressure on the surface of the earth, water is

solid—ice—at or below 32°F. Between 32 and 212°F, water is a liquid. At and above 212°F, water is a gas: steam, spreading into the kitchen above a boiling teakettle.

You might assume that you should be able to see through gases, but not through solids. However, some solids, such as glass, are as clear as air. How come?

To make a long story short, light is absorbed when it hits the molecules of most solids. Some of the light's energy ends up staying in the solid, as heat. Most of the light, however, is reflected: sent back out the way it came. So you see the solid object, but you can't see through it.

But glass is a peculiar kind of solid. Glass molecules absorb photons of light, but then emit photons of light

# ice, are made of tightly can we see through them?

Liquids, Solids + Gases "DANCE" Contest!

1st prize "Slow Dance to Solids!"

2nd prize "FAST DANCE" to GASES!

3rd Prize "Variable speed" DANCE to Liquids!

traveling in the same direction as the original photons. So glass is transparent—light passes straight through.

In water and other nearly colorless liquids, it's a similar story. Most of the light coming through is passed on by the molecules. Some is absorbed, heating the liquid.

In gases, where molecules are often far apart, light can travel a long way without even meeting a molecule. In fact, much sunlight makes it all the way to the Earth by passing through empty spaces between molecules in the atmosphere.

Light that does encounter a gas molecule is scattered. White light enters the molecule, where it is broken up into its rainbow of colors. When the colors emerge, blue light comes out strongest. So gases, such as those in the Earth's sky, may look blue. But they are still considered transparent.

# How come some atoms are radioactive?

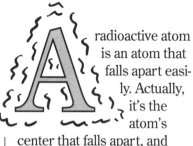

A radioactive atom is an atom that falls apart easily. Actually, it's the atom's center that falls apart, and hurls particles outward.

The center of an atom—its nucleus—is a bundle of protons and neutrons (except for the nucleus of the simplest kind of hydrogen atom, which has one lone proton). Surrounding the nucleus is a cloud of electrons.

Protons have a positive electrical charge; neutrons have no charge at all. The nucleus is positively charged because of its protons.

Electrons have a negative charge. What keeps them whirling around the nucleus is their attraction to the protons. But particles with the same charge repel each other. So inside the nucleus, protons have a tendency to push away from other protons.

This isn't a problem in most small atoms, which have only a few protons. But some

Ralph bought a radioactive toupee...

The Radioactive Toupee
The directions said...

NEAT!

DANGER
Keep in
Lead box

...And he did.

atoms are unstable, especially the larger ones (like uranium-238, with 92 protons). Sometimes, the center doesn't hold. These atoms are said to be radioactive.

"Radioactive" means the atom spews some particles from its center. What's left after a rickety nucleus has spat out some particles is a new nucleus, called a "daughter." The daughter nucleus may be stable, and then everything is fine. But depending on the number of protons left, the daughter may be as unstable as its mother. In that case, the daughter will fling out more particles, and a new daughter will form. This process continues until a stable daughter atom is left.

There are three basic kinds of radiation emitted by unstable atoms: alpha, beta, and gamma. Alpha particles have two protons and two neutrons each. These little bundles are lobbed out of such elements as uranium-238. Compared to other kinds of radiation, alphas are jumbo particles. They can't get through paper, and are too big to penetrate the dead cells on the surface of your skin.

However, that doesn't mean alpha particles are harmless. An intense dose can burn. And if you inhale or swallow an alpha emitter, like some uranium-238, alpha particles can seriously damage the inside of your body.

Beta particles are electrons made inside the nucleus when a neutron is changed into a proton and an electron. The out-of-place electrons are cast out of the nucleus, leaving the protons behind.

Beta particles are only 1/7,000th the size of alpha par-

*Inside an atom's nucleus, protons have a tendency to repel each other.*

ticles, so they can do more damage. They zip right through paper, but are stopped cold by wood. Beta particles can bore into the skin, but will be trapped in the skin's layers. They can cause severe burns, and, if let loose inside the body, extensive internal damage.

The third kind of radiation emitted from unstable atoms is gamma rays: high-energy photons, similar to X-rays. They race through paper and wood; only a thick concrete wall or a slab of lead stops them. Gamma rays will slip through the skin and into the body, damaging cells as they go, and pass out the other side.

---

**FAST FACT**

Reactions in the centers of atoms make energy in both nuclear power plants, where the nuclei are split apart, and in stars, where nuclei are fused together.

---

# How can X-rays take pictures of your bones ?

......................

Remember Superman's X-ray vision? Superman's eyes shot X-ray beams at a door; the beams bored through the door, and he could see what his enemies were up to on the other side. Only doors made of lead could foil Superman.

Well, they got the last part right. Lead is a good shield against X-rays. That's why we wear heavy lead aprons when the dentist X-rays our teeth.

But Superman's X-ray eyes came from the imagination of his creator. Eyes can't shoot beams of light, X-ray or otherwise. Our eyes see when light from other sources, such as the Sun, is reflected back to us from an object.

However, X-rays are indeed a kind of light—but a kind that is invisible to us. (There are many kinds of light that we can't see, including gamma rays, radio waves, and ultraviolet light.) X-ray light has a lot more energy than visible light. That's how it can penetrate wooden doors—or skin and muscle.

Like weakly-thrown balls, photons (particles) of visible light bounce right off skin. But high-energy X-ray photons push right through. To an X-ray, skin cells are just big, watery, see-through sacs.

## FAST FACT

**Although X-ray light is invisible to humans and animals, some animals can see other kinds of light that are invisible to us. For example, rattlesnakes can detect infrared light, and spiders can see the glow of ultraviolet.**

But bone is much denser than skin. Instead of slipping straight through, most X-ray photons are stopped in their tracks when they encounter bone. So X-rays can take pictures of bones through skin like we take photos of a fish through water. Skin is transparent in X-ray light.

Here's how it works: Let's say the doctor wants a picture of the bones in your hand, to see if any are broken. Your hand is sandwiched between an X-ray machine and a piece of film that has never been exposed to light.

The X-ray machine is

## *X-ray light has a lot more energy than visible light.*

turned on, and photons of X-ray light stream through your skin. Some pass by your bones, going right through your hand and into the film. Those that meet bone

screech to a stop. When the film is developed, it shows the outline of your bones. If a bone is badly cracked, some X-rays will make it through the crack to the film, and the doctor will see that you have a broken bone.

Since X-rays can push through skin, they can damage cells. That's why doctors take as few pictures as possible—to avoid injuring healthy cells while they find out what's wrong. The people

# Those Big X-Ray Machines in the Sky

**X**-rays don't just exist in hospitals. They are also a part of nature. Stars, such as the Sun, give off X-ray light as well as visible light. Most of the X-rays, however, are blocked from reaching the Earth by our atmosphere.

Just as scientists photograph distant stars and galaxies in visible light, they also take pictures of the universe in X-ray light. By sending X-ray satellites high above the Earth's atmosphere, scientists have collected X-rays on film. These X-ray photographs have revealed objects in places where space looked dark and empty. Some of these objects, scientists say, are probably black holes (objects with such intense gravity that not even light can escape). Gas and dust pulled into black holes heat up. Hot objects give off light; the hotter the object, the higher-energy the light. The gas and dust being sucked into a black hole reach such tremendous temperatures that they emit one last gasp of X-ray light before they tumble in.

*Most X-ray photons are stopped in their tracks when they encounter bone.*

who take the pictures, X-ray technicians, must see many patients each day. To avoid getting exposed to X-rays over and over again, they stand behind special lead doors while X-raying is in process.

# How come a boomerang returns when you throw it?

Most of us have a movie image of boomerangs: The hero throws the boomerang, it slices through the air with a swishing sound, knocks the bad guy down, and comes obediently back. Our hero smiles; the day is saved.

There is one thing wrong with this picture, however. If a boomerang hits something, it won't come back. Instead, it will bounce off and fall to the ground—like any other thrown stick.

In fact, the boomerang is a kind of "throwing stick." Throwing sticks have been around for more than 10,000 years. Archeologists have found them in ancient Egyptian tombs. The Hopi Indians of Arizona used them to kill rabbits for food and fur.

But unlike the boomerang we know and love, ordinary throwing sticks won't return to the thrower. The only returning throwing sticks come from Australia.

Australian Aborigines—tribal people who lived in Australia before anyone else, as the Native Americans did in the Americas—used non-returning boomerangs for hunting. But they also invented boomerangs that return to the sender.

Some scientists think the Aborigines originally used

*Australian Aborigines invented boomerangs that return to the thrower.*

returning boomerangs to scare water birds into nets. But surprisingly, most think the returning boomerangs were designed as very sophisticated toys.

A familiar, banana-shaped boomerang may range from 16 inches to 3 feet long.

Boomerang makes a comeback, why?

5¢ deposit

Mind control

Fear of the unknown

on ? ? ?

electronic homing device

Usually made of plywood today, it may weigh only 3 or 4 ounces—the same as two small bags of potato chips.

Boomerangs need not be shaped like bananas, however, to work. Returning boomerangs have been carved in the shape of stars, Indian tomahawks, and the letter "H."

What makes returning boomerangs return? One Dutch physicist, Felix Hess, started thinking about that question when he was a little boy. When he grew up, after studying a lot of math and physics in school, he wrote a 600-page book on why the boomerang comes back to its thrower.

A boomerang returns, Hess reports, for two main reasons: the shape of its arms, and the way in which it is thrown.

Think of the two arms of a banana-shaped boomerang as its wings. Like airplane wings, the underside of the arms is flat, and the top of the arms is curved. This shape causes air rushing over the boomerang to lift it up.

But one of the boomerang's "wings" is different from the other. On one arm, the curved top points into the wind. On the other arm, the curved top points away from the wind. It's as if, on an air-

plane, one of the wings were made backward but then put on the plane the normal way. Such a strangely-built plane would have a hard time flying straight. And so does a boomerang.

How it's thrown also helps a boomerang travel in a big circle. The boomerang is held vertically (rather than horizontally, like a Frisbee). The flat side points away from the thrower's body. Then, with a snap of the wrist, it is tossed into the air. As it flies away from the thrower, the boomerang is spinning end-over-end about 10 times a second and traveling forward at about 60 miles an hour.

Soaring into the sky, a right-handed boomerang will begin to lean to the left. To understand why, Hess suggests thinking of riding a bike with no hands. If you lean to the left a little, the spinning front wheel of the bike will begin to turn left, too—even though you didn't touch the handlebars.

With a boomerang, the automatic left turn comes from how the wind is rushing over its spinning arms. The boomerang is flying forward, but it is tugged backward a little each time an arm spins under and back. This combi-

## *The shape of a boomerang's arms is what brings it back.*

nation creates pressure on top of the boomerang, just like the weight you put on your spinning bike wheels when you lean to the left. Gradually, little by little, the boomerang turns to the left. As it traces a big circle, it "lies down," until it looks like a rotating helicopter blade. Floating down out of the sky, it lands at the thrower's feet.

# What causes static electricity in your hair?

**D**ry hair flies up, attracted to a hairbrush. A blanket rubbed against a cat's fur in a dark room sends sparks flying. A jagged streak of light jumps from cloud to ground in a summer storm.

All are examples of static electricity—when ordinary objects, such as hair, fur, blankets, clouds, and Earth become—for a moment—electrically charged.

To understand how it works, we must understand how atoms behave. We know that each atom has a nucleus made of positively charged particles called protons, and neutral neutrons.

Surrounding the nucleus is a cloud of negatively charged electrons. These electrons are attracted to the protons in the nucleus, which is what holds atoms together. This electromagnetic force is like a very powerful glue. Without it, everything in the universe would crumble into a pile of particles.

If an ordinary atom has three protons in its center, then it will have three electrons, too, balancing positive and negative charges. So the whole atom is neutral—it has no charge at all. Since our bodies and everything around us are made of atoms, ordinary objects have no electrical charge, either.

The sparks of static electricity occur when objects temporarily become charged. The charge means their atoms have become unbalanced, with either too many or too few electrons.

You can easily charge your hair when you brush it in a dry room. The

*Static electricity occurs when objects become temporarily charged.*

hairbrush picks up electrons from your hair, and both the hair and brush become charged.

Friction, from the brush dragging through dry hair, is the cause. Friction occurs when two surfaces catch and pull as they rub against each other. Hairs and plastic bristles look smooth. But if you could shrink to atom-size, you'd see a bumpy landscape: hills of piled-up atoms here and there. As you brush your hair, piles of atoms on each hair catch in the valleys on a brush bristle, and vice versa.

Friction lessens when the room is damp, since your hair holds onto more water, which makes it smoother. There is also less friction when your hair is oily. The film of oil lets the brush glide through smoothly. But with dry hair in a dry room, there is a lot of friction. Electrons get torn loose from hair and glom onto the atoms in the brush. Since electrons have a negative

charge, the brush gets a negative charge, too.

Meanwhile, some of the hair has a positive charge,

*Friction is greater in a very dry room.*

having lost some electrons. And since positives and negatives attract, the positively charged hair clings annoyingly to the negatively charged brush. Lift the brush above your head and you can make your hair float upward through the air as it obediently follows the brush. Eventually, the atoms settle down to their normal state, with electrons and protons perfectly balanced.

# How come if your hands something electrical, you

**M**ost materials in the world fall into one of two categories: conductor or insulator. The difference? Conductors allow electric charges, such as electrons, to move freely through. Insulators don't. And electrons, moving in a current, can give you quite a jolt.

Take copper, which is such a good conductor that copper wire is usually used to carry electricity through a house. Each ordinary copper atom has 29 electrons, in a kind of "cloud" around its nucleus. But not all the electrons stay put. What's special about copper (and other metals) is that electrons slip away from their home atoms, to wander like nomads from atom to atom. That's what

identifies a conductor: roaming electrons. So the next time you see the copper bottom of a frying pan, imagine all those electrons meandering through it.

Here's the shocking part: When a copper wire is connected to a working electric circuit, the free, randomly wandering electrons begin to drift together in one direction. This movement is called an electric current—and it is what can shock you.

*Electrons in conductors wander like nomads from atom to atom.*

The electrons moving in a current are slowpokes; in the kind of wire found in most homes, the electrons move a little over 3 feet an hour. That may seem surprising, since most people tend to think of electric current as moving so quickly as to be instantaneous. It seems that way because a copper wire is always full of moving electrons. Once the electrons at your end of the wire start drifting, they have almost no distance to travel. (Think of electricity as a flowing stream instead of a faucet you can turn on and off.)

Copper and other metals aren't the only good conductors; you are, too, as are other living creatures, and the Earth itself. And as you probably guessed, tap water is also a very good conductor.

# are wet and you touch get a shock?

Conductors at Work...

Materials that don't have free-wheeling electrons are called insulators. Good insulators include glass, plastic, and rubber. That's why you can touch the plastic cord of a lamp, even though there is an electric current moving inside. The electrons in the plastic stay put.

If you touch the outside of a plastic wall outlet with dry hands, you probably won't get shocked, since your skin will most likely not come into contact with the bare wiring in the wall. But if your hands are wet, the water can slip into the outlet and come into contact with the current-carrying wire. A current starts flowing through the water and then into you. That's why wet hands and electricity shouldn't be mixed. It's a bit like plugging yourself in to the household current.

# How do magnets attract?

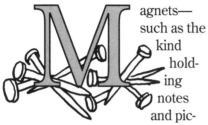

Magnets—such as the kind holding notes and pictures on your refrigerator—have a number of unusual features. First of all, magnets are attracted to iron or steel objects—such as the refrigerator door. They also have poles. Hold two magnets close together. The north pole of one magnet attracts the south pole of another magnet. And the north pole repels—or pushes away—the north pole of another magnet.

Magnetic fields are caused by electric currents — moving electrons. Electrons, which orbit the nucleus of an atom, have a negative electrical charge. The movement of this charge from place to place is called a current.

An electric current produces a magnetic field, which

loops out in a big arc around the electrons' path. For example, when a lamp is turned on and an electric current flows through its copper wire as electrons jump from atom to atom, weak magnetic fields surround the wire. Likewise, strong magnetic fields extend out from high-tension wires strung above fields in the country. Electricity and magnetism are just two sides of one force: electromagnetism.

## Magnetic fields are caused by electric currents.

Even the moving electrons inside each and every atom create tiny magnetic fields. An orbiting electron can be thought of as creating a tiny loop of electric current. But most of the magnetic field in an atom is created by

**FAST FACT**

The mineral lodestone is a naturally occurring magnet. But most magnets have to be specially made by people.

the electron spinning on its axis like a rotating planet.

In most materials—like plastic, for example—the tiny magnetic effects of each atom cancel each other out, because the atoms' poles face in different directions. But in some materials, such as iron, atoms are arranged in special ways that allows the material to become magnetized.

In these materials, atoms are clustered together in groups called magnetic domains. Each tiny domain holds billions and billions of atoms, with all their magnetic fields facing the same direction. So each domain is a kind of tiny magnet.

Ordinarily, the domains themselves point every which

way, cancelling each other's magnetic effects out. So a bar of iron isn't a magnet. But if you could make all the domains line up in the same direction—watch out! The whole bar would suddenly become magnetized, and attract every straight pin, iron nail, and refrigerator in sight.

How can the bunches of atoms be forced to line up like good little domains? Put the iron bar in a strong magnetic field. One by one, the domains will swing around in the direction of the field. As they align, domains will attract atoms from other domains, swelling in size. Soon, many of the domains in the bar will be aligned, and voilà—the bar is suddenly a magnet.

You can demonstrate this yourself with a small iron nail. Put the nail in the magnetic field of a refrigerator magnet. Its domains will promptly line up, and, temporarily, it will become a magnet, too. You can use it to pick up a pin.

# How come scientists say energy can't be created or destroyed?

 ou probably think of energy as something that can be used up. When a car runs out of gas, its energy source is gone. But a scientist would see it differently. She'd say the energy had been transformed. That's because of the law of conservation of energy, which says that energy can't be created or destroyed—it can only change from one form into another. That means that all the energy in the universe was here from the beginning, and will be here as long as the universe exists.

Imagine water poised at the top of a dam. With the dam closed and the water just waiting, we say the water has potential energy. The water's energy is not being used yet.

But then the dam is opened, and the water cascades down, attracted to the Earth by gravity. The water's gravitational energy turns into mechanical energy as it hits a paddle wheel, and the wheel begins to spin. The water is "doing work" on the wheel; it is turning it. The water's potential energy has changed into kinetic energy—energy of motion.

The turning paddle

wheel, part of a turbine at a power plant, causes a generator to produce electrical energy. The electrical energy is carried into your home, where it lights your lamp. When the lightbulb is switched on, it produces light (electromagnetic energy) and heat.

*All the energy in the universe was here from the beginning and will be here as long as the universe exists.*

So the potential energy of the water at the top of the dam did not disappear, but was instead eventually changed into the light and heat energy spreading out into your room, through your windows and walls, and into the universe beyond.

# On the Matter of Energy

One form energy takes is—surprise—matter. Einstein's famous equation, $E=Mc^2$, means that matter can be changed into energy. Look carefully at the equation. The "c" stands for the speed of light—186,000 miles a second. The "2" means that the speed of light is multiplied by itself (or squared). Then you multiply that long number—34,596,000,000—by the amount of matter, "M," you have. And that tells you how much energy, "E," it can be transformed into. As you can see, even a miniscule amount of matter can be converted into a huge amount of energy. A relatively small amount of uranium, transformed into energy, is what produced the tremendous destructive power of the first nuclear bomb.

# How come neon glows ?

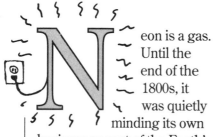

**N**eon is a gas. Until the end of the 1800s, it was quietly minding its own business as part of the Earth's atmosphere. Then Sir William Ramsey, a British chemist, discovered it. Later, others invented neon lamps, and neon signs began popping up everywhere in the 1920s.

When we think of neon, we think of multicolored signs spelling out store or restaurant names. But actually, neon makes only a bright red-orange light. Other gases, such as mercury or sodium, are used to make other glowing colors. In Las Vegas, the streets are ablaze with a slew of trapped gases, luring tourists into casinos and to hear Wayne Newton sing.

Because neon is in the air all around us, at this very moment, you may be breathing a tiny amount of it. But don't be alarmed: In one gallon of air, there's only enough neon to fit inside a poppy

*Liquid neon is clear and colorless.*

seed. To separate neon from the rest of the air, the air must be changed into a liquid.

Just as water changes from a gas—steam—to a liquid when its temperature drops, so does air. Water turns from gas to liquid when its temperature falls below 212° F. But chemists must lower the temperature of the air to −411° F before neon liquifies. They then separate the elements in the liquefied air and end up with a mixture of nitrogen, helium, and neon.

By increasing the pressure and lowering the temperature even further, the chemists remove nitrogen. Finally, neon is separated from helium by a process called *adsorption*, in which molecules attach themselves to the surface of a solid. In this case, neon molecules stick to the surface of charcoal. Some 88,000 pounds of liquid air must be collected to get a single pound of neon.

If you saw a jug of frigid liquid neon, you would notice that it is clear and colorless—definitely not bright red. How, then, does it shine so crimson in the signs?

The neon gas trapped in a sign is made of billions upon billions of neon atoms. Each neon atom has 10 electrons orbiting its center. The tube of gas is connected at both ends to an electric circuit. When the sign is turned on, an electric current flows through the tube: Electrons jump from atom to atom in the same direction. The neon atoms get excited as their electrons get a burst of energy, rather like you would if someone shoved you.

As each electron in a neon atom settles down again, it releases a photon of light—almost like a sigh. When the photons hit our eyes, we see red.

Other gases give off different colors when they are excited. For example, mercury gas, which has 80 electrons in each atom, glows blue when excited.

## Excited neon atoms release red light.

The difference between red and blue light is one of energy. The photons sent off by the mercury atoms are more energetic than those of the neon atoms. Sodium gas, which is used in some highway lamps, gives off bright yellow light, which has more energy than red but less than blue.

As the current flows through the neon sign, some atoms get excited while others return to normal. The atoms themselves are much

like little lights, winking on and off. But because there are so many of them, the gas appears to glow continuously. When the sign is turned off, the neon gas becomes its ordinary, colorless self.

# What is the Doppler effect?

Imagine you are an ambulance driver, threading your way as fast as possible through city traffic. You flip on the siren, which begins a steady wail. As you hurry towards the hospital, you pass people gaping on the sidewalk.

Now imagine you are one of those standing on the sidewalk: You know there's an ambulance coming. You can hear its siren from far off. As the ambulance gets nearer, the sound of its siren becomes louder and more frantic: The wail gets higher and higher. In other words, the pitch changes as the ambulance races toward you.

Then, as the ambulance passes, the opposite effect occurs: The sound of the siren drops in pitch, getting lower and lower as the ambulance disappears.

But the ambulance driver hears no change. To her, the siren always sounds the same. To bystander after bystander, however, the siren grows to a high-pitched wail,

Early Doppler research moved at a snail's pace...

*Sound waves course through air like water waves roll through the oceans.*

and then just as quickly dies.

Is the siren's pitch steady, or changing? Who's right, the driver or the spectators?

Actually, both. What you hear depends on where you are standing. The Doppler effect makes the difference.

What we perceive as sound is actually waves rippling through matter. The siren causes air molecules to vibrate; sound waves course through air like water waves roll through the oceans. Air molecules bunch up, spread out, and bunch up again.

The closer together the waves are, the higher the pitch, or frequency, of the

sound. The farther apart the waves, the lower the pitch.

As the ambulance races toward us, the sound waves it emits are squashed together. The waves are compressed, so we hear a higher pitch. But as the ambulance passes, the waves spread out behind it, and we hear a lower sound.

Inside the ambulance, however, the driver and the siren are moving together, so the pitch remains the same. The frequency an observer hears depends on how the observer and the source of sound are moving relative to each other.

The Doppler effect works on other kinds of waves, too. Take light waves, for example. If the ambulance were emitting, say, yellow light from its front and back instead of sound, the frequency of the light would change as the ambulance approached us and then sped away.

At ordinary, Earth speeds, we wouldn't see much of a change. But if the ambulance could speed up to

near the velocity of light— 186,000 miles a second— we would notice a startling difference.

The driver would see a steady yellow light beaming out on the road in front of her. Because the light waves would become compressed as the ambulance came nearer, bystanders would see the light changing from yellow to high-frequency blue. As it passed, they would watch the light on the back change from blue back to yellow, as the waves spread out again. Finally, they would glimpse the light from the ambulance as a receding speck of low-frequency red light, disappearing on the horizon.

**FAST FACT**

**Frequency is the number of wave crests that pass any point each second. The greater the frequency, the higher the pitch of the sound, or the bluer the light.**

# How can a rocket move no air to push against?

**S**treaming rocket engines lift the space shuttle into orbit around Earth. Other rockets boost satellites and space probes.

When we think of rockets, we think of space flight.

But rockets also whiz around our living rooms at birthday parties. A balloon can be a rocket. How? Blow up a balloon, squeezing the opening shut so air can't escape. Now let it go. The balloon will jet wildly around the room, forced forward by the air shooting out.

Here's another simple rocket: Imagine an open railroad car—with a machine gun mounted on the rear. (Pretend that there is no friction between the car's wheels and the track to slow it down.)

Each time the gun shoots a bullet, the car moves a bit. As the gun fires off its rounds of bullets, the car begins to pick up speed. Spewing out from the rear, the bullets force the car forward. This force is called thrust—and it's what makes rockets work, on Earth or in space. Whenever matter rushes out of an object, and the object moves in the opposite direction, you have a kind of rocket.

To lift objects into space, engineers must design powerful rocket engines. Engineers base their designs on principles of how the universe works, first described in detail by Sir Isaac Newton, a brilliant British scientist who worked in the late 17th century. Newton's laws describe gravity and tell us what happens when things move. His second and third laws are particularly good for understanding rockets.

*Rockets actually work better in the emptiness of space.*

Newton's second law noted that the force of a moving object depends on its mass (how much matter it contains) and its acceleration (its changing speed). So, to make a forceful rocket, make sure it spits out a great deal of high-speed matter each second.

Newton's third law says

# in space, where there is

Giant Sneeze Turns Man's Head into Rocket

that for every action, there will be an opposite and equal reaction. In the case of a rocket, the action force is matter streaming out of the exhaust. The reaction is that the rocket is thrust forward.

The rockets that power the space shuttle use hot gases. But anything thrown out the rear of an object could make a rocket—solid pellets, liquids, or even the individual parts of atoms—electrons, protons, and neutrons.

Many think that a rocket works because its gases push against air. But it is the force of its emissions that thrusts the rocket forward. In fact, rockets operate better in the emptiness of space, because the gas rushing out of the rear can really speed up when there's no air to stand in its way.

Also, there is no friction between the ship and air to slow it down as it starts to move. Finally, an orbiting ship, or a ship far from any planet or star, is practically weightless. So even a very small thrust from the rocket engines can send a big ship gliding quickly forward.

# Is time travel possible? If so, how?

**A**lthough you may never be able to buy a time machine, a kind of time travel into the future is not technically impossible. It would involve traveling at extremely high speeds—in fact, close to 186,000 miles per second (at that rate, you could zip around the world several times in the blink of an eye).

186,000 miles a second is the speed of light—and it seems to be the universe's built-in speed limit. What's interesting is that as you approach the speed of light, time begins to slow.

Physicists like to theorize about what would happen to two twins—one traveling on a speeding starship, the other left behind on Earth. The story, set in the far future, might go like this:

Beth and Bob are twins, both 30 years old. Beth is an astronaut; Bob is a reporter. Beth has just gotten the assignment of a lifetime: She will be a crew member on the first ship to visit a nearby star system. Bob will cover the story for his newspaper.

*As you approach the speed of light, time begins to slow.*

The star and its planets are 60 trillion miles, or 10 light-years, distant. (A light-year is the distance light travels in a year—about 6 trillion miles.)

Beth's ship will cruise at 90 percent of the speed of light. So, judged from here on Earth, it will take more than 22 years to get to the star and back. As those years pass, reporter Bob marries, gains 10 pounds, raises two kids, and gets some gray hair.

But for astronaut Beth, it is a different story. As her ship plows silently through space at enormous speed, on-board clocks run slowly compared to those back home. The clocks don't need fixing, though. Time itself has slowed for ship and crew.

However, nothing *feels* different. A minute seems like a minute, not an hour. Yet with every passing minute, Beth and the others are getting more out of sync with time back on Earth.

After a successful mission, the crew heads back to Earth. As they near our solar system, ship clocks show that almost 10 years have passed. Beth celebrates her 40th birthday as the ship passes Pluto.

Both Beth and Bob knew that time-slowing effects would occur. But they are still shocked when they are reunited. Beth is 40, but Bob is 52. The twins no longer

*A light-year is the distance light travels in a year—about 6 trillion miles.*

look at all alike. Bob sees space travel as a fountain of youth, and feels left behind.

Beth is disoriented: 22 years have passed, and she has arrived in a changed world. In effect, she has traveled 12 years into the future.

This idea of time travel is based on Albert Einstein's Special Theory of Relativity, which describes how time, distance, and mass are affected by motion. Trips taken at speeds even closer to light speed would thrust travelers even farther into the future— centuries, say. Although there may be insurmountable problems with building such fast ships, we have seen the time effects already, even at much slower speeds. Very accurate clocks taken for rides on supersonic planes slow by a fraction of a second.

In his General Theory of Relativity, Einstein predicted that increasing gravity slows time, too. So some speculate that we might make use of the universe's natural structures with enormous gravity—such as black holes—to catapult a traveler into her own past.

# What happens to an object when it approaches the speed of light?

The speed limit on most major U.S. highways is 55 to 65 miles an hour. Although no signs are posted, there also seems to be a speed limit in the vacuum of space—669,600,000 miles an hour.

That's the speed of light. Scientists usually measure it by the second. Light travels 186,000 miles in a second. Light is made of photons—they're what are zipping along at such an incomprehensible speed.

Although scientists call photons "particles," they're very peculiar particles. They have no rest mass, so they have no weight in the usual sense. It's hard to imagine something that is pure energy and no substance being real, but photons are.

It's interesting to compare the incredible speed of photons to that of ordinary objects we think of as speedy.

Take the Pioneer space probe, for example. When it left the solar system on its way to travel the dark stretches between the stars, Pioneer was clipping along at about 37 miles a second. Not bad: Pioneer could make it from New York to San Francisco in about a minute and a half. But compared to a photon's 186,000 miles a second, that's barely crawling.

Or imagine the wanderings of the Sun. Even as you

*Traveling at the speed of light, a spaceship would appear to an observer to have no length at all.*

read this, our Sun, the Earth, and the other eight planets of our solar system are hurtling around the Milky Way galaxy like horses on a merry-go-round, at about 155 miles a second, or 588,000 miles an hour. (And you can't feel a thing!) Still, even that tremendous speed is much less than

# Time=Distance=Spacetime

We talk about time and distance interchangeably. But it seems a strange idea that the passing of minutes, days, and years has something to do with distance. A day, however, is a distance—24,894 miles, the circumference of the Earth, the distance that the Earth rotates in 24 hours. And a year is the distance of the Earth's orbit around the Sun.

Looking into space is looking back into time. Light is the swiftest messenger we have, but it takes time to reach us. So when we look at the Sun, we see it as it was 8 minutes ago, the next-nearest star as it was 4 years ago, and the farthest stars as they appeared billions of years ago.

Gravity, which makes space itself curve like a bowl around clumps of matter, also affects time. Gravity slows time; the stronger the gravitational field, the slower time passes. Even at the surface of the Earth, time slows by a tiny amount—a clock far out in empty space would run more quickly than one near the Earth.

(It's all relative, however. For observers stationed at each clock, time does not seem to pass any more slowly or quickly.) Likewise, people of the same age placed in two different gravitational fields would get out of sync, too. Brought together, they would no longer be the same age.

Near a black hole, which curves space so much that it resembles a hole, time slows to a crawl, just as it does for an object traveling near the speed of light. For an object falling into the hole, time stops—just as it does for an object traveling *at* the speed of light.

Because of the way the universe works, The Theory of Relativity treats space and time as one thing: spacetime.

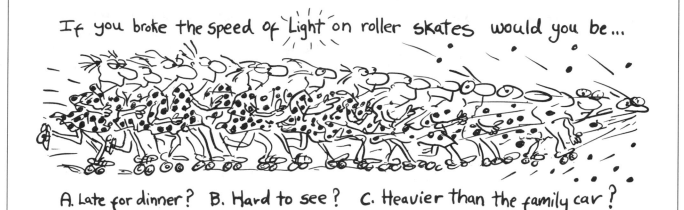

If you broke the speed of Light on roller skates would you be...

A. Late for dinner?   B. Hard to see?   C. Heavier than the family car?

1 percent of the speed of light.

But strange things happen when ordinary objects really speed up. As an object approaches the speed of light, an observer outside would see the object's length and mass change. Even time begins to change.

A spaceship hurtling along at 167,400 miles a second (about 90 percent of the speed of light) would appear to have shrunk to less than half its former length. As the ship sped up, it would appear to shrink still more until, at light speed, it would appear to have no length at all.

Astronauts on board would see the ship and themselves as perfectly normal. Looking out the ship's front window, however, they would see the scene in front of them squashed up.

At 90 percent of light speed, the same ship (and everyone on it) would grow monstrously in mass, becoming more than three times as heavy. Again, no one on board would notice any difference. As the speed increased, so would the mass—until, at light speed, the mass would become infinitely large.

(Scientists know these effects are real, because they've watched the mass of elementary particles increase as they force them to speed faster and faster in accelerators.)

Finally, there are equally strange effects on time. If they could somehow watch a clock on board, observers outside the ship would see the clock slowing down. But from inside the ship, time would seem to pass normally. At light speed, the outside observers would see clocks on the ship stand perfectly still.

# The Great Beyond

It's hard to imagine the size of the universe. Our own solar system seems extremely large, extending more than 4 trillion miles out from the Sun. But the Sun is only one of hundreds of billions of other stars that make up our galaxy, the Milky Way.

Within the Milky Way, distances are vast: Trillions of empty miles separate each star (or pair of stars) from the next. (Scientists speculate that most, if not all, stars may also have orbiting planets.) But vast as it is (some 100,000 light-years across, a light-year being equal to about 6 trillion miles), our galaxy is just an island in the sea of space. There are hundreds of billions of other galaxies strewn across the expanding fabric of space; the universe measures billions of light-years across. Traveling at its normal 186,000 miles a second, it takes light from the most distant stars more than 10 billion years to cross the lonely dark expanses to us.

# Why do stars form pictures?

Have you ever lain on your back on a summer day, watching big, fluffy clouds float by, and suddenly seen what looks like a face or an animal in a cloud? Well, constellations are pictures we imagine we see in the stars. The night sky is like a giant connect-the-dots drawing.

People have been finding pictures in the stars since ancient times. (We know, for example, that the Sumerians drew constellations at least 4,000 years ago.) Not surprisingly, people see what interests them. Cultures in which people spent a good part of their days hunting saw wild animals outlined by the stars. European sailors saw stars patterned in the shape of a compass. In fact, scientists think that one of the most important uses for such pictures was to help people navigate the seas of Earth—to figure out where they were by finding familiar patterns in the sky.

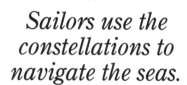

## *Sailors use the constellations to navigate the seas.*

Seeing pictures among the stars also made it easier to study the sky. Astronomers of the ancient world divided the night sky into regions. Each region was made up of a group of stars, called a constellation. Constellations were given names, and people made up stories about them.

Different cultures had different pictures and stories. Some of the scenes people imagined were very strange. For example, take what the Egyptians saw in one large group of stars surrounding what we call the Big Dipper: There was a bull, they said, followed by a man lying down, trailed by a hippopotamus walking on two legs—carrying a crocodile on its back!

Many of the stories of our constellations come from Greek myths. Here's one: The goddess Juno was very jealous of her attendant, the princess Callisto. Jupiter, Juno's husband, was concerned about Callisto's safety. To protect her, he turned the beautiful Callisto into a bear.

But this caused new problems. Callisto's son was out

TEENAGE SKY

hunting one day, saw a big bear, and—not realizing it was his own mother—he took aim. So Jupiter stepped in and "fixed" things again, turning Callisto's son into a little bear. That's how, the myth said, there came to be a big bear and a little bear in the sky. Today the constellations are called Ursa (bear) Major and Ursa Minor.

You've probably heard of the archer Orion, with his starry belt, and Leo, the lion. But there are other pictures in the sky: a chisel, a pump, an easel, a telescope, and a microscope. There's a clock, a chameleon, a whale, and a giraffe. And sweeping across the heavens, there's even a constellation called Berenice's Hair.

In modern star charts, the skies of the Northern and Southern Hemispheres are divided into 88 separate pictures. Scientists believe most of the "modern" constellations date from about 2,600 B.C.

Although the stars in a constellation look like they are near each other, that's an illusion: One star may be trillions of miles farther from Earth than another. But the more distant star may be very bright—so it looks as close as the nearer, dimmer star. Stuck on Earth, we see constellations as flat.

Stars are always being born or dying, and they are constantly moving. So over time, constellations change, too. A million years ago, when its stars were in different positions, the Big Dipper (a part of the Ursa Major constellation) looked less like a dipper and more like a long

**Legend says that Berenice, the wife of an ancient Egyptian king, pledged her beautiful hair to the goddess Venus. But the hair was stolen from the temple of Venus and placed in the heavens as a constellation. Today, we can see Berenice's Hair in the Northern Hemisphere during the summer, below the handle of the Big Dipper.**

spear. A million years in the future, people will probably have come up with different names for the new pictures they see in the sky.

A final thought: From some far-off solar system, our Sun may be a star in another culture's constellation—perhaps a point in the outline of an exotic animal found on *their* home planet.

# Ancient Observatories

If tracking the constellations helped our ancestors navigate the seas, tracking the Sun helped them determine the time of year. Ancient peoples built observatories that used the Sun to pinpoint the summer and winter solstices, which foretell the changing seasons.

Perhaps the most impressive is Stonehenge, a nearly 4,000-year-old structure in southern England. Thirty enormous blocks of sandstone, topped by huge slabs stand in a circle 98 feet across.

On an avenue running out of the circle is a 16-foot-high rock, called the Heel Stone. Each year on the summer solstice, June 21, the Sun rises exactly over the Heel Stone, as if it were a pedestal for the Sun to mount. The first day of winter, spring, and fall are also marked by stones. Other stones track the movements of the Moon through the sky.

Similar structures have been found all over the world. In Chaco Canyon in New Mexico, light pierces a window at dawn on the summer solstice and slowly fills a niche on the wall. Elsewhere in the Southwest, a spiral carved in stone is cut in half by a shaft of light on June 21. On December 21, two shafts of light perfectly frame the same spiral.

# What are galaxies and how many are there?

One of the great mysteries of the universe is why the countless trillions of stars are not simply sprinkled evenly throughout space. Instead, they are gathered into galaxies, like people are grouped into cities, with the vast empty prairies of space stretching out between each glowing cluster.

Our galaxy is called the Milky Way. It is an immense, turning pinwheel of gas, dust, and some 200 billion stars. Between each star and the next often lie trillions of miles of empty space. The Sun, one of the multitude in this city of stars, is on the galaxy's outskirts.

When we look out into space, we are looking through the stars in our own galaxy, like raindrops on a windowpane. All the individual stars we see in the night sky are part of the Milky Way. Ours is a spiral galaxy; from above, the Milky Way would look like a great turning hurricane of stars. The Sun and its nine planets are swept along on one of the arms of stars extending out from the center of the galaxy, just like the arms of a hurricane. (Stars orbit the center of their galaxies like planets orbit stars.) It takes the Sun, speeding along at 588,000 miles an hour, about 200 million years to travel once around this galactic merry-go-round.

From the side, the galaxy looks like a disc with a bulge in the middle. The band of

*On clear nights we may be able to see our neighbor, the Andromeda Galaxy.*

light that stretches across the sky on a clear night (like a dusting of powdered sugar) is part of the disc: our galaxy seen from our vantage point on one side.

If we could get outside of

our own galaxy, we would see the universe as it really is: an inky expanse of blackness, with galaxies strewn about like lit-up islands in a dark sea. The Milky Way, vast as it is, is simply one of about 100 billion galaxies in the cosmos. Though they are each collections of millions of suns, other galaxies are so far from Earth that their glow is dim.

With a small telescope, we can see a few dozen galaxies. Using the best telescopes, we can see many more, and even pick out some of the individual stars in distant galaxies.

On a very clear night, it's sometimes possible to see the Andromeda galaxy, one of the Milky Way's nearest neighbors, without any telescope at all. Like the Milky Way, Andromeda is a spiral. About half of all galaxies are spirals. These galaxies, which resemble spinning pinwheels, are homes to a mix of young, old, and middle-aged stars.

There are also elliptical galaxies: great round balls of billions of stars. Some are almost perfect spheres, others a bit squashed. The stars in an elliptical galaxy all orbit the center, like a cloud of swarming bees. These suns are mostly old, and many are red giants, so elliptical galaxies glow with an orange light. (For more on the connection between a star's color and its age, see page 15.)

Galaxies come in other shapes, too. Some look like spirals without the arms, or like a camera lens. Others have no particular shape; they're called irregular.

Although galaxies may

look calm and still, they can be the scene of violent natural events—the galactic equivalent of earthquakes and volcanoes. For example, in an ongoing fearsome release of energy, a blue-white jet of hot gas shoots into space from the center of a galaxy called M87. The gas jet is some 5,000 light-years long—or about 3 quadrillion miles. Scientists think that black holes at the center of galaxies, gobbling up dust and even entire stars, may be the source of the awesome displays.

Entire galaxies may even collide. Since there is so much empty space between stars, the galaxies don't smash into each other—they mostly slip right through each other. And because galaxies are so impossibly large, these "collisions"

*Sometimes two galaxies collide and merge, forming a bigger galaxy.*

take millions of years, rather than a few minutes. But scientists can make models of galaxies on a computer and speed up the action, showing what happens to two galaxies during a close encounter and how each looks afterward. As the galaxies' stars pass like the proverbial ships in the night, their gravity causes them to pull on one another. Stars are tugged from their former positions, distorting the

shapes of the mingling galaxies. One arm full of stars on a spiral galaxy may be dragged toward an approaching elliptical galaxy, for example.

Some scientists now suspect that today's impossibly large galaxies formed from mergers of smaller collections of stars. For example, a big elliptical galaxy may coalesce from the merger of two spirals. Looking far out into space, past 2 billion light-years—which, is also looking 2 billion years into the past—astronomers see more and more small galaxies, and fewer and fewer big ones. Furthermore, the tiny galaxies are shapeless, not spiral or elliptical. Scientists say it would take 10 to 100 of the little galaxies to construct a single spiral like our Milky Way.

# What are some galaxy names?

. . . . . . . . . . . . . . . . . . . . . . . . . .

Galaxies are great whirling cities of stars. There are at least 100 billion galaxies in the universe, separated by unimaginably vast stretches of mostly empty space. Without using a telescope, we can see only three galaxies from Earth, plus part of our own galaxy, the Milky Way.

Two of these galaxies, called the Magellanic Clouds, were named after the Portuguese explorer Ferdinand Magellan. When Magellan's ships sailed into southern waters in 1519, crew members saw the two dimly-glowing galaxies, and they carried the news back to Europe.

The Magellanic Clouds do look a bit like clouds—soft and diffuse. These two small galaxies actually orbit our much bigger Milky Way gal-axy. So they are our nearest neighbors. How small are they? One galaxy has about 15 billion suns; the other, "only" about 5 billion (as compared to our galaxy, which has about 200 billion stars).

The third galaxy we can see without a telescope is called Andromeda, a spiral galaxy like the Milky Way. The Andromeda galaxy is about 2.2 million light-years away. A light-year is the dis-tance light, speeding along at 186,000 miles a second, travels in a year—about 6 trillion miles. That means Andromeda is some 13,200,000,000,000,000,000 miles from New York, where this book was written. That also means the light from Andromeda's stars takes 2.2 million years to reach us—so we are seeing the galaxy as it appeared 2.2 million years ago.

*The name galaxy comes from the Greek word "gala," which means milk.*

When we look at the Andromeda Galaxy or the Magellanic Clouds without a telescope, we can't see any individual stars. We see only a glowing shape—the pooled light of millions and millions of suns.

Besides these three galaxies, on a dark night we can see part of the Milky Way. A powdery band of stars across the sky is a piece of the disc of our galaxy. The ancient Greeks imagined the band to be milk squirted from the breast of the goddess Hera. The Greek word for milk is "gala," and that is where the word "galaxy" comes from.

*There are about 100 billion galaxies in the universe.*

Other galaxies, which we can only see with a telescope, have equally lovely and unusual names. There is the tiny Sculptor galaxy. And there are Draco, Fornax, Leo I and Leo II, Sextans, Pegasus, Cartwheel, and Sombrero.

However, because there are so many galaxies, most don't have real names, only letters and numbers. In the 1700s, a French astronomer, Charles Messier, made a list of more than 100 fuzzy, glowing objects in the sky, including a number of galaxies. He gave each a number: M1, M2, and so on. (So the Andromeda Galaxy, for example, is also known as M31.)

Later astronomers developed larger catalogs of galaxies and other objects, such as star clusters and nebulae, so some galaxies are known by New General Catalog (NGC) or Index Catalog (IC) numbers. In these catalogs, the Andromeda Galaxy is known as NGC224.

# Why is space black?

*With powerful telescopes, we can nearly see to where the stars "stop."*

On Earth, the sky is bright during the day because air molecules reflect sunlight like billions of tiny mirrors. On the Moon, however, there is no atmosphere, so the sky is dark and the stars are out, even during the day. Likewise, space itself is very empty, with too few molecules to reflect light back to us. So even near the blazing Sun, space stays black.

Even so, the blackness of space involves a genuine riddle, one scientists have been arguing over for hundreds and hundreds of years. Why don't all the stars in our universe together produce an enormously bright glare? Why *is* the sky dark at night?

Thomas Digges, an astronomer, wondered about these questions in the 1500s. Digges believed the universe was infinite, that space stretched on in all directions, forever, and that in that endless space, there were an infinite number of stars.

If space is filled with countless stars, he reasoned, there should be a star everywhere we look. Covered with distant suns, the night sky should blind us with its dazzling light. But it doesn't, and Digges never solved the riddle.

Wilhelm Olbers, a 19th-century astronomer, also puzzled over the problem for years, and the question of why the night sky is dark came to be known as Olbers's Paradox.

Olbers suggested several solutions, but finally decided that the answer was dust. Maybe we can't see the light from very distant stars, he said, because dust in space absorbs it. That would mean that endless numbers of invisible stars exist, veiled only by dust.

But after Olbers's death, scientists calculated that the starlight from all those suns should heat up any dust enough so that it would glow, too. The night sky should therefore be lit up by shining dust. And matters were back where they started: a paradox.

So scientists tried out other theories. Faraway light is dimmer than nearby light, they argued, so very distant stars simply can't be seen. However, if the number of stars were infinite, the light would add up. The sky would still be bright.

# Why is the Night Sky Black?

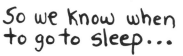

So we know when to go to sleep...

... Because it's the only way to watch fireworks...

... And drive-in Movies!

Clearly, however, darkness rules the night. Something was wrong with the theories. But what? Digges, Olbers, and others assumed there were an infinite number of stars in an infinitely large cosmos. They were wrong.

Astronomer Edward Harrison of the University of Massachusetts in Amherst has written a book called *Darkness at Night: A Riddle of the Universe.* He says that there simply aren't enough stars to cover the sky with light. The night sky isn't lit up, because the stars—and the universe—*don't* actually go on forever.

With the most powerful

*The Moon's sky is dark, even during daytime, because it has no atmosphere to light up.*

telescopes, we are now nearly able to see where the stars "stop." Light can take millions of years to travel to us from far-off stars. So when we look out into space, we look back in time. The best telescopes allow us to see the light that started on its journey toward us some 10 billion years ago.

The universe is only about 15 billion years old. The better our telescopes get, the farther back into time we can look. Edgar Allen Poe, who wrote such spooky poems and stories as *The Raven* and *The Telltale Heart,* was

intrigued by such ideas. In 1848, Poe published *Eureka: A Prose Poem*. In the blackness of space, he wrote, we see the nothingness that existed before the birth of the stars.

According to Harrison, Poe's poem was basically right. "Through the gaps between stars," he writes, "we look back to the beginning of the universe."

# What are pulsars, and how are they formed?

A pulsar is a small, dense whirling dervish of a star that throws off a narrow beam of radio waves. Like the rotating beam of a lighthouse, we detect the radio beam each time it swings toward us. So from Earth, the strange star seems to pulse with energy.

A pulsar is a kind of neutron star. A neutron star is what's sometimes left over after an enormous star ends its life in a cataclysmic explosion.

A medium-size star like the Sun is big enough to hold a million Earths. Giant and supergiant stars may be 10 to 1,000 times as big across as the Sun. A neutron star is one of these enormous stars, collapsed to the size of a *city*.

That's what makes neutron stars so strange. Each contains all the mass of a regular star—but squeezed into an impossibly small space. A single teaspoonful of neutron star can weigh a billion tons.

Here's how it happens: After a star explodes, the leftover matter collapses. As it collapses, its gravity gets stronger and stronger and its atoms are forced closer and closer together. Normally, atoms keep their distance, because the electrons orbiting the outside of each atom repel each other. But in a neutron star, electrons are forced down from their usual orbits into the atoms' centers.

The center, or nucleus, of an atom is made of protons and neutrons. Electrons squashed into the nucleus react with the protons and form more neutrons. Eventually, the star is made mostly of jammed-together neutrons. And a neutron star is born.

Scientists believed that neutron stars existed long before they could prove it. In November 1967, they got their first piece of evidence. An array of radio telescopes in England found a new source of radio waves in space.

Radio waves come from many sources in space. For

## Pulsar Living

Living on a spinning, shrinking star would make it hard to watch t.v.

Everyday, everything would be smaller— your shoes would be smaller, hopefully your feet would be smaller too!

... Maybe your parents would shrink faster than you. ... Then you could make <u>them</u> take out the trash!

*A single teaspoonful of a neutron star can weigh a billion tons.*

example, molecules of water and ammonia, drifting between the stars, emit radio waves. These waves are detected by the dish-shaped antennas of radio telescopes.

The new radio source, however, wasn't like the rest. Jocelyn Bell, a graduate student, carefully studied the markings on the rolls of paper that charted the radio signals as they came in. She was startled when she saw that the new source emitted regularly spaced bursts of radio waves—once every 1.33733 seconds.

When news of Bell's discovery became public, some scientists thought she had stumbled onto a radio beacon left by an alien civilization. But several months later, another pulsing radio source was found. Soon, scientists abandoned the idea that the objects might be artificial. They decided that the sources were collapsed stars, and dubbed them "pulsars," for pulsing stars.

Pulsars, it turned out, were the same neutron stars scientists had been hoping to find all along. Hundreds of the mysterious stars have been discovered since.

But why do pulsars pulse? Scientists say it's because they spin so fast.

All stars rotate on their axes, just like planets. The Sun, for example, takes about a month to turn once around.

Any already-rotating object will spin faster if it shrinks. Imagine a figure skater spinning on the ice. As she folds her arms in to her body, she whirls even faster. So does a collapsing star. A pulsar the size of a city may spin dizzyingly fast, turning once a second. Some may whirl even faster.

Here's where the pulsing comes in. Pulsars have strong magnetic fields. Free protons and electrons on the surface of the star get swept off along the magnetic field lines near the star's north and south magnetic poles. As the particles speed up, they give off photons of energy, from X-rays to radio waves. So as the pulsar spins, the radiation flashes out in narrow beams—similar to the beam thrown off by the spinning light of a lighthouse.

# What is a black hole, objects in space?

**B**lack holes are regions in space where gravity is so powerful that even light can't escape their relentless pull.

There are probably several kinds of black holes, scientists say. One kind may form when a massive old star dies. (Throughout the universe, stars are being born and others are dying every day.) Another kind of black hole is thought to lurk at the center of galaxies. Colossal, dark masses, such objects may be formed from the equivalent of millions of stars. Finally, there may be mini black holes, the size of pinheads or marbles, created when relatively small amounts of mass are squashed down into unimaginably tiny bundles.

The first kind of black hole may form when a star containing 8 to 100 times as much matter as our Sun ends its life in a tremendous explosion. Afterwards, what's left of the star collapses. Tugged by its own gravity, the star matter pulls together, tighter and tighter.

Gravity is simply the attraction of one bit of matter for another. So the more matter there is in one place, the stronger the gravitational force. On the surface of a shrunken star, because so much mass is packed into the small space underneath, the force is incredibly strong.

Eventually, as the shrinking goes on, the star may become an object whose surface gravity is so strong that even light can't escape.

Matter and light sink into the collapsing star—which is why it's called a "black hole."

Scientists haven't yet proved that supermassive black holes exist, but they are coming closer by training their telescopes on the strange centers of many galaxies—including our own—where this second kind of "hole" may be found.

One galaxy that has long intrigued scientists is called NGC4261. Two enormous

# and why does it suck in

BLACK HOLES around the HOUSE

Most hall closets could be hiding a dead star...

Looking for a crushed mountain? Try the kitchen drawer...

How about those 10 million stars lurking in the basement?

jets of matter stream out tens of thousands of light-years into space from the center of this galaxy. (To get an idea of the incredible length of the jets, remember that one light-year is 6 trillion miles.)

Observing the jets, scientists suspected that an enormous black hole lay in hiding at the center of NGC4261. And in 1992, the Hubble Space telescope sent back the sharpest images yet of that

galaxy's mysterious center.

What scientists saw: a dusty, glowing, swirling collection of matter, shaped like a doughnut, hundreds of light-years across. Scientists believe the center of the doughnut may be a monstrous black hole, holding the equivalent in matter of 10 million stars. Other matter circles the hole like water around a drain, falling in as it gets caught by the hole's gravity.

Hard-to-find mini black holes—if they exist—may have formed in the tremendous pressures that scientists think existed in the first second after the origin of universe. Those up to the size of a pinhead would have "evaporated" by now, but there may be slightly bigger ones still lurking in space. (The Earth would become a black hole, if its matter were compressed down to the size of a ping-pong ball.)

# If light has no mass and why can't it escape the

Light is made of particles called photons. Photons are peculiar—scientists say photons have no "rest mass" at all. But photons don't stand still. In fact, photons zip around the universe at the cosmic speed limit—186,000 miles a second. While they have no mass, photons do have kinetic energy—the energy of movement. This energy ensures that photons of light are not immune to the force of gravity.

Here's why: Albert Einstein discovered that mass can be changed into energy. The clearest example is the hydrogen bomb, in which a small amount of mass releases a tremendous amount of energy in a huge explosion.

Since mass can be changed into energy, it follows that energy represents a certain amount of mass. Think of a speeding photon as an object with *all* its mass converted into kinetic energy. The gravity of a black hole tugs the photon down just as if it had the mass that its energy represents.

But there is another, per-

*Since mass can be converted to energy, it follows that energy represents a certain amount of mass.*

*Starlight bends as it passes near the Sun, tugged by its gravity.*

haps easier way to see why photons of light can't escape from a black hole. Einstein's theories explain gravity as a curving of space around masses. The more matter in one spot, the more space is curved there. So a beam of light trying to escape a black hole can't get out—the "bowl" of space around the hole is too steep to climb out of.

Less-massive objects than black holes also have measur-

# therefore no weight, then gravity of a black hole?

able gravitational effects on light. In 1919, Arthur Eddington, a British scientist, proved Einstein was right about massive objects attracting and changing the course of light. Eddington knew that a total eclipse of the Sun was coming. During an eclipse, the Moon comes between us and the Sun's fiery face, blacking it out. With the Sun's glare temporarily dimmed, we can see other stars in the daytime.

Eddington and his colleagues traveled to Africa to get the best view of the eclipse. They found that the Sun bent the light of a far-off star very slightly when the starlight passed near the Sun's rim. This proved that space curves around the mass of the Sun, bending starlight that strays too near.

# Without stars, would there be life?

Imagine the Earth—dark and cold, lost in the nearly limitless blackness of space. Could life evolve on such a world, and survive?

The evidence says no. Although life exists in some very dark nooks and crannies of the Earth, sunlight was crucial to life beginning and flourishing on Earth. And our Sun, as we know, is a star—the nearest star to Earth.

And although we can *imagine* the Earth as a barren, sunless world, the picture is misleading. Planets by definition are bodies that form out of the dust around stars, not all by themselves.

In fact, the lives of animals and plants are completely intertwined with the lives of stars. We owe our existence not only to our own star, the Sun, but to stars that lived long, long ago and far, far away.

*The iron in your blood, the calcium in your teeth, and the nickel in your pocket were all forged inside a distant star.*

Before there were planets and life, there were stars. The first stars probably formed about 13 or 14 billion years ago, when our universe was relatively young.

Stars, like people, are born, get older, and die. During their lifetimes, stars power themselves by fusing elements to make new elements. When a star is young to middle-aged, it fuses hydrogen atoms, making helium. As it uses up its supply of hydrogen, it fuses helium atoms, making carbon.

As time passes, heavier and heavier elements form in the stars' fiery furnaces, including oxygen, neon, magnesium, silicon, and sulfur.

After millions or billions of years, a star uses up its nuclear fuel. Smaller stars end their lives relatively peacefully. Huge stars may explode, briefly becoming so bright that they can sometimes be seen even during daytime on Earth. Exploding stars spew the elements they've formed out into space. These elements become part of the clouds of gas and dust

drifting between the stars. And sometimes, if conditions are just right, these clouds form new stars and planets.

The Sun and its nine planets, including Earth, formed from such a cloud. So the elements that are in and around you—the iron in your blood, the calcium in your teeth, the nickel in your pocket—were forged inside a distant star.

Although that far-off star provided the elements necessary for life, the energy to get life started on Earth came from our star, the Sun. Radiation from the young Sun streamed into the atmosphere

### *Life runs on sunlight, the way a car runs on gasoline.*

of Earth. The Sun's warmth helped create the conditions in clouds for lightning. And lightning, along with ultraviolet radiation, scientists think, may have sparked complex organic molecules in the oceans to make amino acids,

the building blocks of proteins. Proteins, in turn are a crucial part of all living cells. How the first living cells evolved is still a mystery, but proteins must have played a pivotal role.

Once life got a foothold, it ran mostly on sunlight, like a car runs on gasoline. Plants take in photons of sunlight—starlight, really—and use their energy to change carbon dioxide and water into carbohydrates and oxygen. In turn, animals and people breathe this oxygen and eat plants. Animals, in turn, eat other animals. And stars started it all.

# Do scientists still think the universe started with a Big Bang?

The Big Bang is the name of a theory about the creation of the universe. It's a funny name for such an awe-inspiring event, especially if you've ever asked yourself questions like these: If the universe is everything there is, how can it have a beginning? What was there before? If space doesn't go on forever, what's "outside" space? What's outside *that*? And what's "forever," anyway?

These ideas are hard to think about, maybe even a little scary. But they're some of the biggest questions human beings can ask.

For years, most scientists have accepted the idea that the universe did have a beginning—in an explosive event they jokingly dubbed "The Big Bang." About 15 billion years ago, they think, all the matter and space in the universe was collapsed together. The matter now in billions upon billions of galaxies, each with millions or billions of stars, fit into a space infinitely smaller than the period at the end of this sentence.

Scientists believe the universe burst into being some 15 billion years ago, at first as a haze of particles even smaller than atoms. Later, atoms formed, and after perhaps a billion years, galaxies of stars. Since its explosive beginning, scientists say, the universe—space itself—has been expanding like a balloon, getting larger and larger.

*Most scientists believe the universe burst into being about 15 billion years ago.*

But in the past several years, scientists studying the structure of the universe have made some unexpected dis-

coveries. Some of these have shown that there may be problems with parts of the Big Bang theory. (The real world, after all, doesn't always fit neatly into our ideas about it.)

One problem is how matter spread out as the universe expanded. When an object explodes, it tends to throw its contents in all directions equally. So if all matter started out squeezed together and then exploded outward, it should be distributed fairly evenly throughout space.

*All the matter in the universe may once have been collapsed into a space smaller than the period at the end of this sentence.*

The reality, however, is very different. We live in a very lumpy universe. When we look out into space, we see clumps of matter. Enormous galaxies are scattered across the universe, with vast stretches of empty space between them. On a grander scale, the galaxies are grouped into clusters, and the clusters into superclusters. So far, scientists don't agree on how and why such structures formed. But recently, even more serious problems have emerged.

Using the latest instruments, including telescopes orbiting high above the Earth, scientists have discovered new, even more puzzling structures—long chains of galaxies, another challenge to the idea of a nice, even distribution of matter.

To solve all these riddles, scientists are tinkering with the Big Bang theory, fine-tuning it. Their best guess is that gravity, which makes matter clump together, tended to make minor clumps bigger and bigger, helping to create huge, pancake-shaped clouds of hydrogen and helium gas. Under gravity's pull, the clouds shrank together, forming the first collections of stars—the galaxies. Since clouds were already grouped with other clouds by their gravitational attraction, galaxies were born in clusters.

Some scientists have given up on the Big Bang theory entirely. They are working on updating earlier theories of creation, such as the Steady State theories, which assume that the universe has always been here and always will be. In these models, there was no beginning, and there will be no end. Matter is continuously created as time goes on, forming new galaxies of stars.

# The Solar System

**T**he usual picture of our solar system is this: nine planets in nice neat orbits around a constant, ever-burning Sun. But the reality is far more interesting. In addition to the planets, there are dozens of strange moons, some of which are worlds in their own right, and thousands of asteroids. Far beyond the orbit of Pluto, the ninth planet, lurk tens of thousands of comets and, perhaps, other small icy worlds. Tethered to our sun by gravity, these orbit at great distances, almost halfway to the next nearest stars.

And the solar system is chaotic, always changing, sometimes violently. The force of gravity makes neighboring planets pull on one another, changing each other's orbits over time. Violent collisions with asteroids can knock planets over into strange new tilts. Meanwhile, planets undergo shifts in climate, as their atmospheres evolve and change. Presiding over the whole chaotic scene, the Sun is gradually using up its supply of nuclear fuel. Billions of years from now, our star will bloat to red-giant size, and still later, shrink to a cool, burned-out shell of its former self.

# How did the Sun form? what will happen to it?

We depend on our star, the Sun. Every morning, as the Earth turns, the Sun rises in the sky, lighting and warming the landscape. Without the Sun, there would be no life.

But 5 billion years ago, the Sun and its nine planets didn't exist. The atoms in your body and in this page were floating in a cloud of gas and dust between the stars.

Scientists think the cloud's gas, which was mainly hydrogen, was swirling around slowly. As more gas and dust collected, the cloud began to pull in on itself. The force making the cloud shrink was gravity. In the cloud, particles were attracted to other particles and began bunching up.

Meanwhile, the cloud had begun to rotate in one direction. To see how, astronomer William Hartmann of Arizona's Planetary Science Institute suggests this experiment: Stir a cup of coffee every which way. Then drop in some milk. You should see the coffee begin to rotate in one direction.

Something similar happened in the cloud, as random, every-which-way movements gradually added up into a slight rotation in one direction. The enormous cloud was turning in space.

Some scientists add a dramatic twist to the story. They think that a nearby star may have exploded, sending material spewing in every direction. Some of this material may have spread into our gas cloud. And the shock waves from the explosion may have pushed the cloud to shrink even more.

*The light that floods out from the Sun is equal to that of 4 trillion trillion light bulbs.*

As the cloud condensed, it began to spin faster, like a spinning figure skater who pulls her arms close to her body. The faster the cloud turned, the more its shape changed. The cloud's center

# In millions of years,

began to bulge, as more material collected there. And the outer part of the cloud flattened. Soon, its shape resembled a pizza with a ball stuck in the center. The ball was—you guessed it—the infant Sun, a lump of gas several times larger than our entire solar system today. (Scientists call the newborn Sun a "protostar.")

How did the Sun go from being a dark ball of gas to a hot, fiery star? It happened very slowly, over thousands and thousands of years, as the protostar and the surrounding cloud continued to contract under the pull of gravity. In the cloud, atoms collided with other atoms, making heat. Temperatures in the cloud rose, especially in the overcrowded center,

where the collisions were fast and furious. Gases in the protostar begin to glow. Inside the shrinking Sun, the temperature gradually rose—up into the millions of degrees.

At these enormously high temperatures and intense pressures, something new began happening to the crammed-together atoms. Hydrogen atoms began to fuse, or join together, forming

helium atoms.

Each time some hydrogen changed to helium, a little leftover energy—heat and light—was released. Since this was happening throughout the core of the Sun, it added up to a lot of energy, flooding the new solar system with light: The Sun had turned on. It had become a living star, joining the other glowing balls of gas we see in the night sky.

The process that powers the Sun is called nuclear fusion. Fusion is a kind of continuous controlled explosion at the center of the Sun, where temperatures are thought to approach 27,000,000° to 40,000,000° F. In the Sun today, 4 million tons of hydrogen are turned into helium every second of every minute of every day. The light that floods out is equal to that of 4 trillion trillion light bulbs.

But the Sun has only so much hydrogen to fuse, and gradually, the star has been changing. It started out as nearly 75 percent hydrogen, and some 25 percent helium. Today, after billions of years of fusion, the amount of hydrogen in the core of the Sun, where fusion goes on, has dropped to about 35 percent.

As you might guess, stars eventually run out of hydrogen in their core. Like any fuel, it will eventually be used up; there are no hydrogen filling stations for stars. The star

will find itself with a helium center, surrounded by a hydrogen "shell." Hydrogen in the shell will continue fusing into helium, but the star will be on the decline.

FAST FACT

When the Sun was very young, it was 20 times larger and 100 times brighter than it is today.

Like people, stars are born, get older, and finally die. At 4.6 billion years, the Sun is a middle-aged star. Scientists estimate that the Sun has another 5 or 6 billion years of life left.

As our star ages, and the hydrogen in its core disappears, the Sun will fuse the hydrogen closer to the surface. But sooner or later, hydrogen fusion will die out. The helium core will shrink a little. Then a new process will start: helium fusion.

The helium that was created over billions of years will be jammed together, and heli-

um atoms will fuse, forming heavier carbon atoms. The Sun will continue to shine. But over millions of years, the outside of the Sun will expand into the cold of space and then cool from its current 10,000° F to about 5,800° F. The cooler, bigger Sun will give off lower-energy red light. We call such a star a "red giant."

The bloated Sun will swell until it swallows the planets Mercury and Venus. As the Sun looms nearer to Earth, temperatures on our planet will soar. The oceans will boil away into space, and Earth will become a dry, rocky world, like Mercury is today. By then, perhaps, we humans will have left for more comfortable surroundings elsewhere.

When the helium is all used up, carbon will be fused. But nuclear fusion can't go on forever. The Sun will slowly lose some of its gases to space, until only the hot core remains.

From a red giant, the Sun

will collapse into a white dwarf, shrunken, perhaps, to the size of Earth. (Because a white dwarf star is so dense, a teaspoonful of its matter can weigh a ton.) And then, over millions of years, the Sun will cool into a dark, dead cinder—a black dwarf.

Stars more massive than the Sun go through even stranger changes as they age. Running out of hydrogen and helium, they fuse carbon into oxygen. Once the stars have oxygen hearts, they fuse oxygen into neon. Neon fuses into other elements, until finally, atoms such as silicon may

*In the future, the Sun will expand until it engulfs Mercury and Venus.*

be fused into iron. The iron core eventually collapses, and there may be a tremendous explosion. The exploding star, called a supernova, spits its contents into space.

The most massive stars may ultimately shrink into black holes. In a black hole, gravity is so strong that even light can't escape. A black hole is something like a whirlpool in space, sucking matter in and growing bigger as it does. Some scientists speculate that black holes may be doorways to other universes, or may be used as ways to travel in shortcuts across our own universe. (For more on black holes, see page 86.) So although stars die, some are reborn as strange and wonderful new objects.

# Does the Sun spin?

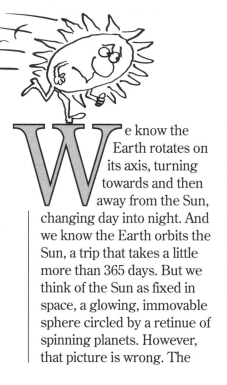

We know the Earth rotates on its axis, turning towards and then away from the Sun, changing day into night. And we know the Earth orbits the Sun, a trip that takes a little more than 365 days. But we think of the Sun as fixed in space, a glowing, immovable sphere circled by a retinue of spinning planets. However, that picture is wrong. The Sun is constantly moving. It's up to the planets and their moons to keep up with the Sun as it traverses space.

First, the Sun is indeed rotating, just like the Earth and the other planets. Second, scientists think the Sun is pulsating—rhythmically swelling up and then shrinking again. And finally, the Sun is moving through space, planets circling it like moths, as it journeys through the dark between the stars.

The Sun spins for the same reason the planets do.

FAST FACT

**If we could weigh the Sun here on Earth, the scale would show it contains about 900,000,000,000,-000,000,000,000,000,000 pounds of matter—mainly hydrogen and helium.**

Along with Earth and the other planets, our star was born from a rotating cloud of gas and dust in space some 4.6 billion years ago. The solar system was born in motion. However, the Sun is not solid like the Earth. It is a ball of glowing gases. And because the Sun is so wispy, it can behave in its own peculiar way as it spins.

For example, different parts of the Sun can, and do, rotate at different speeds. The gases near the Sun's equator, or middle, take 25 days to rotate once around. But the gases near its top and bottom—its poles—take 33 days to turn once around. (The entire solid Earth, of course, takes about 24 hours to turn once around.)

There are many mysteries about the Sun, and one of the strangest is the behavior of its superhot core. The core, scientists think, is spinning on its own, and nearly four times faster than the rest of the Sun.

As it spins, the Sun pulsates, expanding and then shrinking about every 5 minutes. It's almost as if the massive star were breathing. No one knows why the Sun pulsates, but some suggest the expansion and contraction is caused by complicated sound waves traveling through the solar gases.

There may be another kind of pulsing going on in the Sun. Scientists think that gravity causes the Sun to pulse about every half hour. How? Dense hot gases near the Sun's center swell up through the Sun into regions of thinner gases, expanding the Sun a bit. Then gravity pulls the gases back toward the center, and the Sun shrinks again.

# Spying on Our Star

Scientists, stuck 93 million miles away on Earth, have worked hard to come up with new ways to figure out how our star works. They launch rockets with cameras that pick up the X-rays the Sun emits, creating pictures of the star in X-ray light. Satellites circling Earth carry instruments to monitor the Sun's pulsations. And some scientists trek to Antarctica in the summer, when the Sun never sets, to study our star for 3 months at a time.

# How does the Sun keep the planets in orbit ?

Gravity is the most mysterious force in the universe, scientists say—and the least understood. And yet, if it weren't for gravity, the planets would go flying away from the Sun like nine billiard balls.

In fact, if gravity didn't exist, neither would planets. Gravity—the attraction of matter to other matter—is what binds them together into balls to begin with. (For more on how gravity shaped the planets, see page 31.)

The gravity of the Sun is strong enough to keep nine planets, dozens of moons, and thousands of asteroids and comets orbiting it like moths around a porch light. Left on their own, these bodies would tend to move off in a straight line. They orbit instead because their attraction to the Sun continuously pulls their paths into curves. Like a pony tethered to a pole, carrying kids around and around, an orbiting object is tied to the Sun by the invisible threads of gravity.

But as the distance between objects increases, attraction between them weakens quickly. The Sun's pull on faraway Pluto is much less than its pull on Mercury or Venus.

*If it weren't for gravity, the planets would go flying away from the Sun like nine billiard balls.*

Gravity's force decreases (or increases) exponentially. For example, if the Earth were 186 million miles from the Sun—twice its actual distance—the Sun's pull on it would be only one-quarter as strong. Three times further away than now, and gravity would be just one-ninth as

strong. And so on. Move the Earth far enough, and, virtually free from the Sun's grip, it could make a break for the wide-open spaces between the stars.

In addition to distance, the mass of objects—how much matter each contains—affects the force of gravity. The Sun and the Earth are each attracted to the other, but because the Sun is so much more massive, it pulls harder.

Scientists think that the force of gravity actually shapes space. Space around a clump of matter is curved; the more massive the object,

**Scientists think that the force of gravity actually shapes space.**

such as a star, the more space is curved.

How? Imagine holding a bedsheet with someone, the sheet pulled tight. Now imagine putting a heavy ball in the center. The sheet curves around the ball. Other balls placed on the sheet will tend to roll toward the heavy ball. Something similar happens with stars; their mass curves space and keeps other objects, such as planets, "rolling" around them.

# Does the Sun shine on all nine planets ?

· · · · · · · · · · · · · · · · · · · · · ·

The Sun's rays stream out into space in all directions, reaching all nine circling planets. But depending on how far away a planet is, more or less light reaches it.

We can see how this works by looking at distant stars. Most stars in the night sky are as big and bright (or brighter) than our Sun. But because they are so far away, their light is too weak to illuminate the Earth.

On Mercury, the nearest planet to the Sun, the Sun looms huge in the sky, nearly three times the size it appears from Earth. During daytime, the surface may be blindingly bright. But the sky is black, even during the day, because Mercury has virtually no atmosphere to reflect and scatter sunlight (rather like our airless Moon).

When the Sun beats down on Mercury's rocky landscape, temperatures can soar to 800°F. At night, however, the heat freely radiates out into space, and the temperature can plunge to −280°F.

Venus, the second planet from the Sun, is surrounded by an atmosphere made mainly of carbon dioxide gas.

*Even though Mercury is the nearest planet to the Sun, its lack of a real atmosphere makes the sky dark even during the day.*

Floating in this atmosphere are thick clouds of foul-smelling sulfuric acid. The cloud cover makes every day look overcast on the surface.

Although Venus is further from the Sun than Mercury, its surface temperatures are even higher. Why?

Blame the greenhouse effect. Carbon dioxide gas traps heat on the planet, like the glass of a greenhouse keeps plants warm. So temperatures on Venus hover around 900° F.

After Earth, the third planet, comes Mars. On Mars, the Sun appears two-thirds the size it does from Earth. Only one-third as much light reaches Mars as reaches Earth. And the weakened sunlight must filter through a dusty red sky, one that is often filled with the rusty soil kicked up by Martian windstorms. Still, summer days may reach an Earth-like 63° F, and Martian noons can be quite bright.

Beyond Mars are the giant planets, made mostly of gas—Jupiter, Saturn, Uranus, and Neptune. All four are blanketed by thick clouds. And at each of these far outposts of the solar system, the Sun appears more shrunken, its light more feeble.

From Jupiter, for example, the Sun appears only one-fifth as large as it does from Earth, and Jupiter receives only 1/25th the light and heat that we do. From high in Jupiter's clouds, we would see a small, wan Sun. Far beneath its thick clouds, scientists think Jupiter is covered by an ocean of metallic liquid hydrogen. Down on the ocean's surface, they say, we would be floating in eternal darkness, the scene illuminated only by an occasional giant bolt of lightning.

Although sunlight is

weaker still on Saturn, it is strong enough to spotlight the planet's immense ring system. Saturn's thousands of rings are made mostly of ice. Sunlight striking the rings turns them into glittering circles of light. Depending on how Saturn is tilted in relation to the Sun, the rings may cast huge shadows on the planet, plunging most of Saturn's southern half into

*From Jupiter, the Sun appears only one-fifth as large as it does from Earth.*

even deeper darkness. (Imagine an Earth-ring that shaded much of South America, Africa, and Australia, and you'll get the picture.)

Finally, from icy, far-off Pluto, the ninth planet, the Sun is a distant, chilly light, set 3.6 billion miles away. It appears as a very bright star in a dark sky, with little to identify it as Pluto's own sun.

# Is there another solar system besides ours?

Planets, moons, asteroids, and comets surround our sun, like revelers around a bonfire. Together, the Sun and its motley collection of orbiting objects make up a "solar sytcm."

Much as we love and need it, the Sun is just an average star. Look up in the night sky and you will see thousands of others that are just as big and bright, but so far away that they look like twinkly points. Beyond these stars are millions more too distant to see without a telescope—the rest of the hundreds of billions of suns in our Milky Way galaxy.

But our galaxy is not unique, either. Strewn across the empty darkness of space are perhaps a hundred billion galaxies, each made of millions or billions of suns. The universe is an unimaginably big place.

With all those countless stars, why would our sun be the only one surrounded by planets? That's the question scientists ask themselves. The answer seems to be that it's nearly impossible that there aren't planets circling at least some, if not most, of those other suns.

In fact, some scientists have estimated that there may be some 10 billion trillion planets scattered throughout the cosmos. The problem lies in actually finding them,

which is very difficult indeed. Why? Well, compared to stars, planets are small and

*Trying to see a normal-size planet orbiting a nearby star would be like trying to see a speck of dust floating near a 1,000-watt light bulb 2 miles away.*

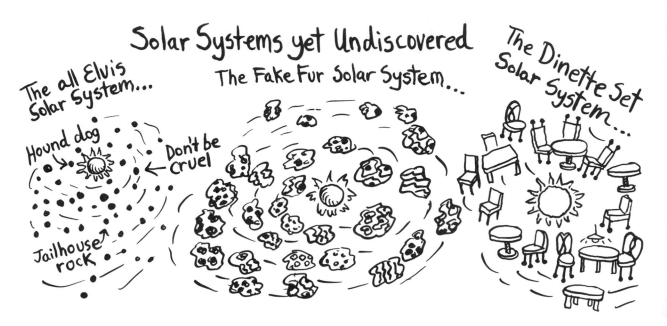

Solar Systems yet Undiscovered

The all Elvis Solar System...

The Fake Fur Solar System...

The Dinette Set Solar System...

Hound dog

Don't be cruel

Jailhouse rock

dark. They don't shine with their own light, although they may reflect light that falls on them from their star.

However, planets around other stars would be too far-off and probably too faint to be be seen with even the most powerful Earth-based telescopes. A normal-size planet orbiting a nearby star would be lost in the glare of its sun's light. Why? Imagine looking at a 1,000-watt light bulb from two miles down the road and trying to see a

speck of dust floating near the bulb. It's just about that bad. So scientists have had to devise other ways of searching for them. The best way, they think, is by looking for their gravitational effects on their home stars.

Because matter is attracted to matter, all objects tug on one another. Stars pull on planets, which is why planets orbit. And planets, in turn, tug on stars. Meanwhile, stars rotate, just like planets, and they also move through

space, pulling their wagon train of planets with them.

Scientists look for wobbles in a star's path as it moves through space. Such wobbles could be caused by unseen planets, as they circle the star and tug it this way and that.

In 1991, British astronomers announced they had found a planet-sized object orbiting a type of star called a pulsar. (A pulsar is a small, dense star that spins very quickly. As the star spins, it throws off radio waves.)

The scientists believed there was something orbiting the star because its radio signals fluctuated, as if the pulsar were wobbling. Some months later, U.S. astronomers discovered a similar wobble in another pulsar, where it seems that two, or even three, unseen planets may orbit.

But in January of 1992, the British astronomers made an unexpected announce-

*Scientists estimate that there may be 10 billion trillion planets orbiting stars throughout the cosmos.*

ment: They were wrong. The team of researchers failed to figure in our own planet's motion around the Sun, which affected the readings on their Earth-bound instruments. This error made it seem like the other star was wobbling.

However, there seem to be no errors in the U.S. study. Their discovery and others like it indicate that we are almost certainly not the lone solar system in the cosmos.

# Is our next-door-neighbor, Venus, similar to Earth?

**S**eparated at birth? Venus has been called Earth's "sister planet." Earth is the third planet from the Sun; Venus is the second. The two planets are similar in size, and in density—the amount of matter contained in each. But there the similarity ends. Venus is more like a twisted sister—Earth's "evil twin," with a crushing atmosphere, inferno-like temperatures, and poisonous clouds.

Venus's thick atmosphere, made mostly of carbon dioxide gas, weighs heavily on the planet. If you were standing on the surface, the atmosphere would press down on each square inch of you with 1,260 pounds of force. (Earth's lightweight air presses with a mere 14.7 pounds per square inch.) A penny dropped through dense Venusian "air" would flutter slowly to the ground, as if falling through water. In fact, trying to walk on Venus would be like trying to take a stroll half a mile under the ocean on earth. If a breeze picked up, you would be swept away as if by a strong ocean current.

Because of its 96 percent carbon dioxide atmosphere, Venus suffers from the greenhouse effect—in spades. Sunlight gets in, but heat can't get out. So the surface stays a toasty 900°F. And as for Venus's clouds, don't even ask. They're a dirty yellow-white, made mostly of sulfuric acid, and smell like rotten eggs. Chemical reactions in the clouds produce acids that can dissolve lead, tin, and rock.

## Venus is dotted with thousands of volcanoes.

Venus is completely covered by heavy layers of these clouds. For many years, Earth-bound humans could only guess at what was underneath them.

As usually happens, whenever we try to imagine what another planet must be like, we picture it as familiar—somehow like Earth. Years ago, some suggested that because it had such thick clouds, Venus was a swampy world, a place where it rained day and night. Reality turned out to be far stranger.

In the late 1960s and early 1970s, the Soviet Union sent a number of space probes, called Venera, to Venus. They showed the planet to be a desolate, rocky place—no watery swamps in sight, and none possible, since water would boil away on the extremely hot surface.

In 1990, American scientists used radar equipment on board the Magellan spacecraft to learn more about what's under the blanket of clouds. Here's how it worked: The spacecraft sent radio signals down to Venus. The radio waves penetrated the clouds, hitting the surface. Some places absorbed the radio waves. Some places bounced them back to the spacecraft. In this way, scientists could map the hidden surface.

There were some surprises: Magellan found that Venus is dotted with thousands of volcanoes. And south of Venus's equator, Magellan found seven flat-topped hills, each more than 8,000 feet high.

The hills are made of

# Airbursts Over Venus

The explosion of a metoroid over Siberia in 1908 shows that even when an object falling in from space disintegrates above the ground, it can do tremendous damage. (For more on this see page 148.)

But Earth isn't the only planet to suffer injuries from such "airbursts." Scientists studying radar images of Venus have found evidence that our neighbor planet, too, has been the victim of exploding falling rocks.

Near the surface, Venus's atmosphere is 50 times thicker than Earth's. So as objects fall through it, it's even more likely that they will be torn apart by friction before they reach the ground. In addition, the denser atmosphere transmits shock waves better—so an object that explodes above ground will have a more deadly impact down on the surface.

What scientists found on Venus (in addition to lots of ordinary craters): some 400 flat splotches, each 18 to 30 miles across. These are the scars, they think, left by meteoroids exploding above the planet's surface.

POW

hardened lava. Scientists say that since Venus is so hot, lava may cool and harden more slowly there than on Earth, allowing it time to pile up into higher lava mountains.

## *The surface of Venus is a toasty 900°F.*

Rivers of lava seem to have flowed across Venus's surface on and off for millions of years, Magellan found. One long channel, apparently etched out long ago by hot lava, stretches for some 625 miles.

On Earth, wind and rain eventually erode and erase newly created features on our planet's surface. On Venus, formations created by lava flows tend to be preserved, showing just how much our strange sister planet has been shaped by volcanoes through the centuries.

# Why is the planet Mars red?

When we look into the night sky, Mars is often easy to find. It is the only planet that seems to shine with a reddish light, making it stand out in a field of twinkling white stars.

Pictures sent back from the Viking lander in 1976 show that Mars looks a lot like parts of Arizona. The ground is rocky. Boulders are strewn among shifting sand dunes. Flat-topped mesas lie under a salmon-pink sky. Even on summer mornings, a light coating of water frost and carbon dioxide snow turns the red rocks white.

Mars is tinted red because the iron oxide minerals in its soil reflect reddish-orange light from the Sun. In other words, Martian soil contains a lot of rusty iron. (So if you want to see the color of Mars up close, just look at a rusty old frying pan.)

Wind spreads the soil particles across the Martian landscape, covering dark-grey volcanic rocks with a layer of rust. Dustdevils—

*To see the color of Mars up close, just look at a rusty old frying pan.*

spinning tornadoes—whip more soil into the air. Dust storms sometimes rage out of control, blanketing the entire planet in a blinding red haze. Even when the air is calm, some red dust is always in the air, tinting the sky pink.

The Red Planet is in many ways different from Earth. It's quite a bit smaller—just over half the size of Earth. And because Mars has less mass, its gravity is weaker—a little more than a third as strong as our planet's gravity. This means that a 100-pound person would weigh only 38 pounds on Mars.

Martian air is very thin—only 1 percent as dense as our atmosphere. Our air is mostly nitrogen and oxygen.

Martian air is mostly carbon dioxide—the gas we use on Earth to make sodas bubbly.

Like Earth, Mars has seasons. Temperatures on Mars range from a frigid nighttime low of –225°F in winter to an almost-warm 63°F on a summer afternoon. On cold winter mornings, carbon dioxide gas freezes in the air, making dense icy fogs.

Earth has the Grand Canyon, but Mars has the *Vallis Marineris* (Valley of the Mariner spacecraft), a string of canyons nearly 3,000 miles long. (If it were carved across the United States, Vallis Mari-neris would stretch almost all the way from the Pacific to the Atlantic Ocean.) Drop a stone into the deepest

*On Mars, water is trapped in the soil, frozen in permafrost, and locked in an ice cap at the North Pole.*

Martian canyons, and the stone would fall and fall—3 to 4 miles down.

Earth has Mount Everest, but Mars has *Olympus Mons,* or Mount Olympus. Towering nearly 15 miles into the Martian air, this spectacular volcanic mountain is almost three times as high as Mount Everest. Its enormous base would neatly cover the entire state of Missouri.

As different from our planet as Mars may seem today, it was once upon a time more like Earth than any other world in our solar system. Photographs show dry riverbeds crisscrossing the Martian surface, and scientists think that water once flowed freely across this desert planet.

The liquid water has been gone for a long time—perhaps 2 billion years. Some of it is trapped in the soil; some is probably frozen deep underground in permafrost. More is tucked away at the planet's north pole, which is capped by a white layer of water ice. (Mars's south pole is mostly frozen carbon dioxide.)

What happened on Mars

---

**FAST FACT**

**Mars has two tiny moons, called Phobos and Deimos. They are named after the mythical horses that pulled the chariot of the Greek god, Mars— the god of war. The names mean "fear" and "panic," which is what most people feel about an approaching war.**

---

to make the water disappear? Scientists think that because its gravity is weak, Mars may

have slowly lost most of its original atmosphere. As the atmosphere thinned, there wasn't enough air pressure to keep liquid water on the surface. Much of it simply evaporated away.

Scientists think that the ancient, thicker Martian atmosphere also contained more oxygen. The evidence: the iron in the planet's red soil. Iron becomes rusty when it reacts with oxygen. The fact that Mars is red shows that it once had a very different atmosphere—perhaps even air *we* could breathe.

# Why does Jupiter have a red spot ?

· · · · · · · · · · · · · · · · · · · · · · · ·

Jupiter is the largest of the nine planets in our solar system—about 278,500 miles around its bulging waistline. This frigid world is shrouded in thick, icy clouds of ammonia and water, floating in an atmosphere that is mostly hydrogen. Down below, scientists think, liquid metallic hydrogen covers the entire planet.

Jupiter also has a large red spot in the clouds below its equator. No, it's not the beginning of planetary measles. The red blotch seems to be a monstrously large storm, nearly 30,000 miles long—big enough to swallow the Earth whole. Like Earth's small hurricanes, the oval-shaped storm on Jupiter rotates. But because it is so large, it takes 6 Earth-days to turn once.

As storms go, this one has had a long life. English scientist Robert Hooke first discerned the spot through a tele-scope in 1664. And the storm had probably been there for some time before he discovered it. Eventually, it was named "The Great Red Spot." And it's still going strong, more than 300 years later.

As the storm rotates, counter-clockwise, fierce winds, upwards of 300 miles an hour, blow past above and below. Why doesn't the Red Spot gradually come apart, scientists wonder?

To try to answer this and other questions, Philip Marcus, a scientist at the University of California at Berkeley, created a model of the Red Spot on his computer. The results were interesting enough that other researchers decided to test the model in a laboratory. How do you build a storm indoors? Scientists at the University of Texas at Austin used a vat of water, which could be rotated—just as Jupiter rotates.

On Jupiter, heat from the inside of the planet makes currents and swirling patterns form in the cream, tan, and orange clouds. The patterns in the clouds look a lot like the patterns that develop in a pan of water simmering on the stove.

To mimic these currents, the Texas scientists pumped

water in and out of the rotating vat. They also dumped red dye in the vat, so they could easily see the patterns in the swirling, spinning liquid.

Out of the chaos, patterns did emerge. Vortices—or whirlpools—began to form in the water. Then, to the scientists' delight, the vortices began to join together. A large oval pattern grew, whirling in the water. They had made a Great Red Spot—in miniature.

This experiment helped to show how the Red Spot on Jupiter could have formed—out of smaller whirling storms linking together. While the Red Spot tends to be pulled

*Jupiter's red spot is a storm 30,000 miles long.*

apart over time, it probably keeps going by absorbing new vortices that form around it. In other words, it stays alive by feeding on smaller storms.

Why is the spot red? Clark Chapman, an astronomer at the Planetary Science Institute in Tucson, Arizona, said that some have suggested that the chemicals phosphorus or sulfur might color the spot. But as yet, he said, nobody really knows.

# Why does Saturn have
# How many are there?

Saturn's rings are one of the most spectacular sights in our solar system. As far as we know, the first person to see them was Galileo, in 1610. Looking through his telescope at Saturn, he saw what he said looked like "two ears" on the planet.

Using a better telescope in 1655, the Dutch astronomer Christian Huygens recognized the ears as a beautiful system of rings, suspended in space around Saturn.

Set against the pale yellow-and-tan planet, the rings glitter in the light that shines from the faraway Sun. Like Jupiter, Saturn is a giant, gaseous world, covered with a hydrogen atmosphere and icy clouds of ammonia and water, which scientists think float over a planetwide ocean of liquid metallic hydrogen.

Saturn's luminous rings are made mostly of water ice. But the ice is not frozen in solid bands around the planet. Instead, each ring is made up of hundreds of thousands of pieces, ranging in size from smaller than the crushed ice in your soft drink to snowballs to boulders to small icebergs.

From far away, the bits of ice, tumbling around Saturn at 45,000 miles an hour, look like they form several wide rings. Before the Voyagers I and II explorer spacecraft flew by Saturn in 1980 and 1981, most scientists thought there were three or four rings of particles. The first pictures sent back came as a revelation.

Instead of a few rings, the photographs showed thousands. There were a few big gaps between the rings, but most were very close together, like the grooves on a compact disc.

The Voyager cameras were too far away to photograph individual ice particles. However, photographs did show how thin some of the

*Each ring is made up of hundreds of thousands of pieces of ice.*

# rings around it?

rings are: You can see the stars through them.

Another surprise: Clearing paths between some of the rings are icy chunks, half a mile to 60 miles across, now called "moonlets" (not to be confused with Saturn's regular moons, of which there are at least 17). These moonlets became known as the shepherds or sheepdogs of the rings. Scientists think that their gravitational force, along with that of Saturn's regular moons, may help define the edges of the rings and their spacings.

While the Voyager space probes photographed the rings, their radios listened to them. Bursts of static were heard. This crackle came from invisible lightning leaping through the rings. The

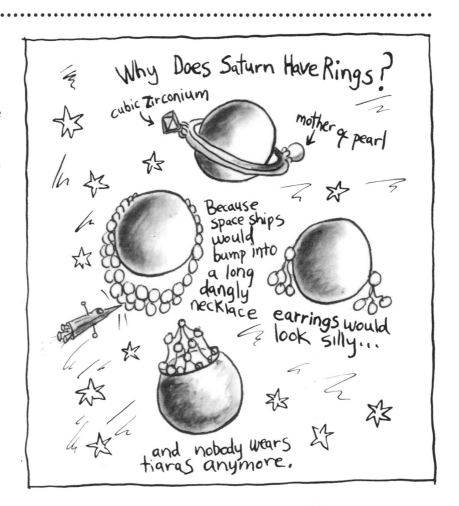

# Ring Once for Jupiter

Jupiter is a ringed planet, too, but it appears to have only one flat ring, about 3,000 miles wide. The ring's inner edge extends down to the top of Jupiter's clouds, some 33,000 miles above what may be the solid center of this gaseous world.

Unlike Saturn's crushed-ice rings, Jupiter's lone ring seems to be made of tiny rocky particles and dust. Scientists think the particles are chipped off Jupiter's orbiting boulders—rocky moonlets. The boulders lose bits of themselves when they collide with micrometeoroids—tiny pieces of rock, whizzing through space. Pulled by the planet's gravity, the boulder bits then settle into orbit around Jupiter. Enough pieces may have been knocked loose from the moonlets to create a visible ring of material.

It is also possible, scientists say, that some of the ring particles were spewed into space out of violent volcanoes on Io, one of Jupiter's big moons.

lightning cannot be seen because there is no air in space to glow.

How did the rings form? Good guesses are welcome. One idea is that the particles in the rings are all that's left of a moon that exploded when it was hit by a comet or asteroid. Another idea is that a comet came too near Saturn and was ripped apart by the huge planet's gravity.

Some scientists also think that as small, nearby moons are hit by meteorites, more particles are added to the rings. To test these theories, scientists hope one day to examine ring material close up, as they have been able to do with Moon rocks.

Although Saturn might seem unique, it is not the only ringed planet in our solar system. Jupiter, Uranus, and Neptune also have rings, but theirs are thin and dark.

# Diamonds Are Forever, But Rings Don't Last

Saturn wouldn't be Saturn without its shining rings. Or would it? Some scientists now think that Saturn's rings, as well as the rings around Jupiter, Uranus, and Neptune have existed in their current form for no more than about 100 million years. But the planets are about 4.6 billion years old. So for at least part of their history, they may have been ringless.

Earlier ring systems may have sprung up and then disappeared. We may never know. But it does seem like rings can't last forever. Gravity and gases cause their downfall.

Here's how: The gases that surround a planet—forming its atmosphere—thin out gradually into the emptiness of space. But even at the distance of rings, there are traces of these gases. And that's the problem. Tiny particles in the ring collide with the gas molecules of the thin atmosphere. So there is a kind of friction between the particles and the gases, called atmospheric drag. This drag slows the orbiting ring particles, causing them to spiral down toward their planet.

Gravity also tugs particles planetward. Overwhelmed by the drag of the atmosphere and the pull of gravity, bits and pieces of the rings eventually tumble down into the skies of their home planets, much like satellites sometimes fall to Earth.

# Why does Pluto switch orbits with Neptune?

At 3.6 billion miles from the Sun, Pluto is usually the most distant planet in our solar system, so it is known as the ninth planet. It is very small, and so distant that scientists don't know all that much about it, but its surface seems to be made mainly of nitrogen ice. Pluto takes about 248 Earth-years to travel once around the Sun. In Pluto's eternal twilight, the Sun is just another bright star in the sky. If you lived on Pluto, you might not even guess that the Sun was "your" star.

However, Pluto is sometimes the *eighth* planet from the Sun, and its neighbor, Neptune, is farthest away. In 1979, for example, Pluto cut across Neptune's orbit, like a car cutting in front of another car.

Pluto's path around the Sun is not the same as the orbits of the other eight planets, which lie roughly in the same plane. That means that they are in concentric circles around the Sun (although no orbit is a perfect circle).

Pluto's odd orbit takes it up and out of the flat plane that the other planets' orbits lie in. So Pluto swings up through the plane of the solar system and then down again, cutting across the path of Neptune. Pluto regains its place as "most distant" in 1999, when its path once again takes it sailing out of Neptune's circle.

Recently, a few astronomers have started

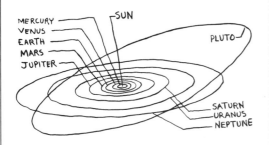

MERCURY
VENUS
EARTH
MARS
JUPITER
SUN
PLUTO
SATURN
URANUS
NEPTUNE

questioning whether Pluto really belongs with the other eight planets at all.

Why? The first four planets in our solar system—Mercury, Venus, Mars, and Earth—are fairly small, rocky worlds. The next four—Jupiter, Saturn, Uranus, and Neptune—are huge, gaseous worlds.

And then there's Pluto. About the size of our Moon, Pluto is impossibly tiny compared to the giant worlds that are its nearest neighbors in the outer solar system. And Charon, its moon, is nearly

## *Pluto takes about 248 Earth-years to orbit the Sun.*

half as big as Pluto itself—it's more like a sister world than a moon.

So here's the theory: Pluto and Charon don't belong in the group of eight planets. Instead, they are just two of many small almost-planets orbiting near the out-

skirts of the solar system. In fact, some scientists think, there may be thousands of "plutos" beyond Pluto and Charon.

Some scientists have dubbed such tiny, cold objects "ice dwarfs." The ice dwarfs, if they exist, would be very far away, very dark, and very hard to find. But if the theory proves true, it will change our view of the solar system. The familiar nine planets may be joined by a swarm of thousands of little icy worlds, each orbiting the Sun at vast distance.

The Casting Out of Pluto + Charon

# How come the Earth is tilted ?

**I**f you could watch the Earth circling the Sun, you might decide our planet has very poor posture. The Earth rides around the Sun leaning to one side, like a sailboat listing in a strong breeze. The Earth is tipped over about 23.5° from straight up-and-down. It got that way, scientists say, in the demolition derby that formed our solar system some 4.6 billion years ago.

The Sun, the Earth, and the other eight planets in our solar system formed from a rotating cloud of gas and dust in space. Scientists think the Earth grew into a planet-size body as particles collided with other particles, adhering together to make bigger pieces. As millions of years passed, the colliding chunks

got bigger, worldlets crashed into other worldlets, and planets grew. (The Earth's moon may have formed when a particularly big body slammed into the still red-hot Earth. For more about this, see page 136.) According to Clark Chapman, of the Planetary Science Institute in Tucson, Arizona, there must have been one final enormous collision that knocked the poor

battered Earth over into its current position.

The tilt makes life on our planet more interesting. It makes leaves turn red in October in Maine. It bakes Ohio in August, sending kids splashing into pools. And it sometimes delivers January snows that shut New York City down. In short, the tilt makes seasons—four of them.

## *The Earth's tilt is what causes the seasons.*

How? Because of the tilt, the North Pole leans toward the Sun for half the year and away from the Sun for the rest. In the Northern Hemisphere, we get more sunlight and warmer weather when the North Pole is tipped toward the Sun. And we get longer nights and colder weather when it is tipped away from the Sun. (In the Southern Hemisphere, just the opposite happens: winter in Boston is summer in São Paulo, Brazil.)

If the Earth were to be pushed straight up on its axis, Chapman said, the seasons would nearly disappear. Since the Earth's orbit around the Sun is not a perfect circle, temperatures would drop a bit as the Earth made its farthest swing from the Sun. Then things would warm up as our planet came closer to the Sun again. But these slight variations would be a far cry from real seasons—fall, winter, spring, and summer. Without the Earth's tilt, these words wouldn't even be in the language.

*Scientists think an enormous impact knocked Earth onto its current tilt.*

# Topsy Turvy World

The Earth is not the only planet leaning to one side. Mars is tipped over by about the same amount, according to Chapman, and it, too, has seasons.

But the planet with the biggest tilt is distant Uranus. Some terrible impact, probably more than 4 billion years ago, when Uranus was very young, knocked Uranus completely over. Today, the whole planet, rings and all, rides around the Sun lying on its side.

Uranus is odd in another way, too: It spins backwards. Uranus turns from east to west. Scientists call its rotation *retrograde*.

At 1.8 billion miles from the Sun, Uranus is a frigid world; the average temperature of the atmosphere is about –350°F. As Uranus makes its long orbit of the Sun—one Uranian year is 84 Earth-years long—first one of its poles, and then the other basks in the Sun. When it is summer at its north pole, the sun shines continuously, day in and day out. Meanwhile, it is winter at the south pole, and pitch black. Each "season" lasts about 21 Earth-years.

When the U.S. space probe Voyager 2 flew past Uranus in 1986, it found some surprises. For example, the temperature of the atmosphere at the shadowed pole was 4° to 6° warmer than the temperature at the sunlit pole.

This may be due, scientists say, to a "seasonal lag" in temperature. Cold objects lose heat more slowly than hot objects. Since Uranus is already cold, it takes a long time to cool further. So a pole that has spent 21 years in light—but is currently in darkness—will take a long time to lose the heat it collected during its years in the sun.

# Where do comets come from, and what are they made of?

Around August 12 each year, meteors streak and flare across the night sky every few minutes, burning up in midair. This light show is called the Perseid meteor shower. In its orbit around the Sun, the Earth has crossed a meteor stream, bits and pieces broken off a comet on *its* journey around the Sun.

Comets (along with rocky asteroids) are part of the debris left over from the formation of the Sun, its planets, and their moons. Comets are made mostly of ice, with bits of rock and dust. Scientists think comets spend most of their time in vast herds on the outskirts of the solar system.

The most distant planet in our solar system, Pluto, is about 3.6 billion miles from the Sun. One collection of comets, called the Kuiper Belt, is thought to lie about 300 million miles beyond Pluto. Another, called the Oort Cloud, may be nearly 100 billion miles out in space.

Take the Oort Cloud—not really a cloud, but a vast gathering of trillions of comets, a little like a herd of lonely cows that goes on and on in every direction. The Oort Cloud is thought to surround our solar system like a halo.

However it's hard for scientists to prove that the comets are lurking out there.

Why? Even if you were speeding through the Oort Cloud, you wouldn't run into many comets. Each one may be separated from the next by millions or billions of miles of empty space. Too far from the Sun to be lit by its light, the comets are nearly as dark as the space around them.

The far-off comets don't

*A comet's orbit around the Sun can take more than a million years.*

have nice tails, either, like the comets in pictures. Reddish-brown, lumpy, averaging about 1¼ miles wide, they look a lot like dirty icebergs.

But a comet's drab appearance changes dramatically when it wanders away from the herd and toward the Sun. As it nears the Sun, a comet gets an instant makeover. Glowing and streaming, the comet may streak above the night sky of Earth, both scaring and delighting people.

What makes a comet split off from the rest of the herd in the Oort Cloud? Gravity gives it a tug.

Here's how. Our star, the Sun, pulls its wagon train of planets, moons, and comets through the Milky Way galaxy, a collection of billions of stars. As the gang of comets is tugged along, it sometimes passes near another sun.

The gravity of the other star pulls at the icebergs. And though the pull is gentle, it can be enough to send comets spinning off in all different directions.

Some take off into the loneliness of deep space, never to return to our solar system. Perhaps they'll travel on to light up the sky of an alien world one day. But other comets are launched on a journey inward, toward the Sun—and the Earth.

The trip is maddeningly slow. It can take a comet several million years to reach the inner solar system, where we are. As the centuries pass in the comet's epic journey, the Sun, once just a star in the comet's sky, looms ahead as a big, bright disk.

The comet begins to feel the solar wind, a stream of

### FAST FACT

A comet loses about 1/10th of 1 percent of its ice each time it passes the Sun as the ice vaporizes, forming a beautiful streaming tail. After about 1,000 trips around the Sun, all traces of a comet's ice will have disappeared, leaving only a collection of pebbles and dust.

radiation from the Sun. Ice crystals and dust particles are torn off the comet, and the ices vaporize, forming a streaming tail of gases. Lit by

the Sun, the gases in the tail glow. As the comet whizzes past the Earth, we may see it flash by in the night sky.

The comet may go in a million-year, slingshot loop around the Sun, traveling way beyond Pluto before once again turning back toward the inner solar system. Halley's Comet, which last showed its face in 1985, passes near the Earth about once every 76 years on its own, shorter loop through the solar system. The comet streaks past Earth, careens around the Sun, whizzes out beyond Neptune, and then takes a hairpin turn, heading our way once more.

# What are shooting stars?

**Y**ou've probably seen what looks like a falling star streak across the night sky. It's as if one star has torn itself away from the others and tumbled to Earth.

But what we are seeing is a meteor. Although from a distance meteors and stars look alike, they actually are very different. Stars are huge, glowing balls of gas, which only look small because they are very far away. (Our Sun is just an average-sized star, but it is big enough to hold more than a million Earths.)

But the meteors that flare so brightly across our skies are solid. They are usually pieces of rock and metal or ice, often only the size of peas, that have broken off from comets, or asteroids.

Like odd pieces of clay around a finished sculpture,

asteroids are part of the rocky debris left over from the formation of the inner planets. One large asteroid group orbits the Sun in the space between Mars and Jupiter.

When asteroids collide, as they have for billions of years, they send rock fragments flying in all directions. These fragments, called meteoroids, keep moving because there is no friction in the emptiness of space to slow them down.

Meteoroids range in size from grains of sand to boulders to house-sized and bigger. In the cold of space, they whiz by, dark and invisible to us. But as meteoroids pass near the Earth, they are sometimes caught by the Earth's gravity. Some hit the Earth's atmosphere traveling at 20,000 to 135,000 miles an hour.

As a typical stony meteoroid is pulled in by the Earth's gravity and tears down through the air, the rock and metal get hotter and

hotter. The heat is caused by friction. (If you rub your hand against carpet, the heat you feel is from friction.) On the space shuttle, special tiles protect the ship and crew from this heat.

Meteors have no tiles to protect them. So small meteors (the most common kind) burn up as they plunge through the sky. They flash briefly by, and then go out like a snuffed candle as they burn to a cinder.

A larger meteor, however, can survive the descent, and then the sky rains rocks.

In the 1980s, a Connecticut family heard a loud noise on their roof. An instant later, a meteorite crashed through the ceiling and rolled under the dining-room table. The astonished family donated their visitor from space to a science museum.

Because stories like this are so uncommon, we might assume meteoroids rarely collide with Earth. Actually, such impacts have occurred many times over the 4.6-bil-

## Lost in Space

*Comets* are icy bodies, measuring from about 3,000 feet to over 60 miles across.

*Asteroids* are stony bodies, measuring from about 3,000 feet to over 600 miles across.

*Meteoroids* are usually fragments of comets or asteroids, ranging from the size of dust grains to more than 300 feet across. When they flash briefly across the sky, burning up as they go, we call them *meteors*. When they land intact on the ground, we call them *meteorites*.

# Extra! Extra! Pieces of Other Worlds Found on Earth!

· · · · · · · · · · · · · · · · · · · · · · · · · · · · · · · · · ·

**J**udging from the kind of rock found in some meteorites, not all are fragments of asteroids or comets. Some appear to be chunks of the Moon. At least eight moon rocks have turned up in Antarctica (the South Pole). One weighs about a pound and a half.

The rocks are nearly identical to those brought back from the Moon by the Apollo astronauts. How did the chunks get here on their own? Scientists think meteorites hitting the Moon shattered Moon rocks and sent them flying out into space. Because the Moon's gravity is so low, the rocks kept going—and some landed on Earth.

Some meteorites may even be little chunks of the planet Mars. And somewhere on Mars, or perhaps Venus, there may be little pieces of Earth—chipped off in the distant past by some huge meteorite that smashed into our planet.

lion-year history of both our planet and our Moon.

On the Moon, we can easily see where meteorites have struck. All those craters are holes made by meteorites slamming into the Moon. (For more on the Moon's craters, see page 142.) Here on Earth, however, most craters have disappeared. They have been covered by the ocean and lava from volcanoes, or erased over millions of years by rain and blowing sand.

# Why do we have eclipses?

When the Sun or the Moon is blocked from view or lying in shadow, we say it is eclipsed. The Moon passes between the Earth and the Sun, partially or totally blocking our view of thc Sun. That's a solar eclipse. Or the Moon passes on the opposite side of the Earth from the Sun, and the Earth shades the Moon like a big oak tree shades the ground. That's a lunar eclipse.

Eclipses happen because bodies in space are constantly changing position. As the Earth moves around the Sun, the Moon moves around the Earth. When, for a few minutes, the Moon, Earth, and Sun line up, there's an eclipse. Total eclipses of the Sun are rarest and the most dramatic.

In a total solar eclipse,

*During a total solar eclipse, the temperature drops and the stars come out.*

something seems to gobble up the Sun, bit by shining bit. As the Sun disappears, Earth's sky darkens, and the stars come out. The air grows rapidly cold. Soon, there is nothing left of the Sun but a thin ring of light hanging far out in the darkness, part of the glowing corona of gases surrounding our star.

Ancient Chinese artists drew a solar eclipse as a dragon devouring the Sun. In real-ity, however, the Sun comes out of hiding after a few minutes, and night turns back to day. The "dragon" was really the Moon, passing between the Earth and the Sun.

To picture what is happening in an eclipse, look at a bright light bulb across the room. Now hold a card in front of your eyes, and move it until the light bulb is covered. The card is nowhere near the lamp, but in passing between the lamp and your eyes, the card hides the light. When you move the card away, the light is uncovered once again.

So it is with the Moon. You see a solar eclipse when the Moon, sliding across the daytime sky, happens to pass in front of the face of the Sun. If the Moon cuts across only part of the Sun, there's a partial eclipse: Some of the Sun's surface is hidden, and for a few minutes, the day gets a little dimmer.

But if the Moon passes exactly in front of the Sun, it covers the Sun's whole face. That's a total eclipse. Total eclipses are quite rare. The Moon's orbit around the Earth takes it a bit above and then below an imaginary line stretching from the Earth to the Sun. That and other variations in the Moon's orbit mean everything lines up exactly only once every year or two.

To see a total eclipse, you must be in the right place at the right time. If you stayed, for example, in Detroit, Michigan and didn't budge, you could see a partial eclipse about every 2 years or so. But you might wait hundreds of years between total eclipses. While lucky Sheet Harbor, Nova Scotia residents got to see total eclipses in both 1970 and 1972, London glimpsed its last total eclipse in 1715— and won't see another until

sometime after the 2700s.

But if you care to chase eclipses, you could see darkness at noon fairly often. A total eclipse was visible from Finland on July 22, 1990. You could have seen an eclipse from the beaches of Hawaii on July 11, 1991, from a ship steaming across the south Atlantic on June 30, 1992, and in Chile or Brazil on November 3, 1994.

A total eclipse visible from the continental United States took place on February 26, 1979. Writer Annie Dillard described what happened in an essay called *Total Eclipse.*

It was morning, and people were sprawled across the hillsides around Yakima, Washington. As the eclipse began, Dillard said, the blue

### FAST FACT

**Although the Moon is only 1/400th the width of the Sun, the Moon is just near enough to Earth that the two appear to be almost exactly the same size. This remarkable coincidence makes total solar eclipses possible, as the face of the Moon covers the face of the Sun as neatly as a pot lid.**

of the sky deepened to indigo. On the horizon, the mountains began to glow with a red light, and the grass on the hillside turned to silver.

Finally, a black cover slid across the Sun. Only a small white ring was left, hanging

in a nighttime sky.

Just before the Sun went out, Dillard writes, something unexpected happened. A "wall of dark shadow" came speeding at the eclipse-watchers. "It roared up the valley. It slammed our hill . . . It was the monstrous swift shadow of the moon." Traveling at 1,000 miles an hour, the approaching shadow caused some watchers to scream.

As the Sun began to reemerge, the wall of shadow "sped away. It coursed down our hill and raced eastward over the plain, faster than the eye could believe; it swept over the plain and dropped over the planet's rim in a twinkling. It had clobbered us, and now it roared away."

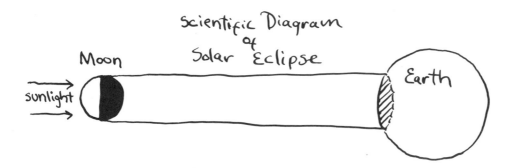

Scientific Diagram of Solar Eclipse

Moon

sunlight

Earth

# Where did the Moon come from?

We call it *the* Moon, as if it were the only moon anywhere, but Earth's moon is only one of many in our solar system. Just as planets circle stars, moons circle planets. Another word for moon is "satellite," which means "companion." Moons are planets' companions on their journeys around the Sun.

Mars has two tiny moons, one shaped like an orbiting potato. Giant Jupiter has at least 16 moons, Saturn at least 17. Uranus has 15 or more. Neptune has upwards of eight. And distant Pluto is orbited by a moon-world called Charon, that is half as big as Pluto itself. Only Mercury and Venus are moon-free.

Unlike our dry, rocky moon, the surfaces of many of the moons in the outer solar system are covered with water ice. You could skate on Europa, one of Jupiter's moons, whose icy surface is as smooth as a billiard ball.

All of these moons, ours included, formed along with the planets, more than 4 billion years ago. They were created in the solar nebula, an immense cloud of gas and dust surrounding the newborn Sun. Over many millions of years, particles in the spinning cloud stuck to other particles, and bigger and bigger objects formed. Eventually, there were many large and small bodies whizzing around the Sun.

With so many objects flying around, there were also many collisions. New planets slammed into each other, sending big chunks out into space. The whole process was like a demolition derby, stretched out over millions of

*Moons are planets' compan- ions on their journeys around the Sun.*

years instead of a day. And when everything sorted itself out, there was a solar system. Orbiting the Sun were nine planets, more than 50 moons, and thousands of asteroids, meteoroids, and comets.

Our moon may have had a particularly violent and dramatic birth. By studying its rocks and comparing them to rocks on Earth, scientists have come up with some good ideas of how we got our moon.

More than 4 billion years ago, the young Earth was still very hot, they say. So hot, in fact, that the surface was molten rock (like the lava flows from volcanoes today).

Near Earth, scientists think, a smaller planet or large asteroid lurked. And the two worlds were on a collision course.

Hurtling towards Earth at perhaps 25,000 miles per hour, the smaller world slammed into ours. The hot, liquid outside of both worlds blasted into space in a tremendous explosion. Some material fell back to Earth, mixing

### FAST FACT

**Studies of rocks brought back by astronauts show that the Moon was once studded with exploding volcanoes.**

# Titanic Titan

Our moon is beautiful, but dead. Its surface is all rock, and it has no atmosphere. Some other moons, however, are very much alive. Titan, a big moon orbiting Saturn, is a good example. It is huge—almost the size of the planet Mars. Titan is surrounded by a thick blanket of gases—an atmosphere. About 90 percent of this atmosphere is nitrogen gas (Earth's atmosphere is 77 percent nitrogen).

But unlike the Earth, Titan's atmosphere has no oxygen; methane takes its place. Titan is very cold—the temperature of its atmosphere is perhaps 300°F below zero. Scientists think there may be rivers or entire oceans of liquid methane on Titan, and methane snowflakes drifting down from Titan's blue skies. Because of chemical reactions with sunlight streaming into the atmosphere, scientists can even imagine frozen *gasoline* sleeting down on Titan.

Could a simple form of microscopic life survive in Titan's frigid seas? To find out, we will have to send a probe from Earth.

*Scientists think the Moon formed from material blasted into space when another world collided with the molten Earth.*

in with the liquid rock. Part of that alien world lies under your feet today.

But most of the blasted-out material stayed in space. It formed a lump of superhot rock orbiting the Earth. Over thousands of years, the lump cooled and rounded. And the silvery moon of poems and songs came to be.

# Where is the rest of the Moon when only half of it is in the sky?

On a clear, cold fall night you go outdoors. The Moon has just risen; it is huge and orange, a Halloween moon.

But a few nights later, the Moon is less round. And as the days pass, it seems to shrink into a cartoon moon: It looks like a crescent, or a pair of horns. Finally, the Moon seems to disappear entirely.

What's going on? Unlike the Sun, which shows us its full, fiery face all day long, the Moon has phases. Each month, the Moon goes through its phases, seeming to blow up and then deflate like a balloon. The truth is, the moon is really an unchanging solid, rocky ball. What changes as the month passes is our view of light and shadows on its surface, day and night on the Moon.

What we call moonlight is actually sunlight reflected off the Moon's gray, rocky surface. As the Moon travels with the Earth around the Sun, it is spotlit by the Sun. As a month passes, we see more and then less of the sunlit half of the Moon because the Earth and the

*What we call moonlight is actually sunlight reflected off the Moon.*

Moon are always changing positions in relation to the Sun.

What we call "phases" are simply the glimpses we get of the sunlit half of the Moon. There's the full moon, when we see one entire side of the

Moon lit. Then, as we see less of the lighted part a few days later, the phase is called a "gibbous" moon. ("Gibbous" comes from the Latin word for hump—and a three-quarters-full moon looks like a hump.)

Next comes the half moon, and then the beautiful crescent moon. Finally, when the side of the Moon we are facing lies in total darkness, we call this phase the "new moon"—a moon waiting to be born. And indeed, as the Earth and Moon move on, we see a sliver of the daylight side, and then more and more, as the whole cycle repeats.

Take a good look when the Moon is just a crescent, and you will see the rest of the Moon, the shaded part, outlined dimly against the sky. To see a full moon every night, you could hop a rocket into space, positioning your ship so that the Earth didn't obstruct your view. Then you would see that even when the Moon appears totally dark to its earthbound audience, the hidden side is lit up like a playing field.

# See for Yourself

You can make your own moon phases (and see how the real thing works) using a tennis or hand ball and a bright lamp. The lamp is the Sun, the ball the Moon, and your head is the Earth.

Turn out all the lights in the room except for the lamp. (Take off the lampshade for the best effect.) Now, hold the ball at arm's length, towards the lamp/Sun. You are looking at the dark side of the Moon.

Now, keeping the ball held rigidly in front of you, turn in a slow circle from right to left. You will see more and more of the lit-up side of the ball—through crescent, half-moon, and more—until the side facing you is fully lit. That's the "full moon," and it should occur when the lamp is behind you.

Then, as you continue to slowly turn, you'll see less and less of the lighted side, until the side facing you is once again completely dark—a "new moon." Now you know why the Moon seems to drastically change shape each month as it journeys around the Earth, changing its position with respect to our planet and the Sun.

**FAST FACT**

It takes the Moon about the same time to complete one rotation on its axis as to orbit the Earth (about 27⅓ days), so the same side of the Moon always faces the Earth. But it's a mistake to think the Moon has one eternally dark side. Both the near and far sides have day and night.

The planets have phases, too. Scientists looking at Mercury and Venus through telescopes have seen them as crescents. And spacecraft sent to photograph other planets have sent back pictures of the Earth as a silvery crescent, backlit by the Sun.

# Why are there craters on and planets like

The face of an 80-year-old human being has been changed by a number of natural processes. Smiling and frowning have etched lines around the eyes and mouth. Sunburns have made wrinkles. Chicken pox or acne may have left a few pockmarks.

The face of a 4.6 billion-year-old planet or moon has also been changed by a number of processes. Plates carrying the world's crust may have slammed together, pushing the crust up into mountains. Magma—hot, liquid rock—has welled up from inside, exploding in volcanoes and cooling back into solid rock. If the world has an atmosphere, wind and rain may have worn down rock

> *The heat of impact of a large meteorite can melt the rocks it smashes into.*

and shifted sand.

The surfaces of planets and moons are also shaped by more violent means. Asteroids, comets, or pieces of either, called meteorites, may whiz in from space, slamming into the surface. Scientists call such direct hits "impact cratering."

An impact can do serious damage to the face of a planet. A meteorite 98 feet wide

traveling briskly—say, at 34,000 miles an hour—would hit the Earth like 4 million tons of dynamite, or several nuclear bombs.

Such a meteorite abruptly dropped out of the sky about 25,000 years ago over what is now Arizona. You can visit the spot where it hit, called the Barringer Meteor Crater, near the town of Winslow. There, a hole more than 600 feet deep scars the desert. The edge of the crater is a raised rim. On the ground around the enormous hole lies the material thrown out by the impact.

Here's what happens when a meteorite or other object hits the solid surface of a planet or a moon. First, a jet of debris shoots up into the air at high speed. Under the impacting meteorite, rocks

# the surface of the Moon, Mercury and Venus?

flatten and shock waves travel out through the rocks around them. (If the meteorite is large, these shock waves can crack and crush other rocks. If the meteorite is *very* large, rocks may melt from the heat of the impact.)

The flattened rocks quickly expand from the heat

and themselves crack apart. Crushed rocks go flying out of the crater. This leaves a blanket of pulverized rocks outside the rim. (You can see this "blanket" at Meteor Crater.) The whole explosive event may last 1 minute.

Over time, the crater's shape may change. Walls may

*Some of the Moon's craters are more than 600 miles across.*

slump. Wind and rain may erode the crater, filling the center with debris. Magma from deep underground may seep up through fractures in the rock, filling the crater and then hardening.

At least 200 craters have been found on Earth. Of course, many more than 200 objects have hit Earth over the 4.6 billion-year life of our planet. But the holes they left have been erased by erosion, magma, and time.

On the Moon, however, there is no wind and rain, because there is no atmosphere. And although the Moon once had spewing volcanoes, its surface is long since quiet. No flowing magma here. So, when something slams into the Moon, the crater it leaves lasts a long time. Some of the Moon's craters are more than 4 billion years old. The largest are more than 600 miles across; they would stretch from New York to Ohio. The smallest could be neatly filled by the head of a straight pin. These craters are made by teeny-tiny meteorites, the size of specks of dust.

# Why is the Moon so far away?

At any given moment, the Moon is between 226,000 and 252,000 miles from the Earth. The Moon's distance varies because its path around Earth is not a perfect circle; it's elliptical, or slightly egg shaped.

In addition, each day the Moon moves a tiny bit farther from Earth—adding up to about 1.5 inches a year. Human beings many centuries from now will see a smaller-looking, more distant Moon. Someday, the Moon may wander off entirely, though that's not likely. A balance of forces keeps the Moon in its orbit around Earth.

Any moving body wants to continue moving in a straight line; this is called inertia. So a circling body wants to escape, to fly off on its own straight course, or tangent. That sense of being pulled away from the center is called centrifugal force. You feel it on amusement park rides that whip you around, or in a car rounding a curve too fast. ("Centrifugal" comes from a Latin word meaning "to flee the center.") The orbiting Moon also wants to flee the center, but it is constantly tugged toward Earth by our planet's gravity. It stays in orbit because its inertial, or centrifugal force, is counterbalanced by the force of the Earth's gravity.

The Moon takes about 27 days to orbit the Earth now. But scientists think that 2.8 billion years ago, the much-closer Moon zipped around our planet in only 17 days.

According to Clark Chapman, a scientist at the Planetary Science Institute in Tucson, Arizona, the Moon may once have been closer still. When the Earth and the Moon formed, about 4.6 billion years ago, Chapman says, the Moon may have raced around the Earth in as little as 7 days. If there had been anyone to see it, the Moon would have loomed monstrously large on the horizon as it rose at night.

*The Moon moves about 1.5 inches away from Earth over the course of each year.*

Surprisingly, it's ocean tides that have been forcing the Moon to give Earth a wider berth. Here's how it works: The Moon's gravity tugs on the water in the oceans of Earth. But the Earth isn't standing still—it's turning. As the water bulges out, the planet spins the bulge away from the Moon.

The gravitational pull of this watery bulge attracts the Moon. But since the bulge isn't directly under the Moon (the spinning Earth has moved it ahead), the Moon is tugged forward. That makes its orbit a little larger.

As its orbit enlarges, month after month, the Moon gets a little farther away. The changes are very tiny, but they add up over millions of years. Theoretically, the Moon could eventually be orbiting so far from Earth that it would feel little gravitational pull from our planet. Then the Moon could move off into its own orbit around the Sun.

However, scientists think that this lonely fate is unlikely. Tides affect the Earth, too.

*Billions of years ago, the Moon may have orbited the Earth in as few as 17 days.*

The ocean's sloshing slows the rotation of the Earth, and over the course of 100 years, the day gets half a minute longer. (Billions of years ago, a day was only about 6 hours long.)

Millions of years from now, the length of a day and the length of a month—the time it takes the Moon to orbit the Earth once—will be the same, and very much longer than 24 hours.

Once the Moon and Earth are synchronized, the tidal bulge will be directly under the far-off Moon. So the moon will start to be tugged back toward Earth. The whole process will reverse, as the bulge lags behind the Moon, pulling it into smaller and smaller orbits each month. And the Moon will loom large once again.

# A Momentous Principle

The more closely a moon or satellite orbits a planet, the more it speeds up.

Why? Any moving object has momentum. A circling object's momentum depends on its mass, speed, and distance from the center of its orbit. (You find the momentum by multiplying these three numbers.)

But the momentum never changes, scientists have found. So as the distance to the center gets smaller and smaller, the orbiting object travels faster and faster, resulting in the same total momentum.

This principle, called the conservation of angular momentum, is also why a figure skater revolves faster when she pulls her arms closer to her body.

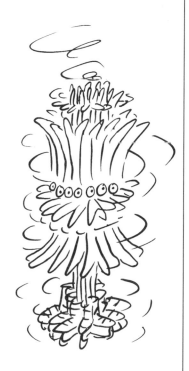

# What would happen if a big meteorite hit Earth?

Although space is very empty, there are still a lot of objects whizzing around our solar system—and no one is at the wheel. There are icy comets, stony asteroids, and meteoroids, which are usually fragments of asteroids and comets.

As these objects follow their own, often unusual, orbits around the Sun, they may cross paths with the Earth. And when this happens, neither can swerve out of the way.

Sometimes, people have even been around to watch such an event. In 1972, a meteoroid weighing about 1,000 tons was filmed as it grazed the atmosphere, narrowly missing Earth.

Decades earlier, we were not so lucky. On June 30, 1908,

in Tunguska, Siberia, a fireball streaked across the early-morning sky, and then exploded in mid-air. A 1,200-square-mile forest of fir trees was knocked flat. Scientists believe that what observers saw was a meteorite or a comet, over 300 feet across, shattering as it plunged through the air.

Luckily, few people lived in Siberia; nonetheless, a trader some 36 miles away from the center of the explosion had his clothes charred and blackened. Had the impact occurred in a city, there would have been a devastating loss of life.

As it was, the damage was not confined to Siberia. The explosion sent a tremendous load of dust into the atmosphere, and the dust quickly spread around the planet, affecting the climate

*In 1972, a 1,000-ton meteoroid grazed the Earth's atmosphere.*

and damaging the Earth's ozone layer.

As we go to school and work and live our daily lives, we usually don't think much about what's going on in the dark of space around our planet. But in 1990, astronomers began using the Spacewatch telescope in Arizona to search the skies for asteroids and meteoroids wandering near the Earth. On January 18,

1991, they saw an asteroid fragment pass silently by. At its nearest, the huge chunk of rock was about 106,000 miles away.

That may seem far—but remember, the Moon is about 240,000 miles from us. So scientists consider the passage of this meteoroid a near-miss. If it had been on a slightly different course and had hit Earth, the 26-foot rock would have exploded with the power of three Hiroshima-type atomic bombs.

Some scientists estimate that, on average, every 100 years or so an object as big as 160 feet across slams into Earth or explodes above our planet. Happily, most land in the ocean or in unpopulated areas.

About every million years, they say, an object as big as 6 miles across may drop from the sky. Then the damage done is equivalent to a million bombs, each packing 13,000 tons of TNT. Such an explosion, even if it occurred in an ocean, would send so much fine dust into the atmosphere that sunlight could be blocked for months. Earth's

**FAST FACT**

Scientists think large meteoroids pass near the Earth once a day, and they are studying ways of detecting threatening objects and then diverting or destroying them.

climate would change drastically. Such an event, some think, is what led to the extinction of the dinosaurs some 65 million years ago. (For more on the dinosaurs' extinction, see page 245.)

# How come the Earth never slows down or stops turning?

The Earth was born spinning. Scientists say it and the other eight planets of our solar system formed from a revolving cloud of gas and dust in space some 4.6 billion years ago. The bits of material in the turning cloud were themselves rolling and spinning, sticking together, forming bigger rotating bodies.

Today, the spinning planets journey around the Sun in the same direction as the cloud from which they formed revolved. Asteroids, the small, rocky bodies left over after the planets and moons formed, also rotate as they orbit the Sun. Some large asteroids take 5 to 18 hours to turn once around.

Our planet takes about 24 hours to turn once. So, since the Earth is about 25,000 miles around, it must be spinning about 1,000 miles an hour at the equator, according to William Hartmann, an astronomer at the Planetary Science Institute in Tucson, Arizona.

*More than 4 billion years ago, days were only 6 hours long. In millions of years, a day may last 1,128 hours.*

The Earth turns eastward. When countries send up satellites, they try to launch them near the equator (from places like Florida), and towards the east. That way the satellite gets a 1,000 mile-an-hour boost—like a speck of dust tossed off the edge of a spinning phonograph record.

Why doesn't the Earth ever slow down—or speed up? The answer: It does.

When our planet formed, it was spinning much faster—at about 4,000 miles an hour, scientists estimate. That means that a day was only about 6 hours long. (If there had been people around back then, they could have seen the Sun rise, and then swiftly set about 3 hours later, followed by a 3-hour night for quick catnaps.)

The Moon was then much closer to the Earth. It has been steadily moving away ever since. The Moon's gravity, pulling on the Earth, causes the oceans to rise and fall. The oceans' sloshing makes the Earth spin more slowly, year by year. Each 100 years, the day gets half a minute longer.

Eventually, a day may stretch to 1,128 hours, according to Hartmann. Because of the effects of gravity and tides, however, the Moon will come closer again, the Earth will speed up, and days will shorten. (For more on this, see page 145.)

> ### FAST FACT
>
> **Days on Mercury are about 2 Earth-months long. Giant Jupiter rotates so fast that a day comes and goes in less than 10 hours. Mars has days most like ours: 24 hours, 37 minutes long.**

# Our Home Planet

**S**een from space, Earth, the third planet from the Sun, is a cloudy, blue-and-white world with one large, silvery companion moon. Compared to the giant gaseous planets of the outer solar system, Earth is rather small and rocky. And unlike any of its planetary siblings, Earth has oceans of liquid water, where scientists think life got its start.

Earth has changed a lot over its 4.6-billion-year lifetime. Scientists think that the Earth formed from a cloud of dust and gas, evolved into a ball of molten rock, and then, after slowly cooling, emerged awash in water. Continents grew, moved, slammed together, broke up. Life appeared, evolved, and took many strange forms—most now extinct. For millions of years, huge and (scientists think) quite intelligent creatures, the dinosaurs, thundered across the planet. Then they were gone.

Now we humans, toolmakers living in every nook and cranny of the planet, have ushered in a new stage in the history of the Earth. Our technology has altered the Earth, in ways we are only beginning to discover. We are just starting to understand the responsibility we share for the caretaking of this, our only home.

# How can you find the the Earth?

Nowadays you can find out the circumference of the Earth using surveying instruments and satellites. But you don't need fancy equipment to measure a planet. You could do what Eratosthenes did more than 2,000 years ago: He figured out the size of the Earth without leaving the grounds of the library where he worked.

Eratosthenes was a Greek scholar who lived in Alexandria, a city in Egypt, between about 276 and 196 B.C. He worked at the Alexandrian Museum, which was part museum, part research center. It had botanic gardens, zoos, an astronomic observatory, and laboratories. Scholars gave talks in the museum's lecture hall; others

*A Greek scholar, Eratosthenes, figured out the Earth's circumference more than 2,000 years ago.*

relaxed, ate meals, and talked in the museum's dining room.

Eratosthenes was head of the museum's library, which had a collection of about 100,000 books, all written on scrolls of papyrus (a kind of paper made from the papyrus reed). He was interested in everything: He had studied

philosophy, history, and the sciences, and he had been a theater critic. Some of his fellow scholars thought he was a dilettante—someone who dabbled in many things, but wasn't really first-rate at any of them.

Eratosthenes had heard from travelers about something peculiar they had seen in Syene, a town far south of Alexandria. At noon on the first day of summer—the longest day of the year— shadows disappeared in Syene. The Sun stood directly overhead; its rays beamed straight down. Looking into a deep well, you could see a reflection of the Sun's disc in the water at the bottom.

However, back in Alexandria, Eratosthenes had seen museum walls casting shadows at noon on the first

# distance around

day of summer. From this simple observation, he was able to calculate the size of a whole planet.

Here's how: Eratosthenes knew that because of the enormous distance of the Sun from Earth, its rays reached both Alexandria and Syene in side-by-side, parallel beams. If the Earth were flat, then shadows would disappear everywhere on June 21. But since, he reasoned, the Earth is curved, the walls and columns of Alexandria—about 500 miles north of Syene—were poking out from the Earth's surface at a

*Earth is about 24,894 miles around.*

different angle.

So at noon on the first day of summer, Eratosthenes measured the shadow cast by an obelisk outside the museum. Since he knew the height of the obelisk, he could imagine a line from the top of the obelisk to the tip of the shadow, making a measurable triangle.

After "drawing" the triangle, Eratosthenes used a simple rule of geometry to find that the top of the obelisk pointed away from the Sun by a little more than 7°.

Since there were no shadows at noon in Syene on that first summer day, the angle in Syene must be 0°, or no angle at all. This meant that Alexan-

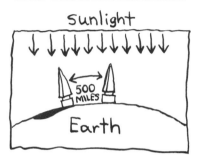

dria was a bit more than 7° away from Syene along the circumference of the Earth.

All circles have 360°, and the Earth's circumference is no exception. The 7° angle between the two cities was about 1/50th of a circle. So Eratosthenes multiplied the distance between Syene and Alexandria—about 500 miles—by 50, getting 25,000 miles for the distance around the Earth. Modern astronomers put Earth's actual circumference at about 24,894 miles. Eratosthenes had

proved himself a first-rate scholar indeed.

Today, there is a whole science, called *geodesy*, devoted to sizing up our planet. Geodesists use special surveying instruments to measure angles of the Earth. They measure gravity to determine the exact shape of the planet, and they make use of the position of satellites in the sky to measure triangles, with a satellite at the apex and two ground stations marking the other two points of the triangle.

# How does the Moon cause tides in the ocean?

**S**pace is mostly empty. But here and there, balls of matter—planets, moons, stars— glide past each other in a kind of dance. As they do their cosmic do-si-do, they tug and pull on each another, causing oceans to rise up and planets to bulge out at the sides. The tugging is caused by gravity—the attraction of matter to other matter.

Ocean tides are the regular rise and fall of the waters, as the Earth experiences this gravitational pull. When the ocean swells to its highest point, as it does about every 13 hours, that's "high tide." When the waters sink to their lowest level, that's "low tide." So when you go to the beach and it's high tide, you are seeing the local effect of worlds wheeling in the dark of space.

The Sun, the Moon, and all the planets of our solar system tug on the waters and land of Earth. But only the Moon and the Sun have significant effects. The Sun, although it's far away (93 million miles), is extremely massive, and therefore exerts a strong gravitational pull. The Moon, although it's small (1/81th the mass of Earth), is very nearby (240,000 miles), and because of its closeness, also exerts a noticeable pull.

*The Moon's gravity causes ocean tides on Earth.*

Although the huge Sun's gravity is stronger, the little Moon has a bigger effect on bodies of water on Earth. The Moon creates tidal forces on Earth because it is closer, and because the pull of its gravity

varies sharply from place to place on our planet. The strength depends on how far away each place is from the Moon at a given moment.

The water currently under the face of the Moon is more strongly attracted to it, since it is nearer, than water on the opposite side of the planet. However, both sides experience high tide at about the same time. Why? On the near side, water tends to be pulled away from the Earth. On the far side, the Earth is pulled away from the water—resulting in a high tide on

*When the Sun, the Moon, and Earth are aligned, as they are when the Moon is full or dark, the tides are extra high and extra low.*

that side, too. As the Moon orbits the Earth, and the Earth rotates, high tides alternate with low tides.

In contrast to the Moon, the Sun is so far away that its greater force doesn't change very much from one side of the Earth to the other. So the Sun doesn't have such a jarring effect on the oceans. However, when the Sun, the Earth, and the Moon are aligned, as they are when the Moon is full or dark, there are especially high and especially low tides on Earth, called spring tides (though they

# Body Tides

**While we see the effects of gravity most easily in the Earth's oceans, the mutual pulling of the Earth and Moon creates *body tides* in each. Both tend to bulge out at their middles as a result, but the smallish Moon undergoes the most stress, stretching out an average of 60 feet. (The amount that the Moon can stretch is, of course,** limited: it is made of rock, and rock isn't very elastic. However, just like on the Earth, some of the rock deep under the surface is hot liquid—molten.)

So when the Moon has the misfortune to be aligned with the Earth and the Sun, it is wracked with moonquakes, as the bigger bodies literally pull it out of shape.

happen year round).

How an ordinary tide starts: Water as a liquid is free to flow. (When you swirl your hand in water, you can see how easily it moves.) The Moon's gravity isn't strong enough to really lift the waters vertically. Instead, what happens is that as the Moon circles the Earth, some of its gravitational force pulls on ocean waters from just ahead of them, making them flow forward and bunch up under the Moon. The force isn't very strong, but it doesn't take much to get water sliding around.

When this several-foot-high bulge is pushed against the land, it thrusts up still higher. Tides may rise 40 feet above sea level in some spots. Meanwhile, water rushing away from other regions cause low tides in those places.

# Is it true that continents one big mass of land?

**B**etter go to the beach while you still can. The Atlantic Ocean, according to some scientists, won't exist in another 300 million years. Eventually, the east coast of the United States will become a new Midwest, with the nearest ocean more than 3,000 miles away.

The continents, which seem so securely fixed in place, are indeed moving. And every 500 million years or so, they jam together in a worldwide collision that pushes coastlines up into mountains. When it happens next, the continents will merge into one gigantic clump of land, surrounded by an enormous ocean. You will be able to drive from Detroit to Paris and on to Beijing. (Of course, if human beings still exist, they will probably have renamed every city, country, and ocean many times over by then.)

*This year, North America and Eurasia will drift about three-quarters of an inch farther apart.*

This picture of continents butting up against each other some future day is based on the theory of *plate tectonics*. What we call the Earth's crust is really a patchwork of plates, which float on a layer of extremely hot, partially liquified rock in the mantle. Like rafts on the sea, the plates slip and slide along the surface of the elastic rock.

The continents—North America, South America, Africa, Eurasia (Europe and Asia), Australia, and Antarctica—are attached to the plates, so as the plates move, so does the land we are standing on. How much? Well, this year the North American and Eurasian plates will drift about three-quarters of an inch farther apart. And the Atlantic Ocean will get that much wider.

Scientists think that the

# move? Was there ever

Plate theory as demonstrated by Jiggles the Clown.

Earth now...

...Earth later.

drift of the continents is part of a cycle that repeats over and over. Continents break up, and then jam back together, about every 500 million years.

But don't take scientists' word for it. Just look at a globe. The continents look like jigsaw-puzzle pieces, and it isn't hard to imagine those pieces fitting together. For example, the jutted-out northeastern coast of South

America fits neatly into the inwardly-curving coast of western Africa.

Put the puzzle pieces together and you have a supercontinent. The last supercontinent, which broke into pieces about 180 million years ago, has been dubbed *Pangaea*, which means "all earth." Pangaea is thought to have been surrounded by an immense, planet-wide sea of water, the ancestor of today's

Pacific Ocean.

There were probably several other supercontinents before Pangaea. Each one lasted about 80 million years, scientists think, before it began to break up.

Scientists say the big breakups are probably caused by two things: heat from inside the Earth, and the Earth's rotation.

Some of the heat rising from deep inside the Earth is

blocked from escaping by the supercontinent. Scientists suggest imagining laying a book on an electric blanket to see why: The part of the blanket under the book becomes a hot spot. As heat builds up underneath, parts of the supercontinent swell and crack.

Meanwhile, the big continent, lopsidedly jutting out from the Earth, experiences a great deal of stress as it is

*The last supercontinent, called Pangaea, broke apart 180 million years ago.*

spun around by our planet. The combination of this stress with the heat fractures eventually breaks the huge land mass up into pieces, as it did 180 million years ago.

However, over millions of years, the Atlantic Ocean floor will sink, and the ocean will shrink, inch by inch. The continents will ram back together, and we will be truly one world—at least for 80 million years.

# How can scientists determine the age of the Earth?

The Earth's history is written in its rocks. At places such as the Grand Canyon, walls eroded by water reveal layer upon layer of rock that was built up over millions of years. Because older rock layers lie under newer layers, geologists get an idea of how the Earth's crust developed.

But knowing deeper layers are older doesn't tell us how old the rocks are. Scientists in the 1800s—trying to figure out the age of the Earth by watching how long it took rock layers to build up in modern times—guessed at the age of the Earth. Their best guesses ranged from a relatively youthful 3 million years to a more ancient 1.5 billion years (or 500 times older). Clearly, a better method was needed.

Scientists would have loved to have a clock that had been first wound up when the Earth formed. By reading the clock, they could read the age of the planet.

Well, it turns out that there are clocks in the Earth—in rocks and trees, and in the ocean depths. The Earth's natural clocks are radioactive elements—elements that decay into other elements as time passes. Determining the age of rocks or fossils using radioactive

*Radioactive elements serve as natural clocks because they decay according to a strict timetable.*

elements is called *radiometric dating*.

Radioactive elements make good clocks because they decay according to a strict timetable. Take the car-

bon test. The carbon test is based on the fact that organisms take in both ordinary carbon-12 and radioactive carbon-14 from air and water. The test assumes that the ratio of one kind of carbon to the other has remained constant in air and water, so plants and animals have taken in the same ratio of the two carbons for thousands of years.

While the amount of carbon-12 in an organism stays the same, carbon-14 decays. Half of it is gone in 5,730 years. So by measuring the relative amounts of the two

carbons left in a once-living organism, scientists get an idea of how old the remains are.

However, none of the dating methods are foolproof, so geologists look for several radioactive elements, such as uranium and thorium, in addition to carbon-14. They often double-check dates by using two different tests on the same material. And sometimes, two tests give two very different dates.

For example, geologists took samples of a coral reef off the island of Barbados. They measured the levels of

carbon in the coral, as well as the amounts of uranium and thorium.

For "young" coral—up to about 9,000 years old—the two methods agreed on the age. But the older the coral, the more different the results. The uranium-thorium test might say a chunk of coral was 20,000 years old, while the carbon-14 test might say it was only 17,000.

Why such a big difference? And which test was right? Scientists believe, in this case, the uranium-thorium test was the more accurate, because carbon-14 tests have given some strange results in the past.

The reason for this may be that the amount of carbon-14 in the atmosphere seems to have been increasing in recent years—which means it could have increased or decreased at times in the past, too. Because it hasn't remained at a steady level relative to carbon-12, carbon-14 can fail as a test for a reliable age.

With a dead tree, scientists can check whether their carbon-14 clock is right. First, they measure the carbon and get an age. Then, they count the tree rings—one for each

*Radiometric dating methods are not foolproof, so scientists try to double-check their findings by measuring levels of two different radioactive elements in the same material.*

year—and see if the ages match.

By measuring the decay of uranium-238, which has a half-life of 4.5 billion years, some rocks on Earth have been dated at about 3.8 billion years. How long before that did the planet form? Scientists got more evidence by testing rocks brought back by astronauts from the Moon. These proved to be about 4.6 billion years old—as did meteorites whizzing into Earth from nearby parts of the solar system. So scientists think the entire solar system, including the Earth and Moon, formed around 4.6 billion years ago.

# How can dinosaur bones more than 65 million

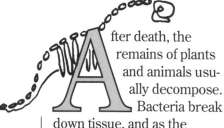

After death, the remains of plants and animals usually decompose. Bacteria break down tissue, and as the months and years pass, the tissue disintegrates.

But once in a while, when the remains are in the right place at the right time, the hard parts—bones, shells, teeth—get preserved. Digging in the dirt, a paleontologist excitedly turns up a 3-million-year-old tooth. What she has found is called a fossil.

A fossil may be an animal's actual tooth or bone or shell, preserved over the centuries. Or it may be a cast, or impression, of the original: a tiny sea creature's skeleton, carved into stone. Still other fossils are replicas of the orig-inal bony parts, sculpted by the Earth from minerals.

**FAST FACT**

By far the greatest number of fossils are sea creatures, because they are buried much more quickly than land animals.

For the Earth to create a fossil—allowing us to see part of a creature from the enormously distant past—the conditions must be exactly right. Most importantly, the remains must be protected from wind and rain. This can happen if the plant or animal is buried by sediment—rock fragments such as sand or gravel. Ash also makes a good cover.

Remains are sometimes protected by sediments in places like lakes, swamps, and caves. The best spots, however, are places where the Earth is (or once was) "geologically active"—such as a volcano that has spewed ash, or near growing mountains. The already-towering Himalayas are growing mountains, a range of land being pushed up as India rams into Asia. (For more on the continents moving, see page 160.) Such mountains shift bits of rock and dirt from their sides and into rivers, which carry the sediments into oceans.

Most fossils are found under bodies of water (or where water once flowed), nicely covered by sediments and safe from the bacteria that live on dry land.

Fossils are made in sever-

# still be on Earth after years?

al ways. Minerals may seep into the pores of a slowly decaying shell or bone and preserve it from further decay. Or acids may dissolve a shell, leaving an impression or cast of the shell in the rock it was pressed against. Sometimes, the Earth creates a duplicate shell. Minerals fill the mold carved into the rock, forming a replica of the original shell.

Fossils come in every size, from the humongous—a Tyrannosaurus rex thigh bone—to the exquisitely tiny. A geology student in

# Forever Amber

While most fossils are made from hard bones and shells and teeth, sometimes an entire tiny animal is preserved—in amber, which is tree resin hardened by time. A wasp, caught some 30 million years ago in the then-sticky resin, may be seen today encased in amber, its spindly legs, veined wings, and faceted eyes perfectly preserved. Amber allows us to see with our own eyes what ancient life looked like. And studying the genetic material of such animals enables scientists to get an even more detailed picture.

Scientists have even been able to extract still-intact DNA (the master "blueprint" molecule in cells) from amber-trapped weevils and other organisms. However, cloning a whole new organism from such ancient material is so far impossible. And re-creating a complex animal like a dinosaur by cloning bits and pieces of its genetic material may never be possible.

**FAST FACT**

The youngest amber is about 1.5 million years old; the most ancient, at least 300 million.

How could a wasp end up in amber in the first place? Imagine a perfect, hot day, somewhere near the equator, millions of years ago. A wasp, alighting unluckily on the oozing bark of a tropical tree, tries vainly to free itself from the sticky resin, and dies. Drop by drop, resin slowly covers its body. Centuries pass; the tree dies and decays, but the chunk of dried resin holding the wasp simply hardens. Eventually water washes away the leftover piece of resin, with the wasp entombed inside. Sediment covers it, and over time, buries the resin deep inside the Earth.

Millions more years pass; many animals and plants disappear—including the wasp's own species, vanished into

the dust of Earth. Meanwhile, the resin hardens into a fossil. Finally, as continents slam into continents, thrusting up land into new mountains, the sediments carrying the fossilized resin are pushed up and up. One day, a paleontologist, digging into a mountain, finds a chunk of smooth, translucent amber. Inside, the wasp waits, held in its golden prison for millions of years.

What else have scientists found when they peered into amber? In a match-box-sized piece, a frozen swarm of more than 2,000 long-extinct ants. Flowers and leaves from the forest primeval, preserved in amber like posies in a paperweight. And, finally, a brood of baby spiders emerging from a delicate white cocoon—their first and last act on planet Earth, long long ago, caught forever in amber like a snapshot of eternity.

*A fossil may be an animal's actual tooth, bone, or shell, or it can be a cast or replica of it.*

Colorado found a fossil of a dinosaur embryo—an unborn baby dinosaur. The fossil embryo was 135 million to 150 million years old, and included tiny foot bones and part of a little backbone and jawbone. Two baby teeth were poking up from the jaw. Scientists think the baby dinosaur probably died just before it was about to hatch.

# How come the center of the Earth is so hot?

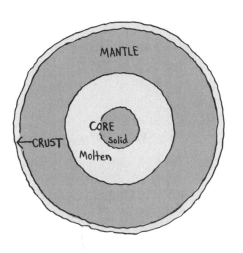

If the Earth were a fruit we could slice in half, we would see a few circular layers inside. The Earth's crust—the outer layer—is like the skin of a fruit. The ground in your yard or in the park is the outside of the crust, which extends down about 15 to 30 miles.

Digging down through dirt or sand, you would eventually hit rock. Most of the crust under the continents is made of layers of granite. At places like the Grand Canyon, where water has worn through part of the crust, the granite layers are exposed to view. Under the oceans, the crust is thinner, extending only about 3 miles below the ocean floor, and is made mostly of basalt, another rock.

Below the crust lies the enormous mantle, about 1,800 miles thick. (If you could drive a car at 50 miles an hour down a tunnel carved through the mantle, it would take 36 hours to get through. A journey to the center of the Earth is impossible, however, because the heat and pressure are too great.)

*Imagine melting warehouses full of iron frying pans and you'll get an idea of what it's like in the Earth's core.*

Scientists don't know much about the hidden mantle, but the upper part of it seems to be made mainly of a rock called peridotite. Peridotite contains such minerals as olivine, pyroxene, and garnet (the red stone we use in jewelry). At least part of the mantle, scientists say, is very pliable. This may be because

molten liquid rock surrounds solid rock grains.

Finally, underneath the mantle, is the Earth's heart, its core, which extends down another 2,000 miles to the very center. Locked away from the warmth of the Sun, it seems as if this core should be even colder than the North and South Poles. Instead, it is searingly hot, at least 4,000° to 6,000° F. The core is so hot that the outer part of it is liquid, made of melted metals. Imagine melting warehouses full of iron

frying pans and you'll get an idea of what it's like in the outer core: hot liquid iron, with some oxygen and sulfur mixed in. As the Earth turns, currents course through this hidden sea.

The Earth's core is very dense. Topped by most of the planet, it is under tremendous pressure, and the matter there is squeezed tightly together.

Because the pressure is so great, scientists think the inner core is a ball of solid iron (with some oxygen and

sulfur) lodged at the center of our planet. Even though the temperature is blast furnace hot, the extraordinary pressure keeps the iron molecules so jammed together that the metal ball *can't* melt. Surrounded by the metallic ocean, the ball, about three quarters the size of the Moon, is like a planet within a planet.

Where did all the heat inside the Earth come from? Much of it was produced some 4.6 billion years ago, from the impact of smaller

# Exploring the World Underfoot

The secrets hidden in Earth can be divined in different ways. The most obvious: Scientists dig down, pulling up samples of rock. So far, they have only been able to tunnel about 5 miles into the crust; they haven't yet reached the mantle. No digging equipment yet built can withstand the tremendous pressure—not to mention temperatures which rise into the thousands of degrees.

Another method is to use seismographs, which detect shock waves that jolt the ground during earthquakes. Seismographs detect waves that travel all the way through our planet, at various depths. Shock waves look different after they pass through hot, liquid rock or metal than they do after they pass through solid rock. The shape of the waves gives scientists a good idea of what the layers of the inner Earth must be like.

Finally, they try to re-create the center of the Earth in their labs. Machines squeeze rock while heating it to very high temperatures, and scientists watch how the rock changes.

bodies slamming together in space to form the Earth. But most of the heat, geologists think, came from natural radioactivity deep in the Earth.

Radioactive elements trapped inside the Earth emit particles, such as electrons. These particles collide with atoms in the layers of rock, transferring some of their energy to the rock's atoms, and the rock heats up.

When the Earth was young, these radioactive elements caused the rock inside the Earth to get very hot indeed. The rock tended to hold onto the heat (think of how hot a rock gets in the sun). And so all that heat remained trapped inside the Earth.

As millions of years passed, the inside of the Earth became so hot that the iron in the rock melted. The heavy iron separated from the lighter metals and sank to the center of the Earth, forming the core.

# What is the ozone layer? How does hurting it hurt us?

**H**igh above our heads, 12 to 30 miles up, ozone floats around the planet. Ozone is a form of oxygen. Most molecules of oxygen in the air are made of two oxygen atoms, linked together—$O_2$. But ozone ($O_3$) has three.

Sunlight makes ozone. As ultraviolet (UV) radiation from the Sun penetrates the atmosphere, it breaks apart ordinary two-atom oxygen molecules. Each freed atom gloms onto a nearby $O_2$ molecule. That makes $O_3$.

The ozone layer is wispy, barely there. If all the ozone molecules spread out over 18 miles of space were squashed down into one solid layer, it would only be about an eighth of an inch thick.

. . . . . . . . . . . . . . . . . . . . . . . . . .

Some ozone also drifts in the air near the ground. When car exhaust and factory smoke are spewed out into the air, sunlight reacts with their chemicals to make ozone.

On a hot, smoggy day, ozone near the ground can reach alarming levels. Breathing ozone is dangerous, because this form of oxygen can damage the lungs. Joggers who gulp in large amounts of ozone-polluted air may find breathing hard and painful. The trees and plants that line exhaust-filled highways often have their growth stunted by ozone.

But ozone at a safe distance—miles above our heads—actually protects our health. Ozone absorbs UV

*Scientists estimate that each 1 percent drop in ozone levels causes a 3 to 6 percent rise in skin cancer cases.*

radiation. UV radiation is what tans our skin, but it's also what makes sunburns—and skin cancer.

In the 1970s, scientists became concerned about the ozone layer. They discovered that chlorofluorocarbons (CFCs)—chemicals used in refrigerators, air conditioners, and aerosol cans—can destroy ozone. These gases escaped into the air with every burst of hairspray and deodorant, and when appliances were repaired or junked.

Floating upward, CFC gases eventually run into ozone molecules, the scientists reasoned. Solar radiation releases chlorine gas from CFCs. Chlorine breaks apart ozone molecules, which reform as regular $O_2$ molecules. Whoops—there goes the ozone layer.

Because of concerns over the ozone layer, the United States banned the use of CFCs in aerosol sprays in 1978. But manufacturers of the chemicals—and some scientists—felt the ozone-destruction theory was flimsy.

Then, in 1985, British scientists made a startling discovery: an enormous gaping hole in the ozone, centered over Antarctica. The hole, which reappears every spring, is about the size of the United States. When the wind's direction changes with the seasons, the hole "fills in" with ozone molecules. But as the ozone molecules rush to fill the gap, ozone levels elsewhere plummet. In the winter of 1992, for example, ozone over parts of Europe and Canada was down by 20 percent.

In the sky above Antarc-

*A hole in the ozone the size of the United States appears over Antarctica each spring.*

tica, researchers found extremely high levels of chlorine monoxide, the chemical formed when chlorine destroys ozone. So it seems that the worldwide use of CFCs is indeed part of the problem.

Scientists estimate that each 1 percent drop in ozone levels causes a 2 percent rise in UV radiation reaching Earth, and a 3 to 6 percent rise in skin cancer cases. UV radiation also damages the body's immune system, making us more vulnerable to infectious diseases, such as malaria. And UV radiation can damage cells in plants, from trees to crops.

Also worrisome is how ozone depletion may change global climate, in ways no one can reliably predict. The ozone layer holds onto heat. As it diminishes, the air at that altitude cools, changing global wind patterns and affecting weather. Droughts, disrupted crop growth, and food shortages and famines may result.

Some scientists estimate that even if every measure were taken globally to end ozone-damaging activities by human beings, it would take 100 years for ozone to reach its former levels.

# If oxygen is so important is the atmosphere only

The Earth's atmosphere is a mixture of many gases. Mostly, it's nitrogen—about 77 percent. Good old oxygen adds another 21 percent. The remaining 2 percent is composed of traces of gases—argon, carbon dioxide, helium, neon, krypton, xenon, nitrous oxide, carbon monoxide, and so on. Water vapor also floats through the air in varying amounts.

Humans are fond of oxygen, since it is the gas that keeps our bodies running. Premature babies, whose lungs may not be fully developed at birth, are sometimes put in incubators with oxygen-rich atmospheres. Instead of 21 percent oxygen, the air inside the incubator is 30 or 40 percent oxygen. Babies with severe breathing problems may be surrounded by air that is 100 percent oxygen, to prevent brain damage.

*Too much oxygen can be as dangerous as too little.*

But too much oxygen can be nearly as dangerous as too little. Too much oxygen in the incubator air, and in the blood, can damage blood vessels in the babies' eyes and cause vision loss.

This illustrates the two-sided nature of oxygen. We must breathe it to live, but oxygen can also be a poison to living organisms.

When oxygen from the air combines with other elements, such as hydrogen and carbon, there's a reaction called oxidation. Oxidation makes organic molecules, which are the basis of life, fall apart.

Oxygen combines slowly with other elements at normal temperatures. As the elements combine, heat is released, but in such small amounts we can't feel it.

But oxidation can happen quickly if the temperature is raised. Strike a match, and the friction between the match head and the strip on the matchbook heats up the match. Oxidizing very quick-

# to life, then why one-fifth oxygen?

# An Oxygen-Free Environment

For a little more than half of the Earth's 4.6 billion years of existence, the air surrounding it was virtually oxygen-free. That was just fine with the first simple life—one-celled bacteria floating in the ocean. They didn't need oxygen to live.

Then, something happened. Scientists think that as the bacteria evolved, some developed the knack of extracting hydrogen from water (which is just hydrogen and oxygen bonded together—$H_2O$). This released oxygen into the ocean and into the air.

Some organisms adapted over time to live with the new gas. They evolved ways to harness oxygen's destructiveness safely inside cells, where it could be used as a powerhouse to break down and extract energy from food. This method of using oxygen is called *respiration*—we do it every day. It was respiration, evolved in response to the oxygen threat, that enabled the evolution of bigger, multicelled organisms—and eventually us.

Over millions of years, oxygen soared from about 2/10ths of 1 percent of the air to its current level of about 21 percent. But ocean-dwelling bacteria may not have been solely responsible for adding oxygen to the atmosphere. Some scientists think that as the Earth's continents crashed together and then broke apart again every few hundred million years, even more oxygen was freed up.

How? As continents split or fuse, sediments (bits and pieces of rock) flood into the ocean and sink to the bottom. Some bits of organic matter that would otherwise be digested by microorganisms drift to the sea floor—and are quickly buried. So the oxygen that would be used to digest the organic materials isn't, and builds up.

Although some organisms adapted to the increasing levels of oxygen, many of the simple forms of life that had evolved on Earth must have perished over time. Other organisms survived by hiding from oxygen in nooks and crannies. Some today live happily in the roots of bean plants, using nitrogen from the atmosphere to make amino acids (the building blocks of protein) for the plants. The deadly botulism organism is another oxygen escapee. If it isn't destroyed by high cooking temperatures, it can thrive in vacuum-packed (airless) canned food, and make us very sick.

ly, the match bursts into flames. In this case, we feel the heat and see the light energy oxidation releases.

In our bodies, oxidation is less dramatic. Red blood cells collect oxygen from the lungs and carry it through the body. In a carefully controlled process much slower and less violent than a fire's combustion, oxygen breaks down molecules in the food we eat. This breakdown frees up energy and water, and leaves carbon dioxide. The carbon dioxide is carted back to our lungs by the red blood cells, and we exhale it into the air.

Getting enough oxygen is crucial. Just as a fire can be smothered by a blanket, we can be suffocated by anything that prevents us from breathing oxygen for as few as 5 minutes. The ideal level of oxygen for us is what we have—the 21 percent in our air. But even at this "ideal" level, oxygen shows its power for destruction. Dry grasslands can catch fire from a single spark.

**FAST FACT**

**When book pages turn brown over time, they are oxidizing—doing a slow burn.**

The balance of oxygen to other gases is maintained by the life cycle in nature: Animals breathe out carbon dioxide; plants use it, and give off oxygen.

However, there is no guarantee that oxygen levels will remain constant forever. The amount of carbon dioxide dumped into the atmosphere is rising, mainly because when fossil-based fuels, such as gasoline, are burned, they leave carbon dioxide. Meanwhile, the biggest plants on our planet, the trees, are being cut down at an increasingly fast rate, with many acres of forests destroyed every minute. This combination means that oxygen in the air is slowly diminishing, and scientists are hard at work to find ways to measure the damage done.

# How's the Weather?

When we ask "what's the weather going to be tomorrow?" we're really talking about what the thin haze of gases around our planet will be up to. Every planet or moon that has an atmosphere—a layer of gas held to itself by gravity—has weather. (Our moon has no atmosphere, and so no weather.)

The Sun heats the atmosphere during the day; at night the earth and air cool, radiating heat into space. Heat makes gas molecules fly apart; cool brings them closer together. Bunches of high-pressure, cooler air stream into emptier pockets of warmer air. The result is weather: an ocean breeze here, a spinning tornado there, a sunny day in Miami, a steady drizzle in Paris.

The atmosphere is spread over the vast area of our entire planet, constantly spinning from warmer day into cooler night. And our tilted planet is meantime traveling around the Sun, slowly changing seasons everywhere. The weather, then, is notoriously hard to predict, as this big, chaotic mass of gases reacts to local and global change. Even the best satellite snapshot of swirling clouds can't always allow us to foresee what will happen next. So when the weather forecaster warns us it will rain tomorrow, we should give her a nod of appreciation if it actually does.

# Why does rain fall in drops rather than gush down ?

Water vapor is an invisible but always present part of the air surrounding the Earth. When a cloud forms, it's as if some of the water has jumped out of hiding. Actually, what happens is that wispy water vapor collects into droplets or ice crystals, which—tumbling and falling in a group—make a visible cloud.

Vapor collects in droplets when there are particles in the air to cling to. Above the ocean, for example, water vapor can soak into salt particles, forming droplets. Or, when the temperature drops to 32°F or below, water can freeze solid around motes of clay dust, blown skyward by the wind. Out of common dirt comes ice crystals. Other debris in the air, such as smoke, can

*Smoke and dust in the air can provide the seeds around which clouds can form.*

also provide the seeds for clouds of water to collect.

Rain is not something "inside" a cloud. Rain is really a cloud falling apart, losing some of itself. This happens when the cloud material— water droplets or ice crystals—grow heavy and fall towards the Earth.

Meteorologists (weather scientists) say there are several ways droplets can grow and become rain. How raindrops are made depends on what sort of clouds they fall from—warm clouds or cold clouds.

Warm clouds are made of tiny droplets of water in the air. Droplets that fall out of the cloud sometimes evaporate before they reach the ground. But sometimes, they are big enough to splash on us in a shower of raindrops.

# Blue Snowmen, Red Rainstorms

It's beginning to rain, and you've forgotten your umbrella. You're wearing a white shirt. You walk faster—you're beginning to get wet and uncomfortable. Then you look down at your shirt—and discover that's it's covered with big red blotches. You look up, and to your surprise, big red raindrops are falling from the sky.

That's what happened to those unfortunate enough to be caught out in the rain on April 9, 1970, in Thessalonika, Greece. Strong winds over the Sahara Desert had hoisted a load of red clay particles high into the sky, and then carried the clay into clouds above Greece. Rainfall washed the clay out of the sky, and for a while, it rained red.

Colored rain is rare, but it can come in many colors. A spring thunderstorm in Dunstable, Massachusetts, in 1959 dumped bucketfuls of chartreuse rain. Apparently, the storm had picked up yellow-green spring pollen.

And on March 9, 1972, blue snow fell in the French Alps, the snow tinted by a load of minerals picked up in the Sahara.

183

There are two ways raindrops grow in a warm cloud. The first: As a tiny droplet falls through a cloud, it bumps into other droplets and these merge, making a bigger drop. This bigger drop may strike (and collect) more droplets on its way down. Soon, it is a large, splashy drop.

The second way warm-cloud raindrops grow is when small droplets latch onto the rear of a falling drop, making it larger. How? One meteorologist suggests imagining a station wagon speeding down a dusty road. Air whooshes around the car and throws dirt against the back window, which is soon coated with a thick layer of dust.

*Some raindrops evaporate before they hit the ground.*

The drop falling through a cloud is like the station wagon, and the droplets around it are like the dust. Air rushing up and around the speeding raindrop pulls tiny droplets into the back of the drop. The raindrop collects more water on its back, getting heavier and heavier. Sometimes, it becomes so heavy that it falls out of the cloud and plops into a puddle on the ground far below.

In cold clouds, raindrops start life as ice crystals. Cold clouds form high in the sky and extend up into regions where the temperature is always below freezing (32°F). Such clouds are a mixture of water droplets and ice crystals. As water evaporates from the liquid droplets, it collects on the crystals, freezing solid. As the crystals grow and gain weight, they become snowflakes and fall through the cloud. But unless it's cold out, the snowflakes don't last long. As they descend into warmer air, the flakes begin to melt, becoming raindrops.

# What makes hail?

**W**hen hail rains down in a thunderstorm, pelting metal roof gutters with a terrible din, it can wreak havoc. Hail can punch holes in the wings of airplanes, reduce a field of wheat to broken stems, and kill horses, cows, and other animals. So much hail can fall so quickly that it may cover the ground like snow, and, carried by rushing rainwater, drift into 6-foot piles.

Small hailstones are often round, bouncing off the ground like tiny gumballs. But hail also comes in strange, irregular shapes—sunbursts, or even a frozen "X." The different shapes are created high in a cloud by air rushing over the freezing contours of each hailstone.

One of the biggest hailstones ever found fell near Coffeyville, Kansas in September 1970. It measured 17 inches around and weighed almost 1¾ pounds. Slabs of ice jutted out at crazy angles from its surface. Hardly a round "stone," this chunk of ice from above was more like a lethal weapon.

*A 1¾-pound hailstone fell in Coffeyville, Kansas, in 1970.*

Thunderstorms are the factories for hailstones. Strong gusts of air carry dust, sand, and other debris up and down in a thundercloud. A hailstone forms when ice freezes around one of the blowing particles. (In some hailstones, the "particle" at the center may even be a dead insect.)

The hailstone gets bigger and bigger as it collects more and more ice on its wind-borne roller coaster ride inside the cloud. Break open a hailstone, and you can see evidence of its trip through the cloud. Rings, like those on a tree stump, mark off layers of ice—one clear layer, then a milky layer, then another clear layer.

Why the different layers? When the ice on a hailstone freezes quickly (at very low temperatures), it traps snowflakes and air bubbles. So the ice looks milky. But at higher temperatures, when ice freezes more slowly around the hailstone, there is more time for trapped snowflakes to melt and air to escape. So the finished ice is clear. The layers reveal the different temperature regions the hailstone traveled through in the cloud.

*To carry a 4-inch hailstone, an updraft in a thunderhead must be blowing at 180 miles an hour.*

Since a hailstone grows as it travels up and down, it also gets heavier and heavier. So you need strong winds to make a really big hailstone. For example, to support a growing, 4-inch hailstone, an updraft in a cloud must be blowing at over 180 miles an hour. These powerful drafts carry the hailstones until they become too big and heavy to support. Then the hail falls to earth.

Since hail grows only on

HAIL BALL HALL of FAME

# Stormy Weather: A Recipe

Take one big bunch of cold, dry air from above the Arctic. Send it sweeping down on a collision course with a mass of hot air moseying up from the equator, full of water. Then watch the storms break out.

Like two cars in a head-on collision, the two air masses smack against each other and flatten out. The long, flat area of their impact is called a *front*.

Remember, warm air rises; colder air tends to fall. A warm front results when a fast-moving warm air mass rides up over the cold air after the collision. Clouds form from the water in the warm air, and it may start to rain.

In other cases, the cold air moves faster, pushing under the warm air after the collision and giving it a boost up. This is called a cold front, with the cold air forcing the warm air to rise much more quickly than it would on its own. The result? Not just clouds, and rain, but often violent storms, including tornadoes.

long trips through clouds, the taller the thundercloud, the more likely it is to make hail. An 8-mile-high thunderstorm has a 50-50 chance of producing hail. A thunderstorm 9 miles high has a 75 percent probability of making hail. But one that is 11 miles high will almost certainly make hail.

A storm making hail may have a greenish cast to it. Why? White sunlight is made of a rainbow, or spectrum, of colors: red, orange, yellow, green, blue, and violet. Hailstones tend to reflect more of the green light in sunlight. So hailstorm clouds take on a sickly green tinge.

# How do snowflakes form?

Snow crystals form in cold clouds high above the Earth. At high, high altitudes, where the temperature can drop to –40°F, water vapor floating in clouds can suddenly freeze into ice crystals. In lower clouds, where temperatures are warmer, water vapor can slowly freeze around blowing particles when the temperature drops to 32°F (freezing).

While we think of snow as being "pure," it turns out that most snowflakes form around tiny bits of dirt, carried into the sky by wind. (Water vapor may also freeze around small particles of smoke.) Using very powerful microscopes, scientists have seen the particles hidden at the heart of snow crystals. In one batch of crystals looked at, more than three-fourths had grown around tiny bits of clay. So snow crystals are often soil—perhaps from your garden—dressed up in ice.

*A snowflake is made of between 2 and 200 separate snow crystals.*

Scientists think there are four basic snow crystal shapes. The simplest are long, spiky needles. The three other basic shapes all have six sides—they are hexagons. (A stop sign has eight sides—it's an octagon.) There are long, hollow columns, shaped like six-sided prisms. There are thin, flat, hexagonal plates. And finally, there are intricate, six-spoked stars.

The basic shape of a snow crystal depends on the temperature at which the crystal formed. The higher the cloud, the colder the cloud. (Above the highest clouds, the air gradually thins out to the cold of space.) High cirrus clouds, drifting through air that is about –30°F, are made entirely of ice crystal columns, which hang like glittering chandelier prisms in the sun.

Differently shaped crystals form at different temperatures. When the temperature in the clouds is about 27° to 32°F, plates form. From 23°

## Rare Crystals

Bahamian Banana Snow, a tropical delight.

French Bread Snow, especially popular if the Brie is falling.

Barking Dachshund Snow, a winter's tale.

to 27°, needles appear. From 18° to 23°, it's columns. From 10° to 18°, plates reappear. And then, from 3° to 10°, the first star shapes grow. Continuing down to temperatures well below zero, plates, columns, and other shapes alternate.

Crystal columns made in high clouds at very low temperatures may fall through warmer clouds and grow stars on their ends. So, in the same way a hailstorm's journey can be traced through its rings, the shape of a snow crystal is a natural record of the temperatures of the clouds it fell through.

And each snow crystal is different, with its own lovely design. Look at a snow crystal and you will see patterns within patterns, stars within stars.

As the snow crystals grow, become heavier, and fall towards Earth, their contours alter. If the crystals spin like tops as they fall, they may be perfectly symmetrical. But if they fall in a haphazard, sideways fashion, they end up lopsided.

Falling crystals clump together, forming snowflakes. Each snowflake is made of from 2 to about 200 separate crystals.

If the air below the snowing clouds is warmer than 32°F, the snowflakes may melt as they fall, turning to rain. (In fact, the rain that splashes down on us often started its journey as snow.) But if the air is cold enough, the flakes will drift to Earth, coating the ground with white.

Once on the ground, the crystals gradually lose their delicate shapes, getting round and nondescript. So if you want to see snowflakes in all their glory, collect them on a dark cloth or mitten as they come down from the sky.

# Why does the wind blow?

Like the other planets in our solar system, the Earth is surrounded by a layer of gas molecules, called an atmosphere. The Earth's atmosphere is made mostly of nitrogen and oxygen gas. Individual gas molecules constantly zip this way and that, but they are clasped to Earth by our planet's gravity.

Winds are the movements of great bunches of these molecules, sweeping along together. A little air will pick itself up and swoop around a tall building, tearing off someone's hat. Or an immense river of air, several thousand miles wide, will flow around our planet.

*Wind is caused by air pressure varying throughout the atmosphere.*

Indoors, with the air barely moving, it's easy to forget

that it's there. But anyone who has put a hand out the window of a moving car knows that air, though invisible, can push hard.

In fact, air is always pressing on us. Air seems insubstantial, weightless. But above our heads, stretching into space, the whole atmosphere of gas molecules weighs more than 5 quadrillion tons (one ton equals 2,000 pounds). Even as you read this, the air around you is pressing on each square inch of your body with about 14.7 pounds of force.

Winds are caused by differences in air pressure from place to place. How? Imagine a dam with water 20 feet deep on one side and 10 feet deep on the other. If the dam is opened, water will flow quickly into the shallow side until both sides are equal.

Something similar happens with air. The air pressure varies from place to place mainly because the temperature varies. Warmer air expands and thins as its mole-

cules spread farther apart. So it tends to weighs less, and its pressure is lower. In cold air the molecules press together, making the air weigh more and exert more pressure.

*Even as you read this, the air around you is pressing on each square inch of your body with almost 15 pounds of force.*

Like water, air usually flows from an area of high pressure to an area of low pressure, as air molecules rush in to fill the spaces where the air is thinner. This rush of air is wind.

Here's an example of how a wind gets started near the

seashore: It's a sunny day. Both the land and the ocean warm in the sun. But the water warms more slowly than the land, since warming surface water constantly mixes with cooler, deeper water. So the air over the land gets warmer than the air over the water.

Air near the ground expands as it warms, making a pocket of low pressure. But as the air expands, it pushes upward. High up, air molecules crowd together—making a pocket of high pressure over the land.

Some of the air high above the sunbathers' heads begins streaming out to sea, where the pressure is lower, and air begins to bunch up over the water. The air pressure over the ocean rises. So air near the ocean surface starts flowing briskly back into the lower-pressure air over the land. As the air sweeps in low over the beach, sunbathers and swimmers are cooled by a newborn sea breeze.

# Does it rain on other planets?

On Earth, we are not surprised to see water drip from the sky. We're used to big puffy clouds forming from water vapor, and then falling apart, drenching us.

On some other planets in our solar system, there are also clouds and storms. But the clouds are often made of chemicals and compounds other than water. Each planet has its own unique atmosphere and weather. (For more about the planets, see the Solar System section.)

Mercury, the planet nearest the Sun, is a cratered, barren world, with daytime temperatures soaring to 800°F. Its atmosphere is so thin as to be nearly undetectable. There are no clouds or rain on Mercury.

But Venus, our next-door neighbor, is thick with clouds, and bursts of lightning zigzag through its heavy sky. Unable to see the surface through the cloud cover, scientists once thought Venus might be wet, swampy, and lush with plants. They now know that our sister planet is rocky and searingly hot—900°F at noon.

On Venus, there is truly "acid rain." The yellow clouds enveloping the planet are made not of water, but of deadly sulfuric acid. But when it rains, the acid droplets falling through the 900°F air boil away before they can hit the surface of the planet.

Mars, fourth from the Sun, may have once been the planet that most resembled Earth. Today, Mars has a thin atmosphere, and its surface,

seen in pictures sent back by the Viking spacecraft, looks a lot like the deserts of the southwestern United States. In the Martian winter, wispy clouds of carbon dioxide drift over the red plains, and frost coats the rocks. Morning fogs may float through the valleys, but this mist is as close as Mars comes to rain.

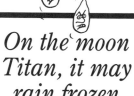

*On the moon Titan, it may rain frozen gasoline.*

However, etched into the Martian landscape are what appear to be river beds, now

Singing in the...

...sulfuric acid — Venus

Ammonia crystals — Jupiter

and frozen gasoline! — Titan

dry. Scientists think that water once swept through these passages. Billions of years ago, they say, Mars must have had a heavier atmosphere. Rain probably fell, in abundance. Today, what water remains is locked in polar icecaps, or trapped in Martian rocks and soil.

Our solar system's fifth planet, giant Jupiter, is as different from Mars as can be. Jupiter is a rotating ball of gases, mainly hydrogen and helium. Deep inside, there may be a small solid core, covered by a hydrogen ocean.

Colored bands of clouds encircle Jupiter. Some clouds may be made of water; most are probably puffy masses of sharp-smelling ammonia ice. Jupiter has its storms, some of them violent, and according to planetary scientist David Stevenson, they may rain (or snow) ammonia crystals. But the ice liquifies and evaporates before it hits the hydrogen sea.

Saturn is another huge, gaseous world, and its weather is thought to be a lot like Jupiter's. The Voyager spacecraft once detected a thunderstorm stretching 40,000 miles around Saturn's equator.

Uranus, yet another

gassy planet, is also covered with a cloudy haze. Some of its clouds, made of methane (natural gas), resemble giant versions of Earth's thunderheads. Shaped like blacksmith's anvils, they tower in the Uranian sky. Drops of liquid methane may fall from the clouds, said Stevenson, but they evaporate on the way down.

Gaseous, far-off Neptune is more mysterious. We know it has clouds of methane ice, but scientists know little about

*Water probably once fell in abundance on Mars, but today, its surface is covered by a cold desert.*

its weather. Frigid Pluto, at 3.6 billion miles from the Sun, is a bigger mystery still.

But the nine planets are not the only places in our solar system to look for precipitation. On Titan, one of Saturn's big moons, methane snowflakes may fall from the moon's reddish clouds, floating down into a vast lunar ocean filled with methane or nitrogen. (Frozen gasoline may sleet down, too.) Someday, our robot explorers may sail Titan's chemical sea.

# How do clouds get electricity to make lightning?

**E**lectricity is something we think is made in power plants, not in puffy masses of water droplets that you can put your hand right through. But there is electricity in clouds, and in this page, and even in you.

Everything is made of atoms, from clouds to trees to human beings. Each atom has a nucleus made up of positively charged protons and neutral neutrons. (Except for the simplest kind of hydrogen atom, which has no neutrons.) Orbiting the nucleus are negatively charged electrons. Positives and negatives attract, so the electrons circle the nucleus like bees swarm-ing around a sweet roll.

The attraction between protons and electrons is caused by the electromagnetic force. So electricity is already present everywhere we look. It's just hidden inside atoms.

*There is electricity in clouds, in this page, and in you.*

Ordinarily, the positive and negative charges balance each other out in each atom. So objects made of atoms—such as you—don't usually have a positive or negative electric charge. And you don't ordinarily go around zapping other people each time you touch them.

Sometimes, the electric charges in an object can become unbalanced. You've probably experienced this, perhaps on a cold winter day, in your toasty-warm home. Let's say the rooms are very dry. You go scuffing across the carpet. And, unbeknownst to you, some electrons in the rug and in your shoes get sheared away from their atoms.

Now *you* are electrically charged. The number of electrons and protons in you don't balance out. Touch a metal

doorknob, and a tiny electric current will flow between you and it. You'll feel the shock.

What happens is that the electrical force—the attraction between positives and negatives—causes your charged body to rebalance itself as electrons flow between you and the doorknob. If it's dark, you can even see a spark. (The bright flash occurs because the electrons emit photons of light as they jump.) If it's quiet, you can hear a tiny crackle.

Electricity is always in and around us, and clouds are no exception. They look harmless enough on a bright sunny day. But just like you in your living room, a cloud can build up a charge. If it does, watch out. When a cloud puts its atoms back in balance, there are fireworks.

What happens is this: In dark, towering storm clouds, there are rushing air currents that cause particles in the cloud—including salt from the ocean, dust, and so on—to slam into each other. Just as your shoes rubbing on the carpet freed electrons, so do colliding particles loosen electrons. The particles then become electrically charged—positively charged if they lose electrons, negatively charged if they gain too many.

For reasons that aren't entirely known, heavier particles tend to get negatively charged, and lighter particles become positive. So the lower layers of the cloud, where the heavier particles fall, become

*A bolt of lightning contains enough electricity to light all the homes and businesses in an entire state—but only for a fraction of a second.*

negatively charged.

The negative bottom of the cloud attracts positively charged protons and repels any stray electrons on the Earth below. Soon, a positive charge builds up on the ground beneath the cloud. Then, just as electrons jumped between you and the doorknob, a tremendous spark—a lightning bolt—connects the cloud and the ground. Electrons zig-zag down, meeting protons on their way up from the ground. And instead of the tiny crackle you heard when you touched the knob, a clap of thunder erupts.

If we could watch the whole process in slow motion, this is what we would see: A dimly glowing bolt, called a *leader,* emerges out of the bottom of the cloud. The leader begins to jerkily move down toward the ground. First it jumps 150 feet down to the right, then 150 feet to the left. (That's the zig-zag pattern we see in the sky.)

The leader's trip down takes only a fraction of a second. At this point, it carries an electric current of about 200 amperes (normal household current is 15 or 20 amps).

But when the bolt gets to within about 60 feet of the ground, a spark suddenly jumps out of the ground to join it. When the two sparks connect, the current races back up to the cloud, increasing to more than 10,000 amps as it goes.

Another leader snakes out and slams down the channel created by the upward stroke. Then another spark shoots back up to the cloud. Temperatures in the channel can reach 50,000° F. The lightning strokes—firing back and forth many times in less than a second—are what we see as a single bolt.

How much power is in a bolt of lightning? Up to 20,000 megawatts, or enough to run all the homes and businesses in an entire state—but only for a fraction of a second.

# Does ball lightning really exist?

**B**all lightning is a glowing sphere of electric current. If it exists—and some scientists still have their doubts—it is very rare. But there are many strange stories about ball lightning's antics.

For example, in 1936, a newspaper in England reported that a ball of fire had cut through telephone wires outside a house, rolled through an open window, and plunged into a barrel of water sitting near the window. As the lightning ball sank into the barrel, eyewitnesses said, the water began to boil.

Ball lightning's rare appearances seem to take place just after an ordinary lightning stroke zig-zags down through the clouds.

The glowing balls may range from the size of a cantaloupe to a beachball, and may be red, orange, yellow, or brilliant white. As the ball comes into view, it may hiss or buzz menacingly.

Judging from observers' reports, there may be two distinct kinds of lightning balls. One kind, often red, seems to float down from the clouds. Then, when the ball first touches something on the ground—say, a tree—it explodes.

The other kind rolls along the ground, and is bright white. The ball is attracted to good conductors of electricity, and may attach itself to the ground, a power line—or even a person.

Scientists don't know much about ball lightning because it is so hard to study.

First, you must predict where it might appear—a nearly impossible thing to do. Then, you must capture the elusive glowing ball on film or video, also a difficult feat as the ghostly ball may disappear before you can point a camera at it.

*Ball lightning may be as big as a beachball, and may hiss or buzz menacingly.*

So what scientists have to rely on is the stories people tell about their strange encounters with the luminous

Close Encounters with Great Balls of Fire...

*I saw one crash a party, and win the dance contest.*

*I chased one down the street for a light.*

*I saw them on tour — they were great!*

balls. With little evidence to examine, some scientists question whether ball lightning really exists. And even those who believe it's real have trouble explaining it.

One big question: Why would ball lightning last as long as it does? An ordinary lightning stroke is over in a flash, as negatively charged particles in a thundercloud connect with positively charged particles on the ground in a fraction of a second.

But ball lightning lasts from a few seconds to a few minutes. How come? One theory is that the ball is a kind of tiny thundercloud, forged by a lightning bolt. Here's the thinking: Dust motes are always floating through the air. Sometimes, scientists think, an ordinary lightning bolt may electrically charge the motes in a region of air. Some motes become positive; others, negative. And then, in a light show lasting for sometimes many seconds,

millions of tiny lightning strokes begin connecting the dust motes, making a glittering lightning ball.

---

*The ball may be a kind of tiny thundercloud, forged by a lightning bolt.*

---

# Where do tornadoes come from?

Tornadoes, although small, are the most powerful storms in nature. Twisting and turning, they snake down from clouds and wreak havoc, exploding houses, tossing cars like baseballs, and pulling trees up by their roots. Storm survivors may find even pieces of straw driven into the side of trees like nails. The sound of an approaching tornado has been described as the roar of a monster freight train.

The United States is the tornado capital of the world, with an average of 700 twisters a year. The country that comes in second on the tornado hit list is Australia, with a measly 15. (Some U.S. states get more tornadoes than others. From 1953 to 1980, Alaska had one lonely tornado, while Kansas—home state of Dorothy and Toto—had more than 1,200.

The recipe for a tornado? Take a big thunderstorm. Add winds blowing from opposite directions, then throw in a strong updraft.

If you were to look at the top of a big thunderstorm, you would see the cloud tops bubbling up and then subsiding as powerful gusts of wind (the updraft) surge up through the clouds. A tornado sometimes forms when the air in the updraft begins to rotate, as opposing winds in the storm spin it around.

This spinning column of rising air is called a mesocyclone. Such a mass of whirling air and cloud, like the whirling water around a bathtub drain, is called a vortex. In the center of the storm vortex, the air pressure drops, as more air is sucked into the spinning part. No one knows just how low the pressure can drop, but some scientists estimate it may fall to half normal air pressure.

Some mesocyclones get stronger, spinning faster and faster as they shrink. As the

## *Wind speed in a whirling tornado can reach 600 miles an hour.*

pressure in the center drops, the whirling air mass takes on the familiar "funnel" shape we know as a tornado. And as more air gets pulled into the funnel, it accelerates upward, stretching the tube.

A tornado may be shaped like a cone, or a thick pillar, or a long, thin, twisty tube. Tornadoes come in different colors, too. When the funnel cloud first dips down from the sky, it may be dirty white or gray. But as it lifts up dust and debris from the ground, it often turns brown or clay-red.

Wind speeds may reach 600 miles an hour. Pieces of wood and metal picked up from the ground hurtle

around in the tornado at the same speeds, becoming lethal weapons. And the extremely low pressure in the center can explode small closed buildings as the funnel passes overhead. Lucky for us, meteorologists are getting better and better at predicting when a tornado will form. If a tornado warning is issued, the northeast corner of a basement or the center of a first floor is the safest place to be. Outside, a ditch or other low-lying area is the best bet.

### FAST FACT

**Why does the U.S. have the most tornadoes? Winds from the west are forced to stream high over the Rocky Mountains. On the other side, they encounter low, warm, moist winds from the Gulf of Mexico. The air masses collide over the central U.S., spawning violent storms, including tornadoes.**

# At the Zoo

L ife on Earth began, scientists say, nearly 4 billion years ago. Organic molecules were the precursors of living cells. By 3 billion years ago, one-celled organisms were joining up into several-celled plants. (By contrast, you have a hundred trillion cells in your body.) And until about 600 million years ago, blue-green algae ruled the Earth. But then life proliferated into many strange forms, eventually giving rise to fish, land plants, and insects. Later came the first reptiles, and then the dinosaurs. As the dinosaurs died out, about 65 million years ago, mammals spread far and wide, birds evolved, flowers grew. And as time went on, monkeys and apes evolved—and finally, just a few million years ago, humans.

Since more complex forms of life evolved as time passed, it's tempting to think of evolution as a ladder, with one-celled organisms on the bottom rung, we humans perched on top, and other animals in between.

But evolution is more like a branching tree. Each animal (and plant) alive today can trace its ancestry back to the same one-celled organisms. Your dog is just as "evolved" as you—it took millions of years for a dog and a person to arrive in their present forms. One branch on the tree of life led to dogs, another to us. And so life continues to evolve, today.

# Why do people say cats have nine lives?

According to the records of one New York City veterinarian, a cat named Sabrina fell from the 32nd floor of a building—and lived to meow the tale. She walked away with a broken tooth and a few other minor injuries.

Amazing as it may seem, Sabrina's story isn't all that unusual. When people fall from great heights, their injuries are severe. Their skulls or backs may break, and they may bleed internally. It's very rare for someone to survive a fall from more than a few stories.

But many cats survive falls that would surely kill another animal, or a person. They may be brought to the vet's office with bloody noses, cracked teeth, and broken ribs, but at least they're alive. So it might seem as if a cat is

literally coming back to life after a deadly accident. Seeing this happen again and again, one might assume cats have many lives.

Of course, cats really only have one life. But they are very, very good at falling. Why? For one thing, cats hit the ground less forcefully than we do. They're smaller than people and they weigh a lot less. So their fall is softer. But being small isn't their only advantage. Cats are better at falling than many other small animals—such as poodles or rabbits.

A cat that starts falling upside down will try to twist around so that it lands on all fours. The excellent balancing equipment in her inner ears lets a cat quickly determine what position she's in and right herself, just as if she carried a gyroscope. And when a cat lands—on its feet—all four legs absorb the impact. Also, the cat's legs are bent when it lands. So the force of the fall doesn't just travel straight through breakable bones, but also spreads through muscles and joints.

But here's the most surprising falling-cat fact of all: Cats are *more* likely to live if they fall from higher places rather than lower ones. Some New York veterinarians found that 10 percent of their cat patients died when they fell from two to six stories above the ground. But only 5 percent died when the fall was from 7 to 32 stories.

Why? Bodies accelerate—speed up—as they fall. All falling bodies, regardless of their mass, accelerate by 22 miles per hour, *each second* as they fall toward the Earth. Starting out at 0 miles an hour, you can be traveling at more than 100 miles an hour after only a few seconds' falling.

If there weren't air, and two objects were falling in a vacuum, they'd hit the ground at the same instant— even if one were a feather and

*Cats are more likely to survive if they fall from higher places than lower ones.*

the other a refrigerator. However, after falling a certain distance through air, an object reaches what scientists call terminal velocity, or final speed, as friction (resistance) from the air slows the fall. How much it slows the fall depends on the falling object's mass and its area— how spread out the mass is. To survive a fall, you want a smaller mass and a greater area.

In real terms, this means that an average-size person

falling six stories will be traveling at about 120 miles an hour when he lands. A cat might be flying earthward at "only" 60 miles per hour.

But the cat has another, unexpected advantage. Once a cat reaches terminal velocity and stops accelerating, it can relax a bit. On a short fall, terminal velocity may not be reached until the very end. But if the cat has enough time—if it is falling from a higher floor—it can spread

*Cats have excellent balancing equipment in their inner ears, enabling them to twist around and land on all fours when they fall.*

out its legs after it reaches terminal velocity. This shapes its body more like a parachute.

And we know what happens when a parachute opens. The uprushing air has a bigger area to push against. Friction increases. And the falling parachute—or cat— slows down. That may be why Sabrina was able to limp away from her tumble from the 32nd floor.

# Why do some animals have four legs while others have only two ?

Each species of animal has its own special shape, and its own special history of how it came to look the way it does. Body shape is determined by animals' ancestors and the environment they evolved in—the climate, how food must be obtained, and so on.

Some animals walk on two legs, some on four (or more), and others use some combination. For example, chimpanzees sometimes lope along carrying an infant in one arm, using both feet and the other hand to propel themselves.

Animals that walk on two feet are called *bipeds*. Those that walk on four feet are called *quadrupeds*. Human beings are bipeds, although as babies we crawl on all fours. And cats are quadrupeds, although they can pull themselves up to stand on their back legs. There are also animals with more than four legs—spiders have eight; centipedes have thirty. And some animals, such as fish and worms, get along just fine without any legs at all.

*Unlike other primates, human beings have straight spines, perfect for standing on two legs.*

However it gets around, an animal must move efficiently in order to survive. If it spends its days in the treetops, it had better have strong arms and hands for hanging on. If an animal's misfortune is to be a lion's favorite dinner, it must be able to run fast, without stumbling.

Each species has evolved its own strategy for moving efficiently. Whether an animal uses two feet for walking or scampers around on all fours is part of this strategy. Looking at one animal—human beings—and how we came to walk on two legs can help us understand this concept.

Human beings are members of a big group of animals called primates, which also includes monkeys, baboons, gibbons, gorillas, and chimpanzees, to name a few. Other primates, as you can see at the zoo, don't walk as we do. Most combine moving on all fours with walking nearly upright. Many also swing through trees, using their arms. Because most primates spend much of their time in trees, but also forage on the ground, they have a variety of ways of moving.

Gibbons, for example,

swing from branch to branch, hanging by their long arms. Their strong grip keeps them safely aloft. When they move along the tops of branches, they run on two legs. Chimpanzees often hang by their arms when having a meal in a tree. On the ground, they walk on their feet and their knuckles. Baboons run along the ground on all fours. Gorillas, like chimps, are

knuckle-walkers. All these ways of getting around work well in the tropical forest environment in which most primates live.

Although human beings are primates, we are shaped differently from our primate relatives. Humans have straight spines, perfect for standing on two legs. (Chimpanzees have spines that bend at an angle to their hips, better for running on all fours.)

Humans have legs that are long compared to our arms. (Gibbons have arms that are long compared to their legs.) We have feet that are built for walking long distances. (Monkeys have feet built for grasping branches tightly.)

We share enough features that we are still part of the same group, but humans, alone among primates, evolved to walk on two legs.

Scientists think what pushed our apelike ancestors towards bipedalism was the food supply. Most of each day was spent gathering food and

*However it gets around, an animal must move efficiently in order to survive.*

then eating it, just to survive. As our ancestors spread out from the African forests to the grasslands, they found new food—small leaves, nuts, seeds, and berries. To collect

enough of these tiny morsels in a day, two-handed gathering and eating was necessary.

It became a great advantage to be able to stand and walk on two legs for long periods. Our ancestors, born "by accident" with straighter spines and longer legs, had this advantage: More of them got enough to eat. So more of them survived, and went on to have children. These children inherited their parents' more upright statures. And gradually, over many generations, humans evolved to spend nearly all their time on two legs, freeing their hands to hunt, gather, and create.

# How can bats catch food dark without bumping

 bat may swoop around a barn at midnight, avoiding poles, rafters, and sleeping cows. But its night vision is nothing special. When it's pitch-black, a bat forced to rely on its eyes would probably bump into as many walls as you and I.

But bats have evolved another way of finding their way through the dark—by listening.

Bats trap most of their food after the Sun sets. During the day, they hang around home—a cave, a hollow tree, or even an attic's rafters. Bats spend a lot of time sprucing up for the night's festivities. They comb their hair with their claws, and lick their wings clean. In between fits of grooming, they doze off.

Around nightfall, bats flap off from their homes in search of food. Some bats munch on fruit. Vampire bats in the tropics feed on the blood of birds, cows, and other animals. But most bats like bugs for dinner.

Bats prefer to trap insects at night for several reasons. Darkness protects bats from animals that would like to eat *them*. And flying at night, their wide, hairless wings are kept out of the hot, drying sunlight.

Bats use sound to navigate the darkness. Like submarines using sound waves, or sonar, to navigate the murky ocean depths, bats send off pulses of sound through their mouths or noses. These pulses echo back, outlining objects in the bat's way. This process is called *echolocation*—the bat uses echoes to navigate its surroundings and locate its prey. A bat's large, oddly-constructed ears help it figure out where the echoes are coming from.

*Like submarines, bats use sonar, or sound waves, to navigate in darkness.*

A bat whooshing through your living room at 3 A.M.

# at night and fly in the into things?

..............................

knows where he's going. Blips of sound bounce off chairs, sofa, and TV screen. At an open window, the sounds travel out into the night, telling the bat where to escape.

The sounds bats send out bounce off tiny objects, too. If by chance dinner—in the form of a tasty fly—should be buzzing around the room, the bat will probably find it. To search for insects, a typical bat sweeps the room with sound, sending out a steady 10 beats a second. When echoes come back from the fly, the sound pulses increase, to more than 25 a second. This gives the bat a better idea of where the fly is as it darts about.

As the bat zeroes in on the fly, it sends out more and

Bat Air Safety

Control to bat, you are approaching a large towerlike object.

211

more sound blips, as many as 200 a second. Then the bat either snatches the fly or swoops nearby and tries again.

Bats are very good at what they do. The hunt may be over in only half a second. Bats may eat a quarter of their own weight in insects in half an hour. Some insects, such as gnats, are miniscule and nearly weightless. So some bats may catch more

*As a bat zeroes in on an insect, it may send out as many as 200 sound blips a second.*

than 1,200 insects an hour— or an insect every 3 seconds. (How researchers figured this out: They weighed bats before a hunting session, and then immediately afterwards, when their tummies were stuffed with bugs.)

Some bats are so skillful at finding objects through echolocation that in the dark they can detect—and not bump into—wires as thin as human hairs.

# How come the black widow spider eats her mate ?

The tiny black widow spider has a bad reputation. Here are some of the rumors about her: She poisons insects. She poisons people. She has her mate for dinner—as the main course. Unfortunately, the stories are more or less true.

Black widows live throughout the world, and all over the United States. It's unlikely that a black widow will set up her house in your house, but just in case, here's what to look for: a shiny black spider, with a red, yellow, or orange design on its abdomen—often in the shape of an hourglass.

Until about 1900, the little black spider went by a variety of names, depending on what part of the country she scuttled around in. People called her an hourglass spider, a shoe-button spider, or just "the poison lady." Around the turn of the century, the name "black widow" became popular—and stuck.

There are striking differences between female and

*Drop for drop, the female black widow's venom is more deadly than rattlesnake venom.*

male black widows. The differences help to explain why the female black widow has such a monstrous reputation.

The male is more dark brown than black, with white stripes running along the side of his abdomen. The design on his stomach is often dully colored and does not usually have a clearly defined shape.

The adult male makes little or no poisonous venom, and what venom he has is weak. It's not even much good for stunning insects.

The female black widow, on the other hand, usually sports a bright design on her belly, and all her poison glands are in good working order. Drop for drop, her poison is more deadly than rattlesnake venom. And the female towers over her little male friends—she's two to three times their size.

### FAST FACT

**Male black widows aren't the only ones for whom mating is a dangerous proposition. Female praying mantises often bite the heads off their beloveds after mating.**

Despite their ferocious-looking fangs, black widows are rather shy. But people avoid them with good reason. The venom that helps a black widow trap tasty insects is also poisonous to humans. Throughout human history, there have been unpleasant stories of what happened when these tiny spiders bit someone.

In 1933, one scientist recorded his ordeal after he was bitten on the finger by a black widow. Pain spread quickly up his arm. His chest ached, and he felt sleepy and headachy. His heart slowed. Soon, his assistants took over writing notes. The pain spread to his stomach, his legs began trembling, and he was taken to a hospital. On the way, he began to have trouble talking, and then breathing. He survived, but it took 8 days for all symptoms to disappear.

The male black widow is in equal danger when mating time rolls around. Finding a female black widow hanging in her web, the tiny male "knocks" on her door, by using his abdomen to make

*A female black widow often has an orange hourglass on her stomach.*

her web vibrate. If she sends a welcoming vibration back through the web, he's proba-

bly safe. Otherwise, watch out. If she's not in the mood to mate, she may pounce on him, wrap him in her silk like a mummy, and keep him around for days of convenient snacking.

If she is ready to mate, all usually goes well. Afterwards, black widow females only eat their sweeties if they are very, very hungry. Otherwise, they let the little guys slink off to parts unknown.

# Why do spiders spin webs ?

..........................

**M**ost spiders spin webs. But some don't. Take tarantulas, for instance. Many of them burrow into the ground, lining their burrows with soft spider silk. They build trapdoors over their burrows, too, the better to catch passing insects.

All spiders, whether they spin webs or not, have a few important things in common. They have eight legs. And insects are their favorite food. (Remember, spiders aren't insects themselves. They are *arachnids*—a group of animals that includes ticks, mites, and scorpions.) There are at least 40,000 kinds of spiders.

Spiders that do spin webs can make simple webs or very elaborate ones. Even

after the web is made, a spider does not live exclusively in its web. It may hang out under a roof shingle, in the corner of a windowsill, or under a rock. The point of a web is to trap insects, and a proper web can take hours to make.

The orb weaver spider, for example, uses several different kinds of silk. It uses a dry thread to build the framework, or scaffolding, of its web. Then it lays on a sticky thread to entrap insects.

The silky thread comes

from glands in the spider's abdomen. Different glands produce different kinds of silk. The spider may combine several kinds to get a line of thread that does what it wants it to.

An orb spider starts its web by tossing out some thread to the wind. The silk blows in the air and catches on a nearby object, such as a branch, allowing the spider to climb the thread and lay a thicker strand of silk along it.

After the spider makes an outline of the web, it spins out a line connecting one side of the web to the other. The spider scuttles to the center of this line and spins out another line, which it anchors to the opposite side of the web.

From there the spider spins more dry lines, radiating out from the center like

spokes on a bicycle wheel. Then it circles the spokes, laying spirals of thread. Finally, it lays down a sticky spiral on top of the dry spiral. The spider gets rid of the dry framework—by eating it. And the trap is ready.

Some webs have more complicated patterns than others. The designs woven into them may be part of the trap, according to some researchers. To us, the patterns may not look like anything special. But that may be because we don't see them in ultraviolet light.

Ultraviolet light comes from the Sun. It is the kind of light that gives us a tan. But its frequency is too high for our eyes to see. So to us, it is invisible light.

But many insects *can* see ultraviolet light—especially insects that feed on flower nectar and pollens. And some spiders may make special webs to attract them.

How? First, the spider spins a web made from silk that reflects very little UV light. Then the spider weaves in a design with a different kind of silk, one that shines in ultraviolet.

What's the design? Well, according to the researchers, the designs look like the patterns that are reflected from many flowers in UV light.

So hungry insects, looking for a meal, see a lovely flower shining ahead of them. Flying in, they are trapped— by a decorated web, inhabited by a hungry spider.

# Why do dogs see in black and white ?

. . . . . . . . . . . . . . . . . . . . . . . . . .

Some ideas get passed around as reality for so long that no one questions whether they are in fact true. One such idea is that dogs see in black and white—that for our canine pals, the world is one big 1950s television show.

But according to Gerald Jacobs, an experimental psychologist at the University of California at Santa Barbara, dogs probably appreciate a deep blue sky as much as any of us.

Jacobs and two other experimenters designed a machine, run by a computer, that both analyzed the light dogs see and spat out beef-and-cheese treats. Then they enlisted the cooperation of two greyhounds and a poodle. The researchers wanted to find out whether our best

friends really do see life in drab shades of gray.

Their experiments proved that dogs see in color. But a dog, they said, is like a color-blind person. Instead of seeing a rainbow of colors, dogs apparently can't tell green from red, or either of those from yellow or orange.

That means your dog's

yellow bowl doesn't stand out when it's sitting in green grass. But a blue ball will look nice and blue and not like any other color.

Many people have problems seeing colors, too. Up to 6 in 100 boys and men in the United States find green hard to see. Few women are color-blind. Most color blindness is inherited along with those genes that make a boy a boy.

The trigger for color blindness may be in the retina, a thin layer of cells that covers the inside of the eyeball. Some of the cells in the retina—called "cones"—send information about color from the eye to the brain. The cones contain pigments, chemicals that absorb different wavelengths, or colors, of light.

In people, the cone pigments are sensitive to three

primary colors: red, green, and blue. Light is absorbed, and impulses travel along the optic nerve to the brain. Somehow, the brain decodes these impulses into all the colors we see.

Some truly color-blind people see only yellow or blue; everything else is gray, black, or white. And others see red and green just fine, but no yellow or blue. A few unlucky people really do see everything in shades of black, white, and gray.

*Dogs apparently can't tell green from red, or either of those from yellow or orange.*

While most people inherit their color blindness, others find that their color vision changed when a disease struck the optic nerve, or when the part of the brain that handles vision is damaged.

Jacobs says that no one is sure what dogs see when they see color. A dog's cone cells may be sensitive only to red and blue, and an orange, a banana, and an apple may all look red to a dog. But at least we know that dogs inhabit a much cheerier world than we imagined.

# How come giraffes

People once thought that giraffes' necks lengthened because they stretched to eat higher leaves. Then, or so the story goes, they passed this change on to their offspring.

We now know that changes in animals and plants over generations—evolution—don't occur that way. The current idea, developed by scientists like Charles Darwin in the 1800s, is that evolution works in two steps. First, there is variation. And then, there is natural selection.

Variation means that sometimes, by accident, an animal will be born that is somehow different from the others of her species. Maybe she's much hairier. Or maybe

her legs are built a little differently, and she can run faster. Or maybe she's exceedingly slow. Variations aren't necessarily good or bad. They just happen in nature.

Natural selection simply means this: The better-suited an animal is to the area it lives in, the better its chances of living a long life and having babies. The babies, then, may inherit the variation that made the parent animal so successful in its local environment.

For example, if you're a fish, one scientist noted, and your pond dries up, and all you can do is flop around helplessly, you probably won't live to have many children.

But let's say you have a special set of fins, which all of your fishy friends think are very funny. And they never seemed much good before— but now you find you can use them to belly-flop your way to the next pond.

Since you've survived to tell the tale, you'll probably have little fish of your own. They'll inherit your strange but useful fins. And they'll be better-suited to life in an area where ponds tend to dry up. As the generations pass, there will be more and more fish sporting the odd fins. That's variation and natural selection at work.

Something like this probably happened with the shorter-necked ancestors of mod-

# have long necks?

ern giraffes. Those who by chance were born with somewhat longer necks could forage from the ground all the way up into the treetops, and find more food—a definite survival advantage, especially when food was scarce. So over generations, the long-necked giraffes crowded out the short-necked ones.

But there are also some

*Long-necked giraffes had a survival advantage over short-necked ones.*

disadvantages to having a very long neck. A giraffe's heart must pump very hard to get blood all the way up to its faraway brain. And animals with very long necks usually can't run as fast, or escape danger as quickly, as short-necked animals. So even the best adaptation has its drawbacks.

# A Moth of a Different Color

Sometimes an adaptation, such as the giraffe's long neck, stops being an advantage. An example is the color of the peppered moth, which lives in England.

In the early 1800s, most peppered moths were light gray. They were nearly invisible on the side of trees, and birds ignored them. Occasionally, a black baby moth was born. But these were easily noticed by the birds, and quickly eaten. So they usually didn't live long enough to have black moth babies of their own.

But as factories were built and pollution filled the air, trees were soon covered with black soot. Now the light gray moths were the ones in danger, and were getting eaten at an alarming rate. The black moths, however, survived and multiplied.

Soon, there were very few gray moths. But now, conditions are changing once more. Pollution is being controlled. Gray moths are coming back as the trees and air of England get cleaner.

# Is a panda a bear? And why are panda babies so small?

When is a bear not a bear? When it's a panda—maybe.

Scientists don't agree on what kind of animals pandas are. The problem is, there are two very different pandas. The familiar black-and-white panda is called the giant panda. Weighing more than 200 pounds, giant pandas have bulky bodies and look like especially cuddly bears.

But the other, less famous panda, is small (only 2 feet long), with rusty red fur and a long bushy tail. This animal, called the red panda, looks more like a raccoon than a bear, from the size and shape of its body to its tail, ringed with dark and light bands.

After studying both creatures, scientists have decided that the small red animal and the big black-and-white animal are close relatives. The way their bodies are designed is similar, and so are their eating and other habits.

Because of the similarities, both are called pandas. But there the agreement ends. Some scientists say the giant panda is indeed a kind of bear. Some say the red panda is, in fact, a kind of raccoon. And still others think the two are part of their own unique family of panda animals.

The giant panda particularly confuses scientists. Instead of galloping, like an ordinary bear, it trots. Instead of roaring, it bleats like a sheep. Unlike traditional bears, it does not hibernate, and it isn't fond of meat.

*Giant pandas eat about 120 pounds of bamboo a day.*

However, studying blood and other cells from giant pandas and comparing them to those of ordinary bears, most scientists have come to

the conclusion that giant pandas really are bears—bears that are specialists at living high in the mountains of China, Nepal, and Tibet. They think that bears, plus raccoons and red pandas, have a common ancestor, an animal that lived 20 to 40 million years ago, which explains their similarities. But the raccoons and red pandas evolved in one direction, and the bears—including the giant panda—evolved in another.

Giant pandas live in thick forests, 5,000 to 10,000 feet up the mountainsides, where they munch on bamboo, which grows in patches around the trees.

Giant pandas eat a lot, swallowing about 30 pounds of bamboo leaves and stems and about 90 pounds of tasty new shoots every day. But no one has accused pandas of being pigs. Unlike animals such as cows, pandas can't digest cellulose, the woody pulp found in bamboo and other plants. So, in order to get as much nutrition from the woody bamboo as possible, pandas must spend nearly all their waking hours busily eating.

(Red pandas also live in Asia, but not as high up. They live in the foothills of the Himalayan Mountains. Like giant pandas, they eat bamboo shoots, but they also eat fruit, nuts, and, occasionally, small animals.)

Giant pandas give birth to one cub at a time. Like traditional bear cubs, panda cubs are born ridiculously small.

Newborn pandas, blind and bald, weigh only about 5 ounces—as much as a small can of tomato paste. Each tiny panda faces the daunting prospect of gaining nearly 900 times its own weight by the time it is 2 or 3 years old.

Why are the babies so tiny? Scientists say there is something special about how bear cubs develop before birth.

When an egg is fertilized in a female panda's body, it apparently floats free in the mother's uterus for a few months, instead of attaching to a wall of the uterus and quickly growing bigger, as

*Instead of galloping and roaring like an ordinary bear, a giant panda trots, and bleats like a sheep.*

most mammals do.

Scientists believe this happens in ordinary bears, as well as in pandas, to ensure that the number of bears born roughly matches the

amount of food available. If a female bear can't find enough food to eat when she's pregnant, the embryo may never become attached and start growing.

But if all goes well, the embryo will become securely fastened near the end of the bear's 4- to 6-month pregnancy. By then, it won't have much time to develop and put on weight before it pops out into the world.

But once out in the world, giant panda cubs grow amazingly fast. By the time it reaches its first birthday, a giant panda is a chubby 80 pounds.

# How did the zebra get its stripes?

A zebra is an almost mythical looking creature, but it is a member of the horse family, along with donkeys, asses, and true horses—the kind we see racing in the Kentucky Derby. Zebras live in Africa, and they stand about 4 feet tall at the shoulder, which is the way horses are measured: from the shoulder to the ground.

Zebras usually live in families, with a stallion, several mares, and some foals. These families often travel together in herds of up to 1,000 zebras. Sometimes, zebras join forces with antelopes, and roam around with them, searching for grasses to eat.

There are three kinds, or species, of zebra, and each has its own peculiar stripe pattern. Grevy's zebra has thin dark stripes and a white belly. The mountain zebra's stripes are thicker, with three very fat stripes crossing its haunches in back. Burchell's zebra has widely spaced stripes that begin underneath, in the middle of its belly, and sweep back over its haunches. Sometimes there are very thin "shadow stripes" in between the thicker ones.

---

*A zebra's stripes confuse predators, helping it escape.*

---

There once was a fourth type of zebra, called the quagga. (It got its name from its neighing cry.) Quaggas looked very different from the three types of zebras left today. A quagga had stripes only on its head, neck, and forequarters (front part); its back was solid brown. So many were hunted and killed that by the early 1900's quaggas had disappeared.

What good are a zebra's stripes? The stripes help confuse a zebra's predators—animals, such as lions, that would like to turn a zebra into dinner—making the zebra harder to catch.

Some animal's colors may match background colors. A green insect may spend most of its time on green leaves, for example. This helps it fade into its surroundings; a predator may not notice it's there.

But other animals, such

as some tree frogs and banded snakes, may have what is called "disruptive coloration." The zebra is one.

Think of an ordinary black horse. Its solid color makes it stand out like a silhouette against most backgrounds. You can easily see the curve of its back, the shape of its body. There's little doubt that it's a horse.

But a zebra is confusing. The black-and-white stripes disrupt, or break up, the smooth contours of the animal's body, concealing the zebra's true shape. When the zebra moves, the pattern may be even more confusing. So a threatening lion may not be so sure that this is dinner after all.

Where did the stripes come from? Scientists think the zebra evolved from a horselike animal with no stripes. They have different ideas about what the zebra's stripeless ancestor looked like, but many argue that it was mostly dark-colored, or black. (So, to answer an old question, a zebra is probably a black animal with white stripes, rather than the other way around.)

The way stripes might have evolved is this: By accidental variation, some of the dark horse foals were born with lighter-colored stripes. Since stripes were protective coloring, they were an advantage. And so striped animals often survived to have striped foals—another example of natural selection.

More and more striped animals appeared as the generations passed. Eventually, there were several distinct species of an animal we call the zebra.

# Why do some animals hibernate in winter?

In the spring, bears are waking up all across the north. They yawn, stretch, shake themselves. They wander around in the sun, perhaps a bit dazed. Soon, they get hungry. After all, many haven't had a bite to eat since the fall.

What's the point of hibernating? Well, a snow-bound winter is no fun for many animals. Food begins to disappear from the frozen ground. The days are short and cold; the nights are long and colder. Searching for the little remaining food can burn more calories than the animal gets back from the food—when and if any is found.

So some animals, like migrating birds, go south for the winter. Others tough it out. Many die. And some—

such as hummingbirds, arctic ground squirrels, and black bears—settle in for a long, chilly rest. By hibernating, an animal reduces its body's energy needs to a minimum.

*True hibernators can reduce their heart rates to as low as one beat per minute.*

If hibernation were simply a matter of going to sleep, then anyone could do it. Pitch your tent in the backyard some December night, close your eyes, and drift off. Next thing you know, it's April. You

get up, stretch, and wander into the house for breakfast.

Obviously this doesn't work. First, you couldn't stay asleep long enough. Second, you'd need water after several days. And third, you'd freeze.

But hibernation isn't really a kind of sleep. Instead, it is a special method of lowering the body's temperature and slowing the heart to conserve energy in times of scarcity and stress.

According to Ralph Nelson, M.D., a professor at the University of Illinois, there is a difference between what scientists call "true" hibernators, little animals such as ground squirrels, and animals like bears, which go into a more shallow form of hibernation each winter.

As it slips into "true" hibernation, the rapidly beat-

*Every few weeks or days, true hibernators wake up to eat, drink, urinate, and defecate.*

ing heart of a small animal, going strong at 150 to 300 beats a minute, may gradually slow to 7 beats a minute or fewer. (The hearts of some California ground squirrels have been clocked at a barely-there one beat each minute.) Body temperature slowly drops from its usual 100°F (close to ours) to the temperature of the air in the burrow the animal has built for itself—even to near freezing, 32°F.

Once it has entered hibernation, an animal is, for a time, dead to the world. If you stumble upon a true hibernator in its nest, Nelson said, "You can toss it in the air and catch it," and it won't twitch a whisker.

However, the little hibernators don't stay "asleep." Every few weeks, or even as often as every 4 days, small hibernators swim up from their hibernation like a patient coming out of anesthesia. They sip water, perhaps grab a bite to eat, urinate, and defecate. They may be awake for an entire day and night. Then they slide back into their barely-alive hibernating state. The little hibernators lose about 40 percent of their body weight during winter hibernation, and some don't make it to spring.

Bears, on the other hand, don't undergo such drastic changes in temperature and heart rate, and they remain aware of their surroundings. A better term than hibernation for the period when bears are inactive, Nelson said, is dormancy.

However, G. Edgar Folk, Jr., a professor of environmental physiology at the University of Iowa, thinks bears may be the best hibernators of all. Unlike the true hibernators, he notes, bears don't have to wake up every few days to drink or eat. Incredibly, some bears can stay dormant for 7 months, with no food, water, or trips to

*Hibernating bears look like they're asleep, but they're actually dangerously alert.*

the bathroom.

Take black bears, for example, which are warm-blooded animals, just like us. They say "good-bye, world" for 4 or more months each year. Sometimes they crawl into caves, or shoehorn themselves into hollow logs. Some bears paw together a nest, flop down on the ground, and lie in the open, collecting snow month after month.

How does a bear survive with no food, no water, and freezing temperatures for months? Somehow, a bear's body drastically changes its metabolism—the way cells use energy to keep the body running.

By a feat of overeating—sometimes bingeing for most of each day—during the summer, the black bear packs on the fat, sometimes 5 inches thick. On a real pig-out—or bear-out—one bear may consume 20,000 calories a day. (For you, that could mean eating 10 breakfasts, 10 lunches, and 10 dinners.)

But all that fat is the key to a bear's survival during hibernation. When a bear curls up for the winter, its body undergoes some changes. Normally, a bear's heart beats about 40 times a minutes as it sleeps. But as a bear drifts into hibernation, its heart slows to about eight beats a minute. And its body temperature drops by as much as 9°F—not as drastic a drop as in the true hibernators, but cause for medical panic if it happened to you.

The dormant bear requires far less energy than usual to stay alive. So instead of eating for energy, the bear's body slowly burns its extra fat.

When fat is burned completely, only carbon dioxide and water remain. During hibernation, a bear doesn't urinate, so it doesn't lose much water. So even without drinking, a bear can get the water it needs to sustain blood and body tissues simply by burning fat.

While bears can perform feats of metabolism that the true hibernators can't begin to match, their sleeping state isn't nearly as deep. A bear's body temperature doesn't fall to that of its surroundings, and the drop in a bear's heart rate isn't as extreme. What this adds up to: Don't try to toss a hibernating bear into the air, or you'll be in for a heart-stopping shock. A hibernating bear may *look*

*During the summer, bears pack on the fat, consuming as many as 20,000 calories a day.*

harmless, but it's actually alert and aware, eyes often open.

Bears are unfortunately nasty creatures, Folk said, and when they are really hungry, they will eat each other. So among other dangers, a dormant bear must keep an

eye open and an ear cocked for any ravenous members of its own species that might be wandering about. If its temperature were to drop to that of its surroundings, and a bear slipped into deep, lost-to-the-world hibernation, it could leave itself exposed to great peril. Therefore, Folk said, evolution has devised a different kind of dormancy for bears—in some ways, more remarkable than "true" hibernation.

Scientists studying hibernating animals hope to use what they've learned to help humans. For example, figuring out what chemicals make animals lower their inner thermostat settings may one day help doctors cool the body for special kinds of surgery.

# Why does fruit get sweeter as it ripens?

What does fruit sweetening as it ripens have to do with hungry bears and birds? Everything. When a fruit is ripe, it sends out urgent messages to animals everywhere. "Hey, look at me! Over here! Yeah, you!" Fruit not only sweetens as it ripens, but it usually changes color, too—the better to attract passing animals.

Why is fruit so interested in animals, and vice versa? First it helps to understand just what a fruit is, anyhow.

Surprise—fruits are a plant's ovaries, like the ovaries in a woman's body. (Ovaries are the organs where egg cells are made.) But although a woman has only two ovaries, a plant may be studded with hundreds of them. Think of an apple tree in the fall, with red globes hanging on every branch.

## *Life on Earth has one basic task: to reproduce itself.*

How it works: Ovaries in flowers, such as apple blossoms, contain ovules, the plant's egg cells. After pollen fertilizes the egg cells, they grow into seeds. Meanwhile, the ovary surounding them develops into a fruit. In the end, what you have is an apple, with little brown seeds in its center, each containing the information required to grow a new plant.

All life on Earth—plants and animals—has one basic task: to reproduce itself. All want to ensure that both their species and their own particular genes—carrying the qualities that make them unique as individuals—survive, and spread far and wide.

But if you are a blackberry bush stuck in the middle of nowhere, how do you get your seeds down the road, let alone to the next meadow?

The answer: You take advantage of the fact that animals walk and fly by, animals that can easily make it to the next meadow and beyond. And you package your seeds in an irresistible way, so they'll gladly transport a few.

Timing is everything: It's pointless to send underdeveloped seeds off into the world.

Why did the Strawberry Cross the Road? ...

... chased by a chicken? ... Bullied by a bear? ... to plant strawberry fields ... forever.?

So plants make use of animals' senses—sight, smell, taste—to get them to pluck fruit only when its seeds are ripe and ready to roll.

Take the strawberry, for example. Until the seeds that speckle the sides of the berry are fully grown, strawberries are green, fading inconspicuously into the leaves of the strawberry plant. A passing bear might not notice the green berries. If it does try one, it will find the strawberry rock-hard and bitter. Unless the bear is *really* hungry, the rest of the strawberries will probably stay put.

But when the seeds are ready, everything changes. The berry turns bright red against its green background—a beacon for passing animals. And the strawberry hasn't just changed color. It has also become softer, and (most importantly) sweeter. A fruit appeals to a bear, and to us, because it tastes so good.

How does the change happen? An enzyme attacks and weakens the fruit's fiber, making it softer and juicier. Some fruits manufacture enzymes that change starch or glucose into fructose and

sucrose (table sugar). Others are flooded with sugar from the parent plant.

Understandably, animals gobble up ripe fruit. Birds fly off and regurgitate the seeds; other animals pass the seeds though their bowels. One way or another, some seeds land on fertile soil, sprout, and grow new plants.

Fruit sweetening as it ripens is a great example of the coevolution of plants and animals on Earth. Plants evolved a way of reproducing themselves that relies on the existence of a hungry animal—with a sweet tooth.

# How do fireflies glow?

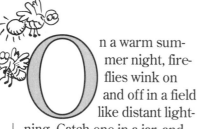

**O**n a warm summer night, fireflies wink on and off in a field like distant lightning. Catch one in a jar, and you can see the firefly's lantern signal in a ghostly, green-yellow light. The light looks strangely cold, and it is: Firefly light, unlike sunlight, produces almost no heat.

Fireflies—surprise—are beetles, and there are more than 2,000 firefly species on Earth. Grown-up fireflies are brown or black and are about a half-inch long.

Baby fireflies hatch out of eggs hidden in the soil. Like many other newborn insects, they are called *larvae*. The larvae don't look much like adult fireflies. Like adults, they are brown; unlike adults, they're quite flat.

Some species of firefly larvae glow all the time.

There is an old song about glowing little glowworms that, "glimmer, glimmer." Well, "glowworm" is another name for a baby firefly.

---

### *Scientists think fireflies flash to attract mates.*

---

Firefly light is made in the insect's abdomen, or lower belly, which contains cells called photocytes. Two chemicals in the photocytes, luciferin and luciferase, react with each other, releasing energy. ("Lucifer" in Latin means "light-bearing.") The energy excites the atoms in luciferin, which give off photons of light.

Behind the photocytes, another layer of cells, filled with a white chemical, reflects the light out at us, like the reflector on the back of a bike.

Other animals (and plants) give off cold light, too. On a dark night in the woods you may see a patch of toadstools, scattered like glowing lampshades across the ground. In the ocean, squids squirt out glowing clouds of chemicals to cloak themselves from prey. And jellyfish flash.

But *why* do fireflies light up? Scientists think the insects blink their lights to attract mates. Each kind of firefly blinks with its own rhythm, so female and male fireflies can make sure they're hooking up with a member of their own species.

Some species of firefly can coordinate their blinking, so a large gathering of fireflies lights up and darkens at

## Give a Firefly a Job...

in a closet...          in a refrigerator...          or hire a whole family for a makeup mirror!

the same instant. In Thailand, for example, fireflies gather in trees, blinking randomly. Soon, however, a pair of fireflies begin to flash together. The pattern spreads throughout the tree: Larger and larger groups send out bursts of light at the same time.

After about 30 minutes, the entire tree is winking on and off, as all the fireflies blink in unison, once each second. It is as if the tree

**FAST FACT**

Some Asian and South American fireflies are so bright that people have kept them in cages to light their rooms.

were garlanded with twinkle lights. Scientists can't explain how the fireflies coordinate their flashing—or why.

Watching fireflies light up, some scientists wondered

if there might be other uses for the chemicals that make them shine.

Inside cells are genes, which tell the cell what to do. Through a complicated series of steps, the scientists managed to isolate the gene that tells a cell to make luciferase, and they inserted it into the cells of tobacco leaves. What they ended up with was a tobacco plant that glowed in the dark.

# How do bees make honey?

The honey we buy in jars and plastic bears at the store is made by honeybees—although bumblebees also make honey. Honeybees build wax honeycombs in handy places like hollow trees. They also inhabit wooden hives that beekeepers build for bees to live in. The beekeepers then harvest the honey stored in the honeycombs.

Each hive is home to between 20,000 and 60,000 bees. Who's who in a hive? One queen, whose only job is to lay eggs, a few drones (male bees), and tens of thousands of workers—all female.

Very young worker bees, just days old, clean the hive and feed the larvae (just-hatched bees). Ten-day-old worker bees take in food collected by older bees, called field bees.

Some field bees perform the more specialized job of scout. Scouts fly out, searching for food (flower pollen and nectar). When they find good flowers, they fly back to the hive. There they do a complicated dance that tells the field bees the direction and distance of the flowers.

Honey is made from a sweet liquid in flowers called nectar. Nectar is 80 percent water, with complex sugars mixed in. (Nectar is the clear liquid that drops from the end of a honeysuckle blossom when you pull it out of its stem.) In North America, honeybees get nectar from flowers such as clover, dandelions, fruit tree blossoms, and berry bushes.

Bees slurp up nectar through their very long tube-like tongues. Bees have a regular stomach and a honey stomach. The honey stomach is used like a backpack to lug nectar from flowers back to the hive. A bee must visit between 100 and 1,500 flowers to fill her honey stomach, drop by drop, with nectar.

The honey stomach holds only about 70 milligrams of nectar. But that nearly equals the weight of the bee. By the time she's ready to fly back to the hive, the bee is loaded down with sweet liquid.

When she gets back to the hive, the bee passes the nectar off to a house-bound worker bee or two, who slurp the nectar from her mouth.

Sometimes the bees feed the nectar to the baby and adult bees, but usually it is made into honey first.

How? First, the house bees spend about half an hour "chewing" it like gum. Enzymes slowly break down the complex sugars in the nectar into simple sugars. (This makes the nectar more digestible, and helps protect it from bacteria when it is stored later on.) Then, the bees spread the nectar, drop by drop, through the honeycombs.

Water in the nectar slowly evaporates, thickening the syrup. The bees make the nectar dry even faster by fanning it with their wings. When the syrup in a cell is the right consistency— just

### FAST FACT

**The eggs that the queen bee lays meet different fates. When unfertilized eggs hatch, their larvae grow into drones (male bees). When fertilized eggs hatch, the larvae fed lightly develop into female workers. A larva fed heavily, and given a little royal jelly (a nutrient that comes from honeybee glands) will develop into a queen.**

gooey enough—it's officially honey, and the bees put a cap of wax on the cell. (The white wax comes in flakes from a bee's wax gland.)

Then the honey is stored until it is eaten. In a year, a colony of bees consumes between 120 and 200 pounds of honey.

Bees make honey only for themselves, of course. But other animals, from ants to bears to pigs, all like to sneak a taste of honey at the nearest beehive. Humans have a sweet tooth for honey, too, dribbling it on biscuits and in hot tea. And even wax is filched from the hive: Beeswax makes the best candles.

# How come some birds can't fly?

A bird that can't fly seems as strange as the idea of a fish that can't swim. Why have wings if you can't use them to soar into the air?

But there are flightless birds all over the world: ostriches running through the deserts of Africa, penguins on the frozen coast of Antarctica, kiwis in New Zealand.

However, compared to the number of flying birds, there are very few of the flightless kind. That's because flying is a great way to survive in a tough world.

If a menacing lion sneaks up on a gazelle, the best the gazelle can do is try to run away. But if a cat creeps up on a sparrow, the sparrow can take off vertically into the air, rising out of reach.

Being able to fly has other advantages, too. You can travel long distances to find food, which gives you an edge over animals who must stay close to home. And you can raise your children in high places, safely out of reach of most other animals.

## *Flying is a great way to survive in a tough world.*

Flying has made birds nature's second-biggest success story. There are some 8,500 species of birds, compared to about 4,000 species of mammals (of which we are one). Insects are the most successful of all—there are nearly a million kinds—but most of them can fly, too.

If flight is such a powerful tool for survival, how come some birds can't do it? Scientists think that some bird species once had the ability to fly but lost it somewhere along the way.

The oldest fossil of a bird found has been dated at 150 million years old. Scientists named the bird *Archaeopteryx*. It was probably pretty scary looking, since it had claws—on its *wings*—and very sharp teeth. From studying its bones, scientists have decided it may only have been able to glide.

*Archaeopteryx*, and the more familiar-looking birds that came later, may have evolved from dinosaurs. In fact, scientists think that very small dinosaurs may have had feathers to keep them warm. Some of these creatures may have been born with peculiar forelimbs, which they could flap to fly short distances. Eventually, quite by chance, some were born with forelimbs more like wings—and an enormously successful advantage.

Birds soon spread across the planet. Some ended up on islands, such as Madagascar or New Zealand. It was mainly on islands that flightless birds came into being.

What happened was this: Some species of birds found

## Some species of birds found island living so easy that they rarely flew.

island living so easy that they rarely flew. There were no menacing predators, and there was plenty of food. Birds born with small or useless wings could survive just

as well as those who could fly. Eventually, species developed, such as the ostrich, with small, useless wings and no real flight muscles.

Some flightless birds, like the ostrich, prospered. Others, such as the dodo, which once lived on islands in the Indian Ocean, didn't last. Human beings killed them for their meat, and pigs made off with their eggs.

Penguins, by the way, are a special case. Their wings evolved for use underwater as flippers, and they are very good at this kind of "flying."

# Why do penguins have fur instead of feathers?

Penguins may look like they have fur. But actually, full-grown penguin bodies are covered with feathers, just like those of other birds. There's a difference, however, in how the feathers grow.

On most birds, feathers grow in narrow strips. On penguins, feathers grow all over the body uniformly—perhaps giving the appearance of fur. And baby penguins are covered with a coat of down (very fine, soft feathers); later, it is replaced by regular feathers.

Although there are at least 17 separate species of penguin, the feathers, or plumage, is similar in each type. Black or dark blue feathers cover penguins' backs. White feathers protect their chests and stomachs.

But penguin faces can be strikingly different. The rock hopper penguin, for example, has punky spiked black feathers on its head, tufted yellow "eyebrows," and bright red eyes.

*A penguin's black and white markings hide it from predators when it swims in the sea.*

Scientists think the basic colors of penguins—the tuxedo look—evolved because it protected them so well from predators, such as seals, in the water.

Penguins glide through the sea on their stomachs. Looking up from below them, a menacing animal would be hard-pressed to pick out a white penguin breast from the glare of sunlight. And looking down from above into the depths, it would be equally hard to see a dark back.

Penguins have been around for at least 55 million years. They seem to have evolved from flying birds. They still have the keel bone, a specially-shaped breastbone anchoring the strong muscles used for flying. And indeed, penguins do fly—underwater.

Penguins flap their wings, pushing against water like other birds push against air. Since air is thin, ordinary birds tend to have wide, thin wings. But water is dense and heavy. So penguins have

## Evolution of the "Tuxedo Look"

For 55 million years penguins have been waiters...

the white plumage gives them a clean appearance from the front...

and in dimly lit restaurants the black provides camouflage from unnecessary requests.

short, hardened wings, shaped like rowboat paddles.

Because penguins spend much of their time in cold water, their bodies are designed to retain as much heat as possible. Penguin feathers have soft down near their roots, which helps trap a layer of air next to the skin.

The ends of penguin feathers are hard, and waterproof. So water rolls off a penguin as if it were wearing an expensive trench coat. Under the feathers is a layer of fat—

sometimes quite thick—good insulation, as long-distance swimmers know.

Like other birds, penguins molt—they lose their feathers on a regular basis. Instead of losing a few feathers at a time, all year round (like most other birds), penguins get rid of all the old feathers at one fell swoop.

A molt takes about 3 weeks. Penguins wait on the land—or on the ice—while their feathers are refurbished. Since they can't go

**FAST FACT**

**Penguins live in large flocks in the Southern Hemisphere, mainly in Antarctica. They eat fish, which they catch with their sharp, pointed beaks.**

into the water for a meal (remember, feathers help trap the air that keeps them warm), penguins may lose half their body weight during the molt.

# How can parrots imitate know what they are

It's thrilling when a pet parrot says her first word—especially if it's your name. Some parrots have even learned prayers or entire poems. But when a parrot talks, you wonder, does it have any idea what it is saying? Is a parrot just a mindless mimic? Or are parrots smarter than we think?

According to researcher Irene Pepperberg, parrots may be capable of much more than mimicry. Unlike many animals, parrots (and related birds, such as parakeets) have vocal tracts that make human speech easy to imitate. Also, Pepperberg said, parrots learn to communicate with others in their flock by imitating adult birds. That helps to explain the behavior of pet parrots, who get rewards for likewise imitating their owners.

*Parrots in the wild learn to communicate with others in the flock by mimicking adult birds.*

But talking is different than understanding. So Pepperberg set up an experiment at Northwestern University to find out how much parrots can really learn. In 1977, she bought Alex, an African gray parrot, at a pet shop. (African grays are the best talkers.) Alex seemed like a rather ordinary, friendly parrot at first. But soon, he showed he was one smart bird.

Alex sits on his perch, and Pepperberg shows him a key on a tray. "Key!" Alex says—and Pepperberg hands it to him. Unlike a pet bird, which may get rewarded with a cracker for saying almost anything, Alex only gets what he correctly names.

In the beginning, Pepperberg said, no one believed a parrot could label objects. But now, Alex can identify more than 100 things, from paper to corn to corks.

Once he was taught the individual names for things, the next step was combining

# words? Do they really saying?

two ideas—not just "key," but "blue key." Alex quickly learned the names for colors. When shown a red key and a green key, he is asked, "What's the same or different?" "Color!" he shouts.

Alex can also answer "shape" or "material" when asked what is different. He has a little trouble with the word "material," Pepperberg said; he pronounces it "matter."

After years of learning, Alex has gotten a little bored. He'll identify a key, take it in his beak, and throw it on the floor. After a session of naming the same old stuff, Alex sometimes asks for something different. After too many keys, Alex may say "I want cork!" He gets it.

The curious bird may also demand, "You tell me what's that!" when shown a

Polly want her cage cleaned, a color TV and you can keep the crackers.

tray of brand-new objects. If asked about the new objects' colors, Alex tends to outdo his usual performance—an attempt, Pepperberg thinks, to acquire the exciting new stuff. In fact, to keep Alex happily naming, she and her coworkers made an expedition to a toy store, where they picked up a whole assortment of little figures and animals.

Still, Alex has his difficult days, sometimes shouting "No!" like a frustrated 2-year-old. And when he really wants to show who's boss, he'll announce, "I'm gonna go

## *Alex the parrot can identify more than 100 things.*

away," walking off from the poor student trying to test him.

Some say Pepperberg's experiment doesn't prove that a parrot can use language. After all, they say, Alex doesn't go around talking about what he's just seen

unless he gets a reward.

Pepperberg responds that although Alex doesn't use language in general, he does use words to express ideas. That must mean, she said, that there is some pretty complex thinking going on in the parrot's brain.

And there is this story: Alex knew the words for banana, cherry, and grape. One day, he saw an apple. "I want banary!" he said. By combining "banana" and "cherry," Alex may have coined a new word for the strange red fruit.

# Why are dinosaurs extinct?

Dinosaurs roamed all over our planet for about 130 million years—100 times as long as we've been around. And then they were gone. About 65 million years ago, dinosaurs everywhere disappeared.

But 65 million years ago was an especially hard time for other life on Earth, too. Flying reptiles also vanished. In the oceans, fishlike reptiles died, as did many kinds of clams and starfish. Even many of the tiny organisms called plankton began dying.

What happened? No one knows for sure, but there have been many theories. Most theories blame changes in our planet's climate, which could have harmed many plants and animals besides the dinosaurs.

One of the most popular theories says that dinosaurs and other animals were wiped out in one terrible catastrophe. A massive asteroid slammed into Earth 65 million years ago, some say, exploding on impact.

*In addition to dinosaurs, flying reptiles and a number of ocean dwellers also disappeared 65 million years ago.*

Studying clay in layers of rock dated as 65 million years old, scientists discovered iridium. Iridium is a metal found only rarely on Earth, since most sunk toward the Earth's core when our planet formed, billions of years ago. Most iridium comes from space, left on Earth when meteorites or asteroids drop out of the sky. Scientists found iridium in ancient clay samples from all over the world. Their conclusion: The iridium fell from a cloud of dust that an impacting asteroid sent up into Earth's atmosphere.

Here's what might have happened: The asteroid, 6 or more miles across, hurtled in from space at more than 60,000 miles an hour. Smashing into the ground, it dug a crater more than 100 miles

Where did they go?

DANGER

They disappeared during a hot air balloon race...

... Sank in the Bermuda triangle...

... they're hiding.

wide. Tons of crushed rock and soil (asteroid and earth, mixed) exploded into the sky.

The dust cloud is thought to have spread quickly around the planet, carried by winds whipped up in the explosion and fireball. Dust blotted out the Sun; day became night. The dark lasted for months. Temperatures dropped worldwide from an average of 66° F to about

14° F. Confined to darkness and freezing cold, many plants, on land and in the seas, died.

The animals that depended on the plant foods soon began dying, too. In a disastrous chain reaction, the animals that preyed on those animals began dying as well. Eventually, most of the dust fell to earth, leaving iridium as its signature.

But many scientists are

skeptical of the "death from space" theory. Why did so many other animals, they wonder, survive? Birds, crocodiles, turtles, snakes, and most mammals lived. Insects, shellfish, and ocean fish, as well as many plants, somehow squeaked through, too.

Some doubt the theory because they believe the dinosaurs disappeared slowly, over millions of years, rather than in a single cataclysm.

And some argue that the iridium in old clay may have come from volcanoes, plumbing the depths of the earth. Exploding volcanoes, they argue, could have filled the sky with ash on and off for centuries, changing the climate and causing extinctions.

One advantage of the asteroid theory is that it can be tested. Scientists have been searching for the telltale crater. Looking at satellite pictures of Mexico, they found a series of lakes arranged in a peculiar half-circle. The lakes, on the Yucatan Peninsula, may outline part of the circular rim of an enormous crater, buried under 3,600 feet of rock. In 1992, scientists obtained rocks from deep inside the circle, collected in the 1950's when a Mexican national oil company drilled there. Dating the rocks, scientists

*The asteroid that triggered the disaster that wiped out the dinosaurs may have smashed into Mexico's Yucatan Peninsula.*

found they were indeed 65 million years old.

Meanwhile, other scientists have been studying fossils of leaves in 65-million-year-old clay. They discovered that the leaves, which came from Wyoming, died suddenly by freezing. The

stage of the leaves' development showed that the deep freeze must have struck in June.

The fossil leaves add another piece of evidence that temperatures plunged as the debris from the impact darkened the sky. However, scientists still disagree over whether this event—if it actually happened—was what finally killed off the dinosaurs.

Some think that massive eruptions of volcanoes over thousands of years, which likewise would have sent gases and debris into the sky, did the deed. But others point out that it may not be necessary to choose between the two scenarios. Exploding volcanoes and a crashing asteroid may both have played their deadly parts. We may never know exactly what happened 65 million years ago.

# If the first land animals mammals come to be?

**M**ammals, of which we humans are one kind, were latecomers to the Earth. They appeared about 216 million years ago, almost 100 million years after the first reptiles showed up. So reptiles roamed the Earth with no competition for nearly a million centuries. Dinosaurs were the biggest reptiles around when mammals began popping up.

Both reptiles and mammals are *vertebrates*—they have backbones. Reptiles are usually cold-blooded—the temperature of their blood changes with the temperature of the air. Mammals are warm-blooded—their blood stays a steady temperature.

(Ours hovers around 98.6° F.) However, dinosaurs may have been warm-blooded—no one's really sure.

What makes mammals different? A clue is in the word "mammal," which comes from the Latin word *mamma*, meaning breast. Mammals have breasts, or mammary glands, which make milk for their babies. Reptiles don't.

There are other differences, too. Mammals are usually completely or partly covered with hair. (Think of dogs, cats, mice, gorillas—all mammals—versus alligators, chameleons, and rattlesnakes—all reptiles.)

Mammals usually give birth to live young—they don't lay eggs. However, there is one exception. The

platypus, which lives along streams in Tasmania and Australia, has webbed feet, fur, and lays eggs—and is considered a mammal.

The platypus is a good example of how mammals probably evolved. It has fur, but it lays eggs—combining a mammal feature with a feature of a reptile. Scientists think that before there were "true" mammals, there were animals that, like the platypus, seemed "half-baked"— not really reptiles, but not quite mammals, either.

The true mammals that first appeared 216 million years ago looked like tiny shrews, scientists think. They ate insects and plants, and probably spent most of their time in trees.

Fur and other signature

# were reptiles, how did

mammal features evolved over millions of years. Evolution works by means of accidental variations and natural selection. Animals born with some hair may grow up and have babies with hair. Over many generations, that fur may prove to be an advantage, retaining body heat and helping warm-blooded animals maintain a constant temperature in cold climates. Animals with fur could look

### FAST FACT

Animals that fell into the not-quite-reptile, not-quite-mammal category lasted for millions of years. Among these were the *therapsids*, which are classified as reptiles but had teeth like a dog's. They may have had fur, were likely warm-blooded, and, like the platypus, probably laid eggs.

for food in cold places as well as warm places, giving them an edge over animals who could survive only where it was warm.

Eventually, animals evolved that had all the regulation mammal equipment. After the dinosaurs died out, mammals spread far and wide. Over millions of years, they differentiated into many families, from cats to whales to people.

# If human beings evolved apes in jungles or zoos

Although we are closely related to modern apes, they didn't turn into us. It's similar to your relationship to a distant cousin. You and your cousin descended from two of the same great grandparents. We and the apes descended from a common relative, too.

We don't have to look into the distant past to see evidence for evolution; evolution is a process going on all around us. Bacteria that were once easily killed by penicillin evolve new forms that are resistant to the antibiotic. The color of moths evolve as the color of their background trees change (see page 222). Animal species change over time, becoming better-suited to their local environments.

And new animal species appear, live for thousands or millions of years, and then vanish.

*Chimpanzees are our closest relatives: We share 98.4 percent of our genes with them.*

Evolution needs time and happy accidents to work its changes. Features that may help a species survive better—such as unusual but more efficient teeth, or a larg-

er brain—can show up in newborn animals accidentally, as random variations. If new features are truly helpful to survival, the fortunate animals that have them may live longer and survive where some others won't. They will live to have offspring, and the changes will be passed along, over generations. If the features are great aids to survival, the animals with them may gradually crowd out the animals without them. Over many years, a whole species will look different.

Human beings are primates, as are more than 100 other species, including monkeys, apes, and gorillas. We primates are more alike than different. We have hands with five fingers and feet with five toes. We have teeth that are

# from apes, why don't turn into humans?

good for eating a wide variety of foods—from tearing off a chunk of meat to grinding up a succulent plant. We give birth to one or a few children at a time. And our children take a long time to grow up.

Our closest primate relatives are the "great apes,"—gorillas, orangutans, and chimpanzees. We are related not because we evolved from them, but because we share a common ancestor with them.

The first mammals, the ancestors of dogs and whales, chimpanzees and humans, and all of the other creatures that feed their young milk, evolved about 216 million years ago. They were tiny, beady-eyed, snouted creatures less than 3 inches long. Scientists think they lived in nests and burrows and ate insects. They weren't much to look at, but after the dinosaurs disappeared, about 65 million years ago, mammals came into their own.

Some 70 million years ago, the first primates (*prosimians*) had appeared.

Small and ratlike, they scampered through the treetops in forests that covered much of the solid ground on our planet. By 30 million years ago, they had been joined by monkeys and small apes, who eventually crowded out the prosimians. Later, apes and monkeys evolved in separate directions, and bigger-brained apes evolved—orangutans, gorillas, and chimpanzees.

Human beings and chimpanzees, our closest animal relative, share a recent common ancestor, an animal that lived millions of years ago and probably looked a bit like a chimpanzee. But chimpanzees and humans also went their separate ways. One evolutionary line led, step-by-step, to us. Another led, step-by-step, to the modern chimpanzee. If you could see a speeded-up movie of evolution, you would see one line that looked more and more like chimpanzees as time went on, and another line that looked more and

more human as time passed.

Not only are chimpanzees our closest relatives, but we are *their* closest relations as well. We share 98.4 percent of our genes with them. We can see some of the similarities ourselves: Chimpanzees are sociable animals who use simple tools (such as twigs to dig out tasty ants), and share food with each other.

## Evolution is a process going on all the time, all around us.

The key to our own human evolution was the grasslands, or savannahs. Some groups of our primitive, apelike ancestors left the forest and began to try making their living on the grasslands.

During the wet season, the grass is green and thick, trees are leafy, and bushes burst forth. But when the rains stop, the trees lose their leaves, and the grasses dry into hay.

Animals that live on the savannah must learn to cope with these changes. Sometimes, there is plenty to eat. Other times, favorite foods nearly disappear. So being able to reach into bushes and comb the ground for nuts and berries can mean the difference between death and survival.

Over time, there were important changes, until a new creature could be glimpsed roaming the savannah. It looked much like an ape, but it walked on two legs, which left its hands free for gathering food scattered on the savannah. Its brain was larger. It wasn't human, but it wasn't quite an ape, either.

These first hominids—humanlike animals—appeared about 9 million years ago. Fossils show what

*All mammals share a common ancestor that evolved about 216 million years ago.*

they looked like. In Ethiopia, scientists found a nearly complete skeleton of a female, which they nicknamed "Lucy." Less than 4 feet tall,

Lucy lived and died millions of years ago. She walked upright, but was probably quite hairy and apelike.

Lucy and her kind eventually died out. Scientists think that they lost the competition for food to later hominids even better adapted to grassland life. These hominids had even bigger brains and made specialized stone tools. They were able to hunt large game as well as gather fruits and vegetables.

Modern humans, known as *homo sapiens*, first appeared about 40,000 years ago. We walk upright, use our hands to make complex tools, and

have devised language to communicate through symbols. We live in complicated social groups. And we have developed a shared culture of ideas and ways of acting that we teach to our children.

Today, we are not confined to the grasslands. We live everywhere on Earth, even in places where we could not "naturally" survive, such as the far North. The apelike creatures that were our ancestors are long gone. We, and the modern great apes, are separate but related animals. Together, we share the Earth.

# Why We Are How We Are

Although we humans come in all colors, shapes, and sizes, we are all members of one species—homo sapiens. Our behavior reflects the ways we are "programmed" to act by evolution, such as looking for a mate, or feeding a hungry stomach, or escaping danger.

But as humans evolved, our brains expanded all out of proportion to our size. (Another primate of the same weight would have a brain only one-sixth as big as ours.) Because we are intelligent, we can also think for ourselves, make choices, and take risks. We can write, compose music, draw, and paint to break down our isolation from each other, to express what it means to be alive. We can build boats and planes to explore every hidden corner of our planet. We can even construct ships to explore our solar system, and vessels that one day, perhaps, will take us to the stars.

# Why does skin come in different colors?

Although we often say people are "black" or "white," those words don't begin to describe the amazing variety of skin tones among human beings. People's skin color depends mainly on where their ancestors lived on the planet. Scientists have tentative theories of how people in different parts of the world developed different skin colors. But no one knows for sure.

Skin color depends on a chemical called melanin. The more melanin in our skin, the darker we appear. When a light-skinned person sits in the sun, his skin produces more melanin. In other words, he gets a tan. (Albinos, whose skin has no melanin, have pinkish skin and eyes. This color comes from blood vessels showing through colorless skin and eyes. Albinos also have white hair, even as children.)

Making more melanin is the skin's way of defending itself against ultraviolet (UV) radiation from the Sun, which can cause skin cancer. (For more on skin cancer, see page 287.) Like sunscreen, melanin absorbs UV radiation, and helps to protect the skin against further damage. The more melanin skin has—the more color—the better its protection from UV rays.

*The extra melanin in dark skin protects against ultraviolet radiation.*

Knowing what melanin does for the skin has given scientists hints at how human skin color might have evolved and changed over millions of years.

Our apelike ancestors were covered with a thin coat of hair, which protected their

Melanin is to the sun like...

A. A glass is to water...

B. A fish is to water...

C. An umbrella is to water.

Answer: C

skin from the intense African sun. As humans evolved over hundreds of thousands of years, however, babies were born with less of this body hair. Why? No one knows. But gradually, our ancestors' light, blotchy skin was exposed to harsh sunlight.

Because dark skin shields better from radiation, humans that happened to have been born with darker skin may have had a survival advantage over their pale-skinned friends. So over time,

as the deeper skin color was passed down to new generations, the skin of humans in Africa grew darker.

As humans branched out and spread further north, however, they found a much colder climate. In Europe, for example, the sunlight was weaker, especially in winter.

This climate led to its own set of survival dangers: Too much UV light is bad for us, but a little is actually necessary. UV light helps our bodies make vitamin D, a vita-

min absolutely necessary for the body to build up tough, straight bones.

The weaker sunlight reaching Europe contained much less UV light than that of Africa. Health problems may have arisen among the first northern humans, whose dark coloring effectively blocked out much of what little UV fell on their skin. Some children may have developed rickets, in which bones become soft or crooked and are easily broken.

So in Europe, humans born with lighter skin had the survival advantage. And once again, over generations, lighter skin tones evolved. In the weak winter sun, such skin remains pale, allowing what little UV light there is to pass through. But in the more intense summer sun, pale skin tans, providing some protection against too much UV light.

As humans spread across the planet, their skin tones

*The earliest humans probably had light, blotchy skin, like the skin of a chimpanzee under its hair.*

tended to reflect the climates they settled in—lightest skin in the very weak sun of Scandinavia, golden-to-medium brown skin in sunnier climates, darkest skin among such groups as Africans and Australian Aborigines. In recent centuries, however, people have moved freely and frequently from place to place, and people of every skin tone mix and mingle in every climate.

# What makes our ears ring ?

Our ears are supposed to pick up sounds from outside, not make them. But sometimes, even in a deathly quiet room, we hear noise—noise that seems to come from inside our heads.

Sometimes it sounds like a radio mistakenly tuned between stations—a high-pitched whine. Other times, it is a steady screech, or a buzzing. One young woman said it was like "a platoon of soldiers marching through my head."

All these describe *tinnitus*—what we call "ringing" in the ears. Often, the ringing starts after you hear an explosively loud noise—such as someone clapping their hands near your ear, or the boom of a fireworks display. Your ears may be ringing

when you walk out of the stadium after a rock concert or after an hour of listening to your headphones with the volume up loud. This kind of ringing may disappear after a night's sleep. But loud noise, especially repeated over time, can permanently damage the ears, causing you to lose some of your hearing.

What makes the sounds of silence? If you could see

into your own ear, you would notice a membrane, called the *eardrum*, stretched across the tunnel leading inside. Vibrations from the air strike the eardrum, making it vibrate, too.

Behind the eardrum is a bony chamber studded with three tiny, movable bones, called the hammer, the anvil, and the stirrup, after their shapes. These bones pick up vibrations from the eardrum and begin quivering.

Deeper in the ear is a fluid-filled channel a little over an inch long, called the *cochlea*. Vibrations from the moving bones make waves in the fluid, like waves in the ocean. Like seaweed underwater, thousands of hair cells undulate in the sloshing fluid.

These hair cells are crucial to our hearing. Somehow, the ripples that pass through the hair cells trigger electrical impulses, which travel along the auditory nerve—the hearing nerve—to the brain. The brain translates these electrical signals into sound—music and voices, the banging of hammers, the chirping of birds.

Hair cells can get hurt by loud noises, or by a knock on the head. They can bruise, get tangled up, or loosen and slip from their roots, impairing or destroying their ability to send electrical impulses through the hearing nerve.

But some hair cells will be hurt in such a way that

*Damaged hair cells in the ear can send signals that the brain interprets as high-pitched ringing.*

they continuously send bursts of electricity to the hearing nerve—even when they no longer respond well to out-

side noises. In effect, these hair cells are permanently turned on. When the brain receives their signals, it interprets them as sound. And so we hear a "ringing," even in a silent room.

Loud noises and head injuries aren't the only culprits. In the common ear disease otosclerosis, an overgrowth of spongy bone in the inner ear prevents the stirrup from vibrating properly, sharply diminishing hearing while increasing "ringing." Colds and the flu can bring on swelling in the ear, causing

hair cells to suffer. High blood pressure can shrink blood vessels, and cholesterol can clog them, letting less nourishing blood through to starved hair cells.

Aspirin often causes tinnitus for a day or so after it's taken. Stimulants like caffeine and nicotine can also prod hair cells into pointless action. And if you ingest large quantities of quinine, an

*Loud noise, aspirin, caffeine, and quinine can all cause tinnitus.*

ingredient in tonic water, it can also cause tinnitus, damaging the ear as it actually accumulates inside.

In fact, so many things cause tinnitus that at least half of us hear strange sounds in our ears at one time or another. Try avoiding the ones that seem to trigger it in you. And, especially, protect your ears—and hearing—from loud noise.

# How come we can hear in a seashell, even after

When you hold a large seashell to your ear, you can hear a distant roaring sound. It is as if the great rumble and crash of ocean waves is somehow trapped within the shell. So when you bring a seashell home from the beach, it's like keeping a memory of the sea alive.

As lovely as this idea is, the sound we hear coming from the inside of a shell is not actually the roar of the sea, captured forever. Instead, the sound is the echo and re-echo of all the noises outside the shell.

Echoes are sound waves that bounce back at us from a smooth, hard surface. When you shout into a cave, for example, you often hear your own voice, a split second later, reflecting off the cave walls and back to your ears.

Think of a sound wave like a wave passing through a field of wheat on a breezy day. Molecules of air get squashed together and spread apart; a wave passing through air is just the rhythmic compression and expansion of bunches of air molecules—a kind of vibration.

But other materials carry sound waves, too. Try shouting on one side of a closed wooden door. First, your vocal cords will vibrate, making the air that comes out of your mouth vibrate. That makes the air in front of you vibrate, which makes the wood of the door vibrate. The vibrating wood makes the air on the other side of the door vibrate, and so on, into the ear of your father, who is standing in the next room. "Don't shout!" he commands.

But when you shout into a cave, the walls don't absorb and carry the wave as the door did. They often richochet it right back at you, like a mirror reflects light. But instead of seeing yourself, as in a mirror, you hear yourself. An echo chamber is a kind of mirror for the ears.

Some European valleys, surrounded by mountains, are famous for their echoes. One note from a bugle may bounce back and forth 100 times before it finally dies away.

Which brings us back to seashells. The best shells for hearing the ocean are those with many inner chambers.

# the sound of the ocean we bring it home?

These chambers are like a series of rooms in an empty house. And because the walls of the shell are so smooth, noises from near the shell, even small ones, echo and re-echo in the chambers. All the echoes from all the noises—people talking, doors slam-

*Sounds echo and re-echo inside a large seashell.*

ming, music playing—blend together into a roar. Adding to the echoes may be your own heartbeat, which the shell picks up and reflects when you hold it against your ear. The wonderful sound effect produced by all these echoes is the roar of the sea.

# How do fingernails grow?

O ur fingernails (and toenails) are made of a protein called *keratin*, which is the building block of our hair as well as our nails. Keratin, as we can tell by tapping our nails on the table, is very tough. In fact, the word "keratin" comes from a Greek word meaning "horn"—the kind of horn you find on an animal's head.

Humans and other large primates evolved from smaller primates that used their more claw-like nails to scrabble up trees. Our nails are vestiges of those nails—and still come in handy for scratching an itch and pulling splinters out of a foot.

The part of the fingernail we polish is called the nail plate. It's like a shield of

## *Nails (and hair) grow more slowly as we get older.*

armor, protecting the tender nail bed underneath. The nail plate is not living tissue like our skin is. No blood flows into the plate, so it isn't "fed" by nutrients the way our skin and other body organs are.

How does a fingernail grow? Take a look at your thumb. See the white half-moon at the base? That's not just an interesting design on your thumbnail. What you are seeing is the *lunula*, a group of cells that manufacture keratin. The lunula is the nail-plate factory. New nail is

assembled and added onto the old nail plate. This pushes the whole nail up and out. That's how the nail grows, even though it's "dead."

The little flap of skin over the half-moon—called the *cuticle*—protects this nail factory from harm. The cuticle keeps bacteria out, and cushions from jabs and jolts.

Reading palms is just for fun. But reading nails can really tell something about your health. If a doctor notices that nails are blue at the base, she may suspect there is a problem with blood flow to your fingers. If nails curl sharply around the fingertips, it may mean a disease of the heart, lungs, or liver. If the nails appear sunken, it may mean you are anemic—that your blood isn't carrying enough oxygen.

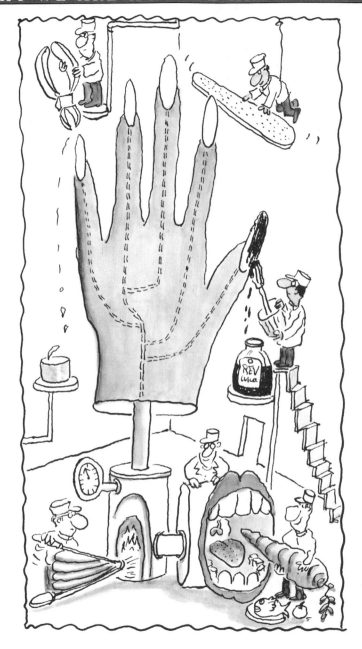

One cause of anemia is a diet low in iron.

Nails, along with hair, grow more slowly as we get older. However, some illnesses, or not getting enough to eat, will also slow nail growth.

## The half-moon on each nail is a tiny nail factory.

It takes about 8 months for the average adult's fingernails to grow an inch. Hair, meanwhile, can grow 4 inches or more in the same time.

If you are right-handed, the nails on that hand will grow slightly faster than nails on the left. If you are left-handed, the opposite is true. Perhaps the reason is increased blood supply to the more active hand. In any case, it seems the more you use your nails, the more it encourages them to grow.

# Why are people's eyes shaped differently?

There is great variety among human faces. We each have our own unique features—no two people, not even twins, look exactly alike. Certain groups of people, however, share some facial features. People whose ancestors came from China look different, for example, than those whose ancestors came from Africa. Scientists think many of these variations evolved because of the different climates human beings found themselves trying to survive in.

Everyone's actual eyeballs are shaped pretty much the same, whether African, European, or Asian. But most Asian people have a fold of skin over the corner of their eyes, called an *epicanthic fold*. Asian's eyelids also carry more fat and so are thicker than the eyelids of most Europeans or Africans. The fold and the thicker lid mean that more of the eyeball is covered. Scientists guess that the eye covering may be part of a symphony of facial features, including high cheekbones and flatter noses, that may better protect human beings against extremely cold air. (Flattened nostrils provide more skin surface for air to flow over, good for warming cold air and filtering dusty air before it reaches the more sensitive upper nose.)

There is some support for this idea: Native people in the coldest regions of Asia—

*Scientists think many variations among facial features evolved according to the different climates human beings found themselves in.*

northern China, Mongolia, and Siberia—have the largest eye folds and flattest facial features.

The epicanthic folds and high cheekbones of the Indians of the Americas, many of whom live in the sweltering tropics, also had their origin in the cold. Tens of thousands of years ago, scientists think, people from Asia crossed over into what is now Alaska by walking across the Bering Strait, a narrow body of water which was then

*Everyone's actual eyeballs are shaped pretty much the same— it's the eyelids that are different.*

partially frozen.

Once on the continent of North America, people gradually explored and settled farther and farther south, until they reached the southernmost tip of South America. Other groups of Asians colonized tropical Indonesia and the balmy Polynesian Islands of the South Pacific. That's why today we see traces of the facial features of northern Asians in Alaskan Eskimos, Peruvian Indians, and Fiji Islanders.

# How come we have two of everything?

When we look at an object, each eye receives light bouncing off the object and sends a message to the brain. The brain combines the images from the two eyes into one picture.

Why, then, do we have two eyes? Why should the brain have to go to the trouble of sorting out visual messages from two eyes, only to re-create one image? Why not have one eye, in the middle of the forehead—like Cyclops?

Two eyes give us something that one eye can't: stereo vision. Our eyes are set about 2½ inches apart. So each eye sees an object from a slightly different angle.

Test this by holding an object, such as an alarm clock, about 10 inches in front of your face. Look at it with both eyes. Now close the right eye and look. Then close the left and look. The clock will appear to shift as you view it from the two different angles.

## *Seeing with two eyes helps us perceive depth.*

The right eye sees more of the right side of the clock, and the left eye sees more of the left side. If you were to simply lay one image on top of the other, they wouldn't match.

But the brain takes the two different images, combines them, and makes one three-dimensional image. Seeing with two eyes help us to perceive *depth*. When you close one eye and look at the clock, it looks much flatter.

This kind of seeing is called *binocular vision*. Just as we do with a pair of binoculars, we view the world through two lenses.

The eyes of many other animals are positioned differently than ours. A white-throated sparrow has an eye on each side of its head. Each eye sees a completely separate area stretching out on the left or the right—a wide-ranging field of view, good for noticing tasty insects or menacing predators.

Adult insects have compound eyes. The eyes are

# eyes but see only one

made of facets, like a diamond, and each facet is a lens. A housefly's eyes have 4,000 facets each. When the fly looks at a flower, each facet sees a tiny part of the flower. Then the fly's brain combines the thousands of images into one whole flower image, like small tiles combine to make a mosaic.

With a compound eye, objects are seen most clearly at very, very close range. If you hold a clock too close to your eyes, it blurs out of focus. But if you were a fly, your sharpest focus would occur when you were crawling on the clock's face. After all, insects are small—and what's most important to them is what's happening within inches, not feet.

**FAST FACT**

The eyes of birds of prey, such as eagles and vultures, are set to look forward, similar to human eyes. But their eyes act as telescopes, letting them see small objects at great distances.

# How Our Eyes See

When light bounces off an object it first zooms into the *cornea*, the clear shield covering the eye. The cornea focuses the light as it enters. Then the light zips into the colored *iris* just behind it, through an opening called the *pupil*.

The pupil, the black spot in the center of the iris, gets bigger in the dark to let more light in, and tiny in bright sunlight. (You can watch your pupil change size by standing in front of the bathroom mirror in the dark for a minute, and then flicking on the light. You will see your pupils do a rapid shrink.) Muscles in the iris push and tug on the pupil to make it behave.

Light that makes it through the pupil passes on through the *lens*, which is behind the iris. The rubbery lens takes over focusing from the cornea, as muscles sculpt its shape to focus light coming from objects at different distances.

The light streams on through the eye's dark inner chamber like the light from a movie projector in the back of a dark-ened theater, and strikes a screen. The screen is called the *retina*, and it contains some 135 million cells specially sensitive to light.

More than 95 percent of these cells are the *rods*, thin cells that enable us to see in dim light. The rest, called *cones*, work best in bright light, and help us see colors.

As they are struck by light, the retina's nerve cells send signals to the brain through the *optic nerve*, the eye's "rear door." The brain combines the images from the two eyes into one picture.

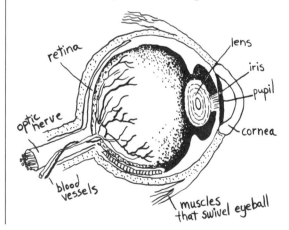

# Why do mosquitoes bite people? And why do the bites itch?

Not all mosquitoes bite. Male mosquitoes spend their days peacefully drinking nectar from flowers. Female mosquitoes like nectar, too. But in most mosquito species, females must also drink blood before they can lay their eggs. And large, lumbering human beings are a good source of a blood meal.

Mosquitoes notice people by our movement, by the heat our bodies radiate, and by the way we smell. When a mosquito flies near your ear, the humming sound you hear is the beating of her tiny wings. Scientists say the buzzing—

so maddening to us on a hot, sleepless night—is very attractive to mosquitoes of the opposite sex. And it's not your imagination—many species of mosquitoes *do* do most of their blood hunting at night. After dark, hosts tend to be conveniently asleep, and far less likely to respond with a killing swat.

Landing lightly on your skin, the mosquito taps with the tip of her proboscis, like someone knocking at a door. (The proboscis is rather like a snout.) Then folding back her hairy lip, she neatly pierces the skin with her feeding stylets (named after a tool used in surgery).

Probing in the skin for

blood vessels (small veins and capillaries), the mosquito searches for blood. In less than a minute, she is usually successful, sucking blood through one strawlike mouthpart while injecting her saliva into you with another. Special substances in the saliva keep your blood from clotting while she feeds.

## Only the female mosquito bites.

A mosquito can swallow about four times her own weight in blood before her

stomach bloats unbearably. If *you* have the stomach to watch her dine on your arm, you can see the blood through the wall of her abdomen. A full mosquito, one scientist said, looks like a tiny red Christmas tree light.

However, it's a better idea to knock the mosquito away. Along with their saliva, mosquitoes may accidentally inject you with one of more than 100 different viruses or parasites. (Since they travel from host to host, they pick up infections as well as blood.) One of the most serious is malaria, with about 300 million people infected around the world, mostly in tropical climates.

Once she is full, the mosquito pulls her mouthparts out of the wound and flies off. If this is your very first mosquito bite, you won't even know you were briefly someone's meal. But if you've been bitten before, your body has become sensitized to the proteins in mosquito saliva. The bite will swell and itch—an allergic reaction. If you get bitten *many, many* times, your body may get used to the proteins. For example, some researchers who study

*A mosquito can swallow four times her own weight in blood.*

mosquitoes have been bitten so often that they are desensitized, and their mosquito bites no longer itch.

A mosquito drinks blood for its amino acids—the building blocks of protein. She needs lots of protein to make eggs. After a blood meal, a female may lay 100 eggs. Without blood, some mosquitoes still produce fertile eggs, but usually less than ten— and perhaps only one.

While we may feel we are being "eaten alive" on a warm evening, humans are not actually mosquitoes' favorite food. Human blood contains little of the amino acid isoleucine, which mosquitoes need to build their egg proteins. A mosquito might prefer to take a drink of buffalo or rat. But as humans elbow out other animals and their habitats, many mosquitoes have come to depend on us. We give them places to live (old bottles and cans, spare tires), and warm bodies to feast on. We're not buffaloes, but we'll have to do.

# Mighty Mite

Other insects make skin itchy, too. One of these is the itch mite, which causes a skin condition called *scabies*. Like the mosquito, only the females are interested in us. But don't blame them—they're just trying to find a warm, safe place to lay their eggs.

The tiny female mite crawls around on the host's skin, looking for sheltered places— between the fingers, or under a fold of skin. Once she finds a spot she likes, the mite digs a trench, burrowing under the top layer of skin.

In the little dark tunnel she has made, the mite lays her eggs. Days pass. Then the secret spot where the mite has taken up residence becomes very itchy.

Most people can't help but scratch, and all that scratching injures the skin. So although the mite did little damage herself, the skin around the burrow becomes cut and crusted.

What causes the itchiness? Scientists believe it's the body's allergic reaction to the mite's feces, which accumulate in the tunnel under the skin.

# Why do people yawn, contagious?

Yawns are more contagious than the common cold. Seeing someone else yawn, you'll almost certainly yawn, too. Just reading about yawning can set you off. Are you yawning yet?

If you are, you're in good company. Human beings yawn all day long. We yawn when when we wake up in the morning. We yawn when we go to bed at night. We yawn a lot when we watch television, studies show. And we even yawn when we are jogging briskly through the park.

Human beings aren't the only creatures that yawn. Many other animals, from lions to fish, open their jaws wide in yawns, too.

When we see people yawn, we often think they are tired or bored. But when Siamese fighting fish yawn, watch out! Male fish begin to yawn when they see other males. More yawning follows—about one yawn every 10 minutes. Then fish attacks fish, and the battle explodes. Other animals, such as monkeys and lions, yawn when they are hungry.

Why do people yawn?

*Some animals, including monkeys and lions, yawn when they are hungry.*

The common explanation is that we yawn to gulp in extra oxygen—for example, in a stuffy room. But Robert Provine, a psychologist who studies yawning, says that isn't true. People given pure oxygen yawn just as much as people breathing ordinary air.

Provine said no one knows exactly why people yawn or why yawns are so contagious. But he is trying to find out.

Over the years, Provine has run a number of yawning experiments at the University of Maryland. In one, he had volunteers sit alone in a quiet room and think about yawning. When they felt a yawn coming on, they pressed a button. When the yawn ended, they did the same. Provine found that the

# and why are yawns

average yawn lasted about 6 seconds. One person who concentrated hard yawned 76 times in half an hour.

Next, Provine videotaped himself yawning or smiling. When shown the tape, only about one of every five viewers smiled when they saw Provine smile. But more than half of the viewers yawned right along with the psychologist. The conclusion: Yawning appears to be much more contagious than friendliness.

When we yawn, the head tilts back, the jaw drops, the eyes squint, and the brow wrinkles. Provine pointed out that when we stretch, we usually yawn, too. Yawns, he said, may be a stretch for the head and neck. But yawning also briefly stops oxygen-carrying blood from leaving the brain.

So yawning may simultaneously wake us up as well as calm us down.

You can see for yourself that yawning isn't just about taking a deep breath by doing an experiment of your own, Provine said. Seal your lips at the beginning of a yawn and try to breathe through your nose. It's just about impossible. If a yawn were simply a deep breath, your nose would work as well as your mouth.

Yawns are so contagious, Provine said, that our brains are probably "programmed" to respond to a yawning face. Since early humans lived in groups, yawning may have been a way to synchronize the group's behavior. A yawn setting off another and another might mean it's bedtime—or hunting time.

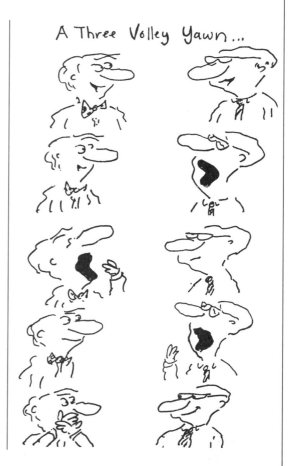

A Three Volley Yawn...

# Why do people get seasick or carsick?

You are on your way to camp, on a hot bus crowded with noisy kids. The bus follows a long, winding road through the trees and up into the hills. As it shifts and lurches around each curve, your stomach shifts and lurches with it. Strangely enough, every time you glance *down* rather than out the window, a wave of nausea threatens to overwhelm you.

If some bus trips make you feel this way, you're in good company. Astronauts on the space shuttle and passengers on the Queen Elizabeth 2 ocean liner share your malady. But whether you're sick at sea, on a turning ferris wheel, or all over the back of your family's station wagon,

you're the victim of the same syndrome—motion sickness.

We don't get sick when we walk down the street. Why, then, do we sometimes feel so miserable traveling down the same street in a taxi, or on a city bus?

The problem is caused by the difference between what we feel and what we see when we are in a moving vehicle. Inside your cabin on an ocean liner, for example, you feel the sinking and rising of the boat on the waves. You register the motion inside your ears, as the fluid in your inner ears shifts with the motion. Your ears signal your brain—correctly—that you are moving.

But to your eyes, the room around you appears to be standing still. Your eyes

send information to your brain that nobody's going anywhere. The mismatch between the information coming in from the sides and front of your head drives the brain a bit crazy. Which should it believe?

Stress hormones, such as adrenaline, start pouring into

*Motion sickness is caused by the difference between what you see and what you feel in a moving vehicle.*

your body, as your brain breaks out into the nervous system equivalent of a cold sweat. The stomach muscles get some extra electrical jolts, and they start contracting faster than usual. Finally, you may throw up.

Nine out of ten people get motion sick at least once in a while. To minimize motion sickness:

• Don't travel on an empty stomach. That just increases queasiness. Eat a small meal before you go.

• In a car or bus, look out the window and watch the road passing by. (So your eyes as well as your ears know you are moving.) Don't read or focus attention on objects inside the vehicle. The best place to sit is in the front of a car or bus, since you can see the road ahead and to the side. Likewise, on an ocean voyage, you will feel better on deck than in your closed cabin. After a few days of travel, as your brain figures out what's going on, your sea-sickness should lessen. (That's what happens on the space shuttle, too.)

• You can take motion sickness drugs, such as Dramamine. But they can make you drowsy, and the drugs themselves make some people feel dizzy and queasy.

• You can try "sea bands," elastic bands which you wear on your arms; a plastic button presses down on a special spot on your wrist. According to the theory of acupressure, this eases motion sickness—as well as morning sickness in pregnant women. Such pressure does seem to make some people feel better, though no one knows exactly why.

# What causes claustrophobia and other phobias?

**P**hobia comes from the Greek word "phobos," meaning fear. And that's what a phobia is—a condition producing attacks of fear or anxiety. But a phobia isn't the normal fear felt when something truly frightening happens, such as a mugger brandishing a knife and demanding all your money. Phobias produce fear in situations that don't seem to warrant it.

On a sunny summer day, the Brooklyn Bridge walkway is the place to be for hundreds of strolling New Yorkers. But if you suffer from *gephyrophobia*—the fear of crossing bridges—walking across the Brooklyn Bridge may be a terrible ordeal.

What might this feel like? As you try to cross, a feeling of panic builds; your heart starts to race and you may feel dizzy and nauseated. The feeling of terror may make you afraid you are losing your mind. Your only thought is to

*Phobias produce fear in situations that don't seem to warrant it.*

get off the bridge. Once you do, you feel safe, and the panicky feelings quickly subside.

*Claustrophobia* is the fear of being in closed or confined places, such as elevators, subway cars, or small, windowless rooms. The worst fear: "What if I can't get out?" A claustrophobic person can reason with herself that nothing awful is happening as a subway train waits between stations, but her anxiety threatens to overwhelm her. She is literally afraid of fear itself, of the panic attack that washes over her.

Where do phobias come from? Some have their roots in a childhood experience. One 9-year-old boy was attacked by a swarm of hornets; today, as an adult, he is afraid of all insects, especially those that fly.

Stenophobia... Fear of Narrow Spaces

Other phobias start in adulthood, and seem to spring from nowhere, as when a formerly outgoing executive suddenly became fearful of driving to work. Psychologists say stress can trigger phobias in some people, who may have inherited a tendency to become phobic from their parents. And phobias are common; at least one out of every nine Americans has one.

Experts say there is no single cause for phobias, but the good news is that they can be treated. The most common treatment densensitizes the phobic person by taking him, step by step, through the places or situations that cause panic.

Meanwhile, there are as many unusual phobias as there are different people. Do you avoid farmyards, and pale at the sight of Frank Perdue? If so, perhaps you suffer from *alektorophobia*—the fear of chickens. When Santa Claus comes, do you run the other way? Perhaps you have *pogonophobia*—the fear of beards.

When you open your lunchbox, are you struck with *arachibutyrophobia*—the fear of peanut butter sticking to the roof of your mouth?

Do you avoid cleaning out your refrigerator, because of *blennophobia*—fear of slime? Do you dislike the *Tonight Show*, with Jay Leno? If so, you may suffer from *geniophobia*—fear of chins. And by now you may have developed *sesquipedalophobia*—the fear of long words.

# What causes hiccups?

**H**ave you ever gotten the hiccups and then become the victim of lots of free home "cures?" While you are *hic*-ing uncontrollably, your brother jumps from behind you, screaming "BOO!" Or your sister blows up a paper bag and smashes it gleefully in your face.

Then a well-meaning aunt appears. She makes you stand over the sink and drink water with the glass tipped away from you. "Drink from the wrong side of the glass," she urges. Meanwhile, you are spilling water down the front of your shirt. And you are still hiccuping.

Clearly, hiccups have a mind of their own. Everyone gets them occasionally, especially after a big meal or consuming alcohol. But despite the fact that people hiccup in hundreds of different languages, scientists aren't precisely sure why.

Hiccups happen when a big muscle near your stomach goes into spasms. This muscle, called the *diaphragm*, helps us breathe. Normally, its movements are rhythmic and regular. When the diaphragm slips out of its normal pattern, breathing changes.

The out-of-control diaphragm makes you take in a big gulp of air. As the air fills your lungs, the brain sends an urgent message to your throat: "No more of this!" And your vocal cords promptly snap shut.

It's rather like a tug-of-war. The diaphragm tries to get you to inhale, while the mouth and throat do their valiant best to keep too much air from entering. And with each jerky movement of the diaphragm, the rush of air makes a weird noise as it hits the vocal cords. That's the *"hic"* in hiccup.

---

*Hiccuping is like a tug of war between your diaphragm and your throat.*

---

Most hiccuping is perfectly normal and stops after a little while, as the diaphragm settles back into its normal steady rhythm. Hiccuping for more than a few minutes, though, can get painful. Your throat hurts, and you get tired of being jerked like a puppet by the *hic-hic-hic*. Usually, however, the hiccups stop as abruptly as they started.

But for some people, hiccuping is like a chronic disease. They hiccup continuously, for weeks at a time. Their bodies become exhausted, just as if they were running a race. The hiccuping interferes with jobs, schoolwork, and talking, eating, and sleeping. By studying these hiccup sufferers, researchers are finding clues to what makes all of us hiccup.

Doctors gave a small group of hiccuping adults a medicine that is normally used to control high blood pressure. The drug keeps calcium from being absorbed by brain tissue. The medicine stopped the hiccups in five of seven people tested. According to the researchers, the fact that the drug worked may mean that hiccups are caused by a temporary overload of calcium in the brain.

For most of us, hiccups are simply a brief but embarrassing nuisance. We would no more take high-powered medicine for hiccups than we would for sneezing. And since none of the home remedies have proven to be "cures," the next time someone attempts to try out their favorite cure on you, just say, "I'm—*hic*—waiting them out—*hic*—thank you."

Hiccups, the International Language

GERMAN  FRENCH  ENGLISH  CANINE

# Why does hair turn gray?

Our hair and skin are both colored by a chemical called melanin. Gray hair is hair that is not getting its usual supply of melanin.

Melanin is made by special cells in the skin called *melanocytes*. (One out of every 10 skin cells is a melanocyte.) A melanocyte has a funny shape; instead of being round, it looks like an octopus.

Inside the melanocyte, amino acids, which come from the proteins we eat, are transformed by an enzyme, making a load of melanin. The melanin travels out into the cell's "tentacles." These tentacles jut up against the walls of other, ordinary skin cells. Using the tentacles like feeding tubes, the skin cells absorb some melanin. That's what gives skin its usual color. The more melanin in skin, the darker it is.

Hairs grow out of special tubes in the skin called follicles. Follicles are made of skin cells, too. So melanin gets into the hair as well as the skin.

Hair loses its color when its normal supply of melanin is cut off. This happens in two ways: The melanocytes may begin to make less and less melanin. And their tentacles may shorten, so that they no longer reach the hair cells.

Melanocyte production slows as we grow older. So some hairs, getting only a tiny fraction of their coloring pigments, begin to look grayish. (Skin loses a little of its pigment, too, but not as noticeably.) But when melanocytes around the hair simply vanish—as they tend eventually to do—the affected hair turns completely white. Why white? Because that's the natural, untinted color of the keratin

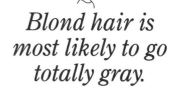

*Blond hair is most likely to go totally gray.*

Going, Going ... Gray!

protein that makes up a strand of hair.

(Sometimes, what we see as a solid gray head of hair is really a kind of optical illusion—dark hairs and white hairs mixed together, appearing gray like pepper mixed with salt.)

When *you* get your first gray hair often depends on when your parents and grandparents did. Some people find their first white strand as early as age 14. A study of men in Australia showed that by age 25 to 34, 22 percent had some gray hair. And after age 55, 94 percent had some gray. However, some lucky people grow old with their natural hair color intact. Surprisingly, people with blond hair are those most likely to go totally gray. On the other hand, gray hairs are more noticeable in dark hair.

Scientists aren't sure why melananocytes tend to disappear over time. Perhaps particles called "free radicals," which are produced when the body uses oxygen to burn fuel, hurt melanocytes.

But scientists do know that diseases, including malaria, typhus, and even the flu, can damage melanocytes. So can an overactive thyroid gland, diabetes, and certain kinds of radiation. And a poor diet, especially one lacking in vitamin B-12, can also cause hair to lose color. Sometimes, melanocytes will swing back into action when the diet improves, and hair will saturate with color once again.

# Why do people develop as they get older?

The wrinkles and lines on our faces are mainly the result of two things: living on the surface of a planet and being sociable animals.

What does the Earth have to do with it? No matter where you are—in school, in an office, or on a mountaintop—our planet's gravity is tugging on your skin, pulling it down. In addition, when you are outdoors, UV radiation from the Sun is pushing through the outer layer of your skin, damaging the skin structures underneath.

On top of all this, you are constantly folding and refolding your skin—by smiling, frowning, raising your eyebrows. As the years go by, these creases are worn into your face, leaving a visible mark of all the conversations you had, all the tears you cried.

*Wrinkling has three main causes: the Sun, gravity, and facial expression.*

Some people develop very few wrinkles. This may be partly due to heredity: If your parents and grandparents had few lines, you probably will too. If you have natu-

rally dark skin, you'll also be less prone to wrinkling, since your skin coloring helps protect you from the Sun's radiation. Monks who spend most of their lives in dark, quiet monasteries show how well protected skin ages. They don't go out into the Sun much, and they are contemplative and relaxed, rather than animated, much of the time. So the smooth, relatively undamaged skin of a 90-year-old monk may allow him to pass for 50.

Why not 30, or 20? Because even a sheltered monk can't escape the force of gravity. Skin droops under gravity's relentless pulling, leaving us with saggy jowls and baggy eyes. Also, over time, some tissue under the skin dies but is not replaced

# wrinkles in their skin

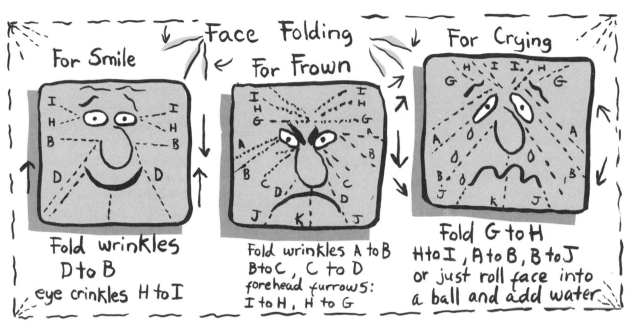

For Smile

Fold wrinkles
D to B
eye crinkles H to I

Face Folding
For Frown

Fold wrinkles A to B
B to C, C to D
forehead furrows:
I to H, H to G

For Crying

Fold G to H
H to I, A to B, B to J
or just roll face into
a ball and add water

by the body. Cheeks and temples sink in. The skin becomes too large for the tissue it once covered tautly, and falls in loose folds instead.

Most of us can't live like monks, or wouldn't want to. For us, the main culprit in wrinkling is exposure to the Sun. UV radiation damages

*Cigarette smokers tend to wrinkle at younger ages than nonsmokers.*

part of the *dermis*, the inner layer of skin. In the dermis, collagen fibers, made of protein, hold the skin's structures together. UV light makes collagen fibers clump together, weakening the skin support. Also, radiation may make skin thinner. And, just as a thin letter is easier to fold than a thick stack of pages, thinner skin folds more easily.

Since we fold our skin with every expression we make, sun-damaged skin is easier to wrinkle. But it's easy to protect skin from UV radiation. Don't sunbathe, and don't spend too much time in the sun without wearing a sunscreen, which keeps radiation from penetrating the skin.

Smoking cigarettes can also wrinkle your face. Scientists compared the skin of people who smoke with others who don't. Here's what

*UV radiation may make skin thinner, and thinner skin wrinkles more easily.*

they found: Smokers wrinkled at younger ages than nonsmokers. And the more

cigarettes smoked, the more lined and wrinkly the face. People who smoked a lot were five times more likely to have extra wrinkling than those who didn't smoke at all.

Scientists think smoking hurts the collagen in skin. Also, smoke gets in your eyes—making you squint, which causes crow's feet, those lines spreading out from the sides of the eyes. Finally, sucking on cigarettes gives smokers little "whistle" lines above their lips.

# How do we get skin cancer?

Sometimes, severe burns or even tattooing can cause skin cancers. But most of the time, skin cancer is triggered by something we are all exposed to every day: that huge source of radiation in the sky, the Sun.

Part of the light coming from the Sun is invisible light—UV radiation. UV is very high-energy light; it can penetrate the skin, damaging cells as it goes.

In the past, people got too much sun by working outdoors, in open fields and on city streets, with their sleeves rolled up or shirts off. But since the 1930s, there has been a new source of too much sun—deliberate tanning.

Around that time, it became fashionable for everyone, including students and office workers, to try and darken their skin if it was

Recipe For Trouble ...Serve (all suspicious growths to a dermatologist.)

Take one teenager, Cover with baby oil... Bake for five or six summers, then broil...

BABY OIL

light. People with pale skin were said to look pasty, sickly. Tans, on the other hand, were associated with the outdoors, fresh air, sports, and the leisure time to lie on the beach or beside a resort pool. The deeper the tan, the better.

## Even a dark tan will not protect you from all UV radiation.

In much the same way that cigarettes were associated with a healthy, active life, so were tans. But the truth was just the opposite. Otherwise healthy people began getting lung cancer from smoking. And otherwise healthy people began getting skin cancer after years of sunburns and countless hours spent lying motionless in the summer sun.

How? Tanning is the skin's attempt to protect itself. First, dead cells on the skin's surface absorb some UV light. Then, living cells in the skin start producing extra melanin, the pigment which colors our skin, which soaks up more UV. That's why sitting in the sun makes light-skinned people tan.

However, even a good tan stops only half of UV light from penetrating the skin. The longer you sit in the sun, trying to get browner, the more UV radiation enters your skin cells. Burns, and sometimes cancer, are the result.

The most common, and least serious, form of skin cancer is basal cell carcinoma. Basal cells are cells in the deepest layer of skin. More than 400,000 people in the United States get basal cell cancer every year. It used to be mainly a disease of old age. But now, physicians are worried because the rate is rising among younger people—including teenagers. Luckily, basal cell carcinoma is quite treatable, usually by removing the cancerous area.

The biggest worry is melanoma, which is cancer in the melanocytes. It is the most serious form of skin cancer. Left untreated, it can be deadly, easily spreading from the skin to organs like the lungs and brain.

## The good news is that skin cancer is almost entirely preventable.

Experts say that the United States is in the middle of a "skin cancer epidemic," created mainly by a national obsession with tanning. Making our love affair with the Sun all the more dangerous is the thinning of the ozone layer, which allows even more UV radiation than usual to reach the ground.

# Crazy Cells

Our bodies are constantly repairing and reinventing themselves. Every minute, 10 million cells divide and copy themselves, in a process strictly controlled by the genes at a cell's heart.

But when cells divide crazily, and lose their ability to function normally—as a liver cell, say, or as a skin cell—that's cancer. The cells grow into a tumor instead of a useful body part.

Skin cancer, usually caused by the Sun, is one of the most common cancers, and thankfully one of the most treatable. Doctors say we should take a good look at our skin, especially if we've had a lot of sunburns. What to look for: moles or brown areas bigger than a pencil eraser; a new growth that's pearly, black, or multicolored; a sore that doesn't heal after 3 weeks. If you find a suspicious spot, see your doctor; he or she can tell you if it's anything that needs treatment.

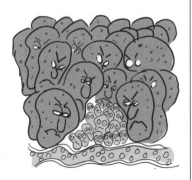

(For more about the ozone layer, see page 173.)

But on the bright side, researchers say skin cancer is almost entirely preventable. Cover up when possible; pick one-piece swimsuits over skimpy bikinis; wear a good sunscreen and a hat. Above all, don't sit out broiling in the sun, hoping for a tan.

# How come tears come out

Upset about something? Have a good cry. Most people say when they cry, they feel better afterward—sometimes *much* better. That is a clue, many scientists think, to the mystery of tears.

Above the outer corner of your eyes, just below your eyebrows, are the lacrimal glands—the tear glands. They are only the size of almonds, but these tiny factories can churn out a flood of tears.

The lacrimal glands are always making tears—even as you read this. These tears wash over your eyes to keep them clean and clear. The tears well out of little passageways in the outer corner of your eyes. Each time you blink, your eyelids spread the tears over your eyes, like windshield wipers spread washer fluid.

Then the tears flow away down drains in the inner corner of your eyes, through another passageway, and into the area behind your nose, where they are absorbed into the body.

If you get a lot of dust in your eyes, however, it's a different story. Tears start flowing faster, to keep up with the cleaning job. There may be so many tears that they begin to overflow your bottom lid, instead of neatly draining away. "My eyes are watering," you complain.

But these tears are quite different from the tears we make when we cry. Those tears are caused by strong emotions or intense pain. Half of all crying, according to researchers, is caused by sadness. But people also shed tears when they are very happy, angry, or afraid.

What's the point of these

*Scientists studying crying have found tiny amounts of stress hormones in tears.*

noncleaning tears? They seem to make us actually feel better. Here's how.

Tears are made mainly of water, oils, salt, and sodium bicarbonate (baking soda). That's why the tears streaming down our cheeks taste salty. But our tears aren't the saltiest: Seagulls, which catch and eat saltwater fish, build up a lot of salt in their bodies. Their tears help carry the extra salt, which could be

# of our eyes when we cry?

harmful, safely out of their systems.

If birds get rid of excess salt through their tears, it's natural to wonder whether people are getting something harmful out of our bodies when we cry. The answer seems to be yes.

When we feel strong emotions or pain, our brains work overtime producing chemicals to carry signals of our excitement or distress, and our bodies produce special stress hormones. Scientists studying crying have found that tears actually contain some of these chemicals and hormones. The crying helps us get rid of the chemicals produced by our strong emotions.

As the chemicals slowly drain away, we may begin to feel calmer. After crying, many people say they feel "refreshed," like a rain has come and cleared the air. So although we don't want to float away on a sea of tears, a little crying now and then may help us heal.

A few Alternative Uses...

Seasoning for cakes

Window Cleaning

Filling up the birdbath

# Why do people have like O, A, and B?

**B**lood type varies from person to person in much the same way as hair color. Your blood type is one of four major groups: A, B, AB, or O. Which group you belong to depends on what proteins are found in your red blood cells and in

*People with type O blood are called "universal donors"—they can give blood to anyone.*

the plasma (mostly water) they float in.

The proteins in the cells are called *agglutinogens*. The proteins in the plasma are called *agglutinins*. The agglutinogens come in two varieties, A and B. The agglutinins also come in two varieties, called *a* and *b*. (Don't worry—it gets less confusing.)

Here's how it works. Emily has type A blood, with A agglutinogens in her cells and *b* agglutinins in her plasma. Lily has type B blood—B agglutinogens and *a* agglutinins. Jeff has type AB blood, with both A and B agglutinogens in his red cells and *no* agglutinins in his plasma. Juan has type O blood. He has *no* agglutinogens in his cells, and both *a* and *b* agglutinins in his plasma.

Your body treats blood containing agglutinogens different from yours as a foreign invader. If Emily, with her type A blood, were given a transfusion of type B blood, her *b* agglutinins would make the incoming blood cells

# different types of blood,

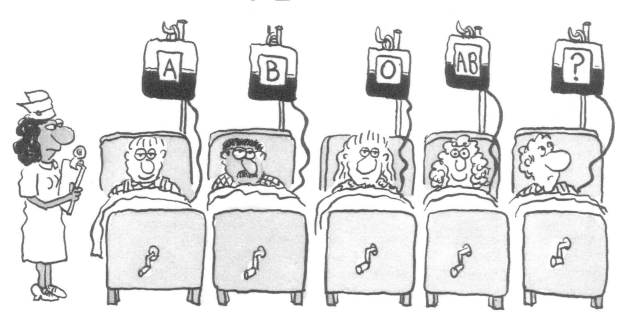

clump uselessly together. Unable to move freely throughout her body, the cells could not deliver oxygen to body organs such as the brain—endangering her life. Likewise, type B blood rejects type A, and for type O's, both A *and* B are out. To prevent any mistakes, patients are tested for blood type before they receive blood.

None of the blood types, however, has a bad reaction to type O (which, you'll remember, has no agglutinogens in its red cells to offend other types). So people with type O blood, like Juan, are called "universal donors"— they can give blood to anyone.

And since AB blood has both A and B proteins, it's equally comfortable with all the other types of blood. So a person with AB blood who needs a blood transfusion can safely receive any other type. That's why people like Jeff are known as "universal recipients."

Just like hair color, you inherit your blood type from your parents. And like hair color, blood types vary among populations, depending on where people originated.

Because so many people around the world get blood tests for one reason or another, scientists have found how blood types vary from place to place.

In the United States, 41 percent of Caucasians have type A blood, compared to 27 percent of African-Americans. Nearly all Indians in Peru have type O blood. In Central Asia, type B is the most common.

Why blood types vary is not entirely clear. But scientists have found some interesting connections between blood types and certain illnesses. People with type O blood, for example, are more likely to get ulcers than people with other types. And type A people have a higher risk of stomach cancer.

Strangely enough, the blood group proteins are very

*If you have type O blood, your body might mistake invading bubonic plague bacteria for friendly cells.*

similar to the proteins found on the surfaces of some bacteria and viruses. If you are infected by microbes with surface proteins that look like your own blood proteins, then your immune system might mistake the invading organism for a friendly body substance— allowing it to sneak by.

Here's an example. The surface proteins of the bacteria that cause bubonic plague are very similar to the blood

group proteins on type O blood cells. Scientists suspect, therefore, that people with type O blood may be particularly susceptible to bubonic plague.

Scientists think bubonic plague started in Southeast Asia and spread west. When it reached Europe, it killed a quarter of the population in the 14th century; it was known as the Black Death. Central Asia, which has the longest history of bubonic plague, has the lowest frequencies of type O blood in the world. This indicates that having type O blood was a disadvantage in plague-stricken areas, and that those with A, B, or AB blood had a definite survival advantage. Scientists think that the connections between blood type and disease may one day help explain the origin and survival of different blood types among human beings.

# Why do we have trouble getting to sleep sometimes?

Every night, all around the planet, hundreds of millions of people are tossing and turning. They have *insomnia*—a word that comes from the Latin *insomnis*, meaning "sleepless." For some people, insomnia is only an occasional problem. For others, every night seems like a battle to get enough rest.

There is no one cause for insomnia. But often the problem is stress. Maybe a big test is coming up at school, and you're not sure you're ready for it. Maybe you had an argument with a friend that day. Or maybe your life is too hectic—you go from school to sports practice to music lessons, with no quiet time to relax by yourself. You may be exhausted from working and playing so hard, but ironically, that's when you may have the most trouble sleeping. You're simply too "wound up."

Insomnia can also be caused by depression—a sad, hopeless feeling that won't seem to go away. People who are depressed often wake up very early in the morning and can't get back to sleep.

Plenty of less serious things can cause insomnia, too. If you come home from school or work feeling sleepy, and take a nap, you may find you can't get to sleep at your regular time that night.

*A near-bedtime jogging session can make you toss and turn.*

Here's another cause of insomnia: hard exercise. If you exercise during the morning or afternoon, you'll probably sleep better than usual that night. However, hard exercise makes the body release adrenaline and

THE SANDMAN'S NIGHT OFF

A.F.L.C.I.O.
SANDMAN'S
Union
Local 444

other natural stimulants. So if you do hard exercise right before bedtime—for example, go jogging, or play basketball—you may feel so wide-awake and energetic that sleep won't come for hours.

What we eat or drink can keep us awake, too. Coffee, tea, and some soft drinks (such as regular Coke and Pepsi) contain caffeine, a stimulant. Drinking these

after dinner may keep you awake later than you'd like.

And here's a surprise: Alcohol causes sleeplessness. Alcohol can make people feel drowsy, but when they go to bed, they may sleep fitfully, and wake up groggy and tired.

Jet lag plays havoc with sleeping schedules. When you fly from one time zone to another—say, from California

to Maine—your body's natural rhythms are thrown off. Maine clocks say it's bedtime; your stomach says it's 3 hours earlier—dinner time. It can take days to readjust.

Sometimes, insomnia is caused by things we do right before bed—like watching an exciting television show or eating a big, spicy meal.

To get a good night's sleep, try to take some of the

stress out of your days. Leave time to relax; try not to worry so much. If you can't sleep at night, don't nap during the day.

Don't drink anything with caffeine in the hours before bedtime. Don't do strenuous exercise then, either. If you want a snack, make it light and bland—cookies and milk is the old standby.

If you can't sleep, and you've been lying awake for

**FAST FACT**

Experts recommend that insomniacs use their bed for sleeping only, so that the only activity the bed is associated with is sleep. Reading, watching TV, or talking on the phone should all take place elsewhere.

awhile, sleep disorder experts recommend getting out of bed and doing something quiet, such as reading, in another room. Then, when you really feel drowsy, go back to bed.

And if you think you might be depressed, your parents, family doctor, or a therapist may be able to help you feel better. As you shake the depressed feelings, you'll find you rest easier, too.

# How and why do we dream when we are sleeping?

 ntil 1952, no one knew what was going on—physically—in a dreaming brain. Most scientists thought that like the sleeper, the brain was quiet and inactive during sleep.

Then a Chicago graduate student, Eugene Aserinsky, used an electroencephalograph (EEG) to "listen" to the brain of his sleeping 8-year-old son. (An EEG detects the tiny electrical currents produced in the working brain. It traces the wavy patterns of electricity on an unrolling sheet of paper.)

What he found was a surprise. Every few hours, as the child slept, the EEG pen suddenly zigzagged crazily across the paper. Meanwhile, the boy's eyes seemed to jerk back and forth under his closed eyelids. Finally, Aserinsky woke the boy during one of these strange intervals, and the child told his father he had been dreaming.

Aserinsky had discovered *rapid eye movement* sleep, or REM sleep, the period when

---

**FAST FACT**

We dream about 20 percent of the time we're asleep. We remember a dream most easily if we are awakened during it.

---

most dreams occur. (When your cat or dog is sleeping, and its eyes begin to twitch under the lids, your pet is probably dreaming. Often, a paw will twitch too, and a dog may bark softly or growl in its sleep.)

Between periods of REM sleep, electrical waves are slow and even, as you might expect from a sleeping brain. But during REM sleep—during dreaming—the electrical pattern is remarkably similar to that of someone who is wide awake.

However, as we all know, dreams are very different from waking life. Nightmares are overrun with ghosts and monsters. And even in good

Field of Dreams

dreams, events are strange and jumbled. In a dream, you may happen upon glittering loose change on the ground. But when you try to pick it up, you find it has turned into worthless pebbles.

Dreams seem to have a funny, jumpy structure. On awakening, we may wonder what one thing had to do with another. *During* the dream, however, things seem to make a weird kind of sense. Martin Seligman, an experimental psychologist at the University of Pennsylvania, has developed a theory of why this is so, and how it may explain what dreams are for.

According to Seligman, a burst of electricity in the brain during dreaming causes an image to pop up in the dream. A new burst produces a new image, and so on, for the 10 to 30 minutes of a typical dream. The first image might be of a giant tree; the second, an old house. The mind, trying to make sense out of nonsense, weaves each strange new image into a "story." The story will be joyful or sad or frightening, depending on the emotional state of the dreamer.

This process of plugging anything and everything into a narrative "plot" also works when the stimulus comes from outside the body. An alarm clock rings on your night table. Instantly, in your dream, a bell rings, telling you it's time to collect your books; class is over. Somehow, the brain is able to quickly fit outside sounds and sensations into the story.

Over the years, scientists studying sleepers in the laboratory have learned more and more about how we dream. But *why* we dream is still unknown. However, Seligman thinks the theory of dream structure "hints at reasons why we dream." Perhaps dreaming gives us, and the other animals who dream, practice in making sense of

*Cats and dogs dream, too. You can tell by your sleeping pet's twitching eyes.*

the world. Each day, we must sort out and interpret events and emotions—we must piece together the stories of our lives. And each night, we practice.

This could explain, Seligman says, why infants spend such a large part of the day sleeping and dreaming. They may be learning the skills they need to understand a vast new world of images, ideas, and feelings.

# Index

# Special Thanks

Since in the world there are no complete or permanent answers, science is most truly about knowing what questions to ask. Thanks to the curious people who provided the wonderful questions:

Julie Allmer
Joseph Amato
Lara Balarezo
"Bebi"
Teddy Blackburn
John Boits
Paul Broadwater
Melissa Blye
Alex Caliman
Nicholas Capobianco
Katie Carbonari
Victor Caridade
Joshua Cayenne
Howie Chang
Michael Chang
Vanessa Christiani
Melissa Cody
Brendan Colfer
Lauren Comer
Carmine D'Ambrosio
Christina de La Cruz
Sasha Dos Santos
Richard di Monda Jr.
Melissa Dvorak
Jennifer Edler
Datisha Edwards
Nikii Edwards
Joey Esposito
Peter Ferreri
Bennett Fins

Luke Fitzgibbon
Jason Fong
Suzanne E. Fountaine
Justin Francavilla
Randall Galera
Melissa Greco
Michael Greenman
Christopher Grimm
Mark Gross
Brett Gurwitz
James Harlacker
Bob Hatten
Sidney Hecker
Billy Hennessey
Justin S. Hirschorn
Erin Hogan
Mahendra Indarjit
Nicole Jackson
Erica Jim
Kristie Keller
Stephen Kelly
Josh Kelner
Billy Kleiber
Eugene Koch
Kris Krasinski
Arathi Kumar
Philip Kushner
Emily Landsman
Katie Larson
Cheryl Lauer

David Lavigne
Angie Lin
Thomas Lin
Philip Mak
Laura Marchetti
Kera Massimina
Ruben C. Matos III
Meredith McHale
Keri McKenna
Paul Medford
Tina Maria Melfi
Robyn F. Meyer
Lainie Miller
Lily Moy
Brian Murphy
Stew Nacht
Joeseph C. Norris
Sonia Angelica Novia
Edwin Ortiz Jr.
Jill O'Shaughnessy
Tara Jean Ostermann
Michael Ostrick
Hiral Oza
Rupal Oza
Angela Patrano
Amy Pellicane
Jonathan Pier
Jenny Pithkongathon
Nutan Prabhu
Ben Rhatigan

David Riddick
Paul Robertson
Manuel Robinson
Janet Rosen
Kristin C. Roussillon
Philip Sachs
Rosie Sciacca
Barry Seiden
Natasha Sewgobind
Rachel Shapiro
Adrian Sinnott
Danielle Skinner
Nadia Smith
Afra Sokissian
Sean Starke
Dominic Suarez
Jefferey Tang
Yungia Tang
Kara Turrisi
Janine Utell
Jennifer Varghese
Roy Walker
John Walsh
Stephen Wayne
Laurence Wohlgemuth
Diane Yager
Richard Yorek
and Rosalyn Esan's
    third-grade class